Android™ *Phones*
FOR
DUMMIES®

by Dan Gookin

WILEY

John Wiley & Sons, Inc.

Android™ Phones For Dummies®

Published by
John Wiley & Sons, Inc.
111 River Street
Hoboken, NJ 07030-5774
www.wiley.com

Copyright © 2012 by John Wiley & Sons, Inc., Hoboken, New Jersey

Published by John Wiley & Sons, Inc., Hoboken, New Jersey

Published simultaneously in Canada

For general information on our other products and services, please contact our Customer Care Department within the U.S. at 877-762-2974, outside the U.S. at 317-572-3993, or fax 317-572-4002.

For technical support, please visit www.wiley.com/techsupport.

Wiley also publishes its books in a variety of electronic formats and by print-on-demand. Not all content that is available in standard print versions of this book may appear or be packaged in all book formats. If you have purchased a version of this book that did not include media that is referenced by or accompanies a standard print version, you may request this media by visiting http://booksupport.wiley.com. For more information about Wiley products, visit us www.wiley.com.

Library of Congress Control Number is available from the publisher.

ISBN: 978-1-118-16952-0 (pbk); ISBN: 978-1-118-22655-1 (ebk); ISBN: 978-1-118-26440-9 (ebk); ISBN: 978-1-118-23244-6 (ebk)

Manufactured in the United States of America

10 9 8 7 6 5 4 3

WILEY

About the Author

Dan Gookin has been writing about technology for over 20 years. He combines his love of writing with his gizmo fascination to create books that are informative, entertaining, and not boring. Having written over 125 titles with 12 million copies in print translated into over 30 languages, Dan can attest that his method of crafting computer tomes seems to work.

Perhaps his most famous title is the original *DOS For Dummies,* published in 1991. It became the world's fastest-selling computer book, at one time moving more copies per week than the *New York Times* number-one bestseller (though, as a reference, it could not be listed on the *Times'* Best Sellers list). That book spawned the entire line of *For Dummies* books, which remains a publishing phenomenon to this day.

Dan's most popular titles include *PCs For Dummies, Word For Dummies, Laptops For Dummies,* and *Troubleshooting & Maintaining Your PC All-in-One For Dummies.* He also maintains the vast and helpful website www.wambooli.com.

Dan holds a degree in Communications/Visual Arts from the University of California, San Diego. He lives in the Pacific Northwest, where he enjoys spending time with his sons playing video games indoors while they watch the gentle woods of Idaho.

Publisher's Acknowledgments

We're proud of this book; please send us your comments at http://dummies.custhelp.com. For other comments, please contact our Customer Care Department within the U.S. at 877-762-2974, outside the U.S. at 317-572-3993, or fax 317-572-4002.

Some of the people who helped bring this book to market include the following:

Acquisitions and Editorial

Sr. Project Editor: Mark Enochs

Acquisitions Editor: Katie Mohr

Copy Editor: Rebecca Whitney

Technical Editor: Tim Stiffler-Dean

Editorial Manager: Leah Michael

Editorial Assistant: Amanda Graham

Sr. Editorial Assistant: Cherie Case

Cover Photo: Portions of front cover image are modifications based on work created and shared by Google and used according to terms described in the Creative Commons 3.0 Attribution License.

Cartoons: Rich Tennant (www.the5thwave.com)

Composition Services

Project Coordinator: Nikki Gee

Layout and Graphics: Claudia Bell, Sennett Vaughan Johnson, Corrie Niehaus

Proofreaders: Melissa Cossell, BIM Indexing & Proofreading Services

Indexer: Infodex Indexing Services, Inc.

Publishing and Editorial for Technology Dummies

    Richard Swadley, Vice President and Executive Group Publisher

    Andy Cummings, Vice President and Publisher

    Mary Bednarek, Executive Acquisitions Director

    Mary C. Corder, Editorial Director

Publishing for Consumer Dummies

    Kathy Nebenhaus, Vice President and Executive Publisher

Composition Services

    Debbie Stailey, Director of Composition Services

Contents at a Glance

Table of Contents

Part II: The Phone Part 63

Introduction

*I*t may be a smartphone, but it makes you feel dumb. Don't worry: You aren't alone. As technology leaps ahead, it often leaves mortal humans behind. I mean, what's the point of owning the latest gizmo when the thing intimidates you to the point that you never use all its features? When that latest gizmo is a modern necessity, like a cell phone, the problem becomes more complex because you always have the thing with you as a reminder.

Relax.

This book makes the complex subject of Android cell phones understandable. It's done with avuncular care and gentle handholding. The information is friendly and informative, without being intimidating. And, yes, ample humor is sprinkled throughout the text to keep the mood just right.

About This Book

I implore you: Do not read this book from over to cover. This book is a reference. It's designed to be used as you need it. Look up a topic in the table of contents or the index. Find something about your phone that vexes you or something you're curious about. Look up the answer, and get on with your life.

Every chapter in this book is written as its own, self-contained unit, covering a specific topic about using your Android phone. The chapters are further divided into sections representing a task you perform with the phone or explaining how to get something done. Sample sections in this book include

- Typing on your phone
- Phoning someone you call often
- Adding your phone to Google Voice
- Uploading a picture
- Borrowing music from your computer
- Creating a mobile hotspot
- Dialing an international number
- Saving battery life

Every section explains a topic as though it's the first one you read in this book. Nothing is assumed, and everything is cross-referenced. Technical terms and topics, when they come up, are neatly shoved to the side, where they're easily avoided. The idea here isn't to learn anything. This book's philosophy is to help you look it up, figure it out, and get back to your life.

How to Use This Book

This book follows a few conventions for using your phone, so pay attention!

The main way to interact with the typical Android phone is by using its *touch-screen,* which is the glassy part of the phone as it's facing you. Buttons also adorn the phone, all of which are explained in Part I of this book.

There are various ways to touch the screen, which are described in Chapter 3.

Chapter 4 discusses text input on an Android phone, which involves using something called the *onscreen keyboard.* Your phone may also feature a phys-ical keyboard. Lucky you. It may even have the newfangled Swype keyboard for superfast text entry. And when you tire of typing, you can always input text on your Android phone by dictating it.

This book directs you to do things on your phone by following numbered steps. Every step involves a specific activity, such as touching something on the screen; for example:

   3. Choose Downloads.

This step directs you to touch the text or item on the screen labeled Downloads. You might also be told to do this:

   3. Touch Downloads.

Because this book covers a variety of phones, alternative commands may be listed. One of them is bound to match something on your phone, or at least be close to what you see:

   3. Touch the My Downloads command or the Downloads command.

In a few places, you might see text that's displayed on a computer. In these instances, the text is shown in a `monospace font`.

 Various phone options can be turned off or on, as indicated by a gray box with a green check mark in it, as shown in the margin. By touching this box on the screen, you add or remove the green check mark. When the green check mark appears, the option is on; otherwise, it's off.

The bar codes in the margins are there to help you install recommended apps. To install the app, scan the bar code using special software you install on your phone. Chapter 18 discusses how to add software to your phone, and in Chapter 26 I discuss how to use the Barcode Scanner app to read bar codes.

Foolish Assumptions

Even though this book is written with the gentle handholding required by anyone who is just starting out, or who is easily intimidated, I have made a few assumptions.

Number one: I'm assuming that you're still reading the introduction. That's great. It's much better than getting a snack right now or checking to ensure that the cat isn't chewing through the TV cable again.

My biggest assumption: You have an Android phone. It can be any Android phone from any manufacturer supported by any popular cellular service provider in the United States. Because Android is an operating system (just like Windows for a PC), the methods of doing things on one Android phone are similar, if not identical, to doing things on another Android phone. Therefore, one book pretty much covers a lot of ground.

Specifically, this book covers the Gingerbread version of the Android phone operating system. It's version 2.3, which you can check on your phone by following these steps:

1. **At the Home screen, press the Menu soft button.**
2. **Choose Settings, and then choose About Phone.**
3. **Look at the item titled Android Version.**

   The number that's shown should be 2.3.x, where the x is another number. Even if the number is 2.2.x, you're good to go for this book.

Don't fret if these steps confuse you: Review Part I of this book, and then come back here. (I'll wait.)

More assumptions:

I also assume that you have a computer, either a desktop or laptop. The computer can be a PC, or Windows, computer or a Macintosh. Oh, I suppose that it can also be a Linux computer. In any event, I refer to your computer as "your computer" throughout this book. When directions are specific to a PC or Mac, the book says so.

Programs that run on your Android phone are *apps*, which is short for *applications*. A single program is an app.

Finally, this book assumes that you have a Google account, but if you don't, Chapter 2 explains how to configure one. Do so. Having a Google account opens up a slew of useful features, information, and programs that make using your phone more productive.

How This Book Is Organized

This book has been sliced into six parts, each of which describes a certain aspect of the typical Android phone or how it's used.

Part I: Have a Little Android

This part of the book serves as an introduction to your Android phone. Chapters cover setup and orientation and familiarize you with how the phone works. Part I is a good place to start — plus, you discover things in this part that aren't obvious from just guessing how the phone works.

Part II: The Phone Part

Nothing is more basic for a phone to do than make calls, which is the topic of the chapters in this part of the book. As you may have suspected, your phone can make calls, receive calls, and serve as an answering service for calls you miss. It also manages the names of all the people you know and even those you don't want to know but have to know anyway.

Part III: Mobile Communications

The modern cell phone is about more than just telephone communications. Part III of this book explores other ways you can use your phone to stay in touch with people, browse the Internet, check your e-mail, do your social networking, exchange text messages, engage in video chats, and more.

Part IV: Amazing Android Phone Feats

This part of the book explores the nonphone things your phone can do. For example, your phone can find locations on a map, give you verbal driving directions, take pictures, shoot videos, play music, play games, and do all sorts of wonderful things that no one would ever think a phone can do. The chapters in this part of the book get you up to speed on those activities.

Part V: Nuts and Bolts

The chapters in this part of the book discuss a slate of interesting topics, from connecting the phone to a computer, using Wi-Fi and Bluetooth networking, and taking the phone overseas and making international calls to customizing and personalizing your phone and the necessary chores of maintenance and troubleshooting.

Part VI: The Part of Tens

Finally, this book ends with the traditional *For Dummies* The Part of Tens, where every chapter lists ten items or topics. For your Android phone, the chapters include tips, tricks, shortcuts, and things to remember, plus a list of some of my favorite Android phone apps.

Icons Used in This Book

This icon flags useful, helpful tips or shortcuts.

This icon marks a friendly reminder to do something.

This icon marks a friendly reminder *not* to do something.

This icon alerts you to overly nerdy information and technical discussions of the topic at hand. Reading the information is optional, though it may win you a pie slice in *Trivial Pursuit.*

Where to Go from Here

Thank you for reading the introduction. Few people do, and it would save a lot of time and bother if they did. Consider yourself fortunate, though you probably knew that.

Your task now: Start reading the rest of the book — but not the whole thing, and especially not in order. Observe the table of contents and find something that interests you. Or, look up your puzzle in the index. When these suggestions don't cut it, just start reading Chapter 1.

My e-mail address is dgookin@wambooli.com. Yes, that's my real address. I reply to all e-mail I receive, and you get a quick reply if you keep your question short and specific to this book. Although I enjoy saying "Hi," I cannot answer technical support questions, resolve billing issues, or help you troubleshoot your phone. Thanks for understanding.

 You can also visit my web page for more information or as a diversion: www.wambooli.com.

Occasionally, there are updates to technology books. If this book does have technical updates, they will be posted at:

www.dummies.com/go/androidphonesfdupdates

Enjoy this book and your Android phone!

Part I
Have a Little Android

The 5th Wave   By Rich Tennant

"You can do a lot with an Android phone, and I guess dressing one up in G.I. Joe clothes and calling it your little desk commander is okay, too."

Silent mode
Sound is ON

Airplane mode
Airplane mode is OFF

Sleep
Low power, instant on, wireless off

Power off

The era of the personal robot is still a few years away. Thank goodness! That length of time could mark the end of the human race as we know it. Robots are admittedly evil, at least according to every science fiction book and movie on the subject. So please treasure these last few years before the robot apocalypse begins.

While you're treasuring your time, you might find yourself armed with an Android cell phone. It isn't a robot (yet), and it isn't intent on destroying your life (yet). Still, it's something with which you're probably unfamiliar. Therefore, I've written this part of the book to get you up to speed and oriented with your new Android phone.

That Phone You Own

*I*t may have a fancy name, like a character in a science fiction novel or a sports hero. Or it can simply be a fancy number, perhaps with the letter *X* thrown in to spice it up. No matter what, the phone you own is an *Android* phone because it runs the Android operating system. Before getting into this detail, let me specify that the adventure you're about to undertake begins with removing the thing from the box and getting to know your new smartphone.

Liberation and Setup

The phone works best when you remove it from its box. The procedure differs depending on whether you're a technology nut or someone desperate to make a phone call. I prefer to gingerly open the box, delicately lifting the various flaps and tenderly setting everything aside. I even savor the industrial solvent smell. If you prefer, you can just dump everything on the tabletop. But be careful: Your phone may be compact, but it's not cheap.

Several useful items might be found inside your Android phone's box. Some of them are immediately useful, and others you should consider saving for later. Even if you've already opened the box and spread its contents across the table like some sort of tiny yard sale, take a few moments to locate and identify these specific items:

- The phone itself, which may be fully assembled or in two or more pieces
- Papers, instructions, a warranty, and perhaps a tiny, useless *Getting Started* pamphlet
- The phone's battery, which might already be installed inside the phone
- The phone's back cover, which also might already be on the phone
- The charger/data cable or USB cable
- The charger head, which is a wall adapter for the charger/data cable
- Other stuff, such as a SIM card holder or MicroSD card or other scary electronic tidbits

The phone itself may ship with a clingy, static, plastic cover over its screen, back, or other parts. The plastic thingies tell you where various features are located or how to install the battery. You can remove all plastic, clingy sheets at this time.

You might have been given, in addition to the items described in the preceding list, a bonus package of goodies from whoever sold you the phone. If the outfit is classy, you have a handy little tote bag with perhaps the Phone Company's logo on it. Inside the bag, you might find these items:

- A smart-looking, leatherette belt-clip phone holster
- A micro-USB car charger
- A car windshield mount
- Headphones
- Screen protectors
- A phone case
- A desktop dock or multimedia station
- Even more random pieces of paper

The most important doodad is the phone itself, which might require some assembly before you can use it; refer to the next section for directions.

You can safely set aside all this stuff until you put the phone together. I recommend keeping the instructions and other information as long as you own the phone: The phone's box makes an excellent storage place for that stuff — as well as for anything else you don't plan to use right away.

If anything is missing or appears to be damaged, immediately contact the folks who sold you the phone.

✔ The phone's box contains everything you need in order to use the phone. Anything extra you buy merely enhances the phone-using experience.

✔ See the later section "Adding accessories" for a description of various goodies you can obtain for the typical Android phone.

✔ If the *Getting Started* pamphlet is written in Spanish, turn it over. Often times the English and Spanish instructions are contained in one booklet but are written on opposite sides.

Phone Assembly

The vast majority of Android phones come disassembled in their boxes. The primary thing that's missing is the battery, which must be installed into the phone. The phone's back cover must then be attached. Only if your phone has no removable battery does it come fully assembled, and even then it may have a MicroSD card (memory) that you must install.

The most extreme assembly involves Android phones that require the battery, SIM card, and MicroSD card to be installed. The following sections offer a general idea of how everything fits together.

Oftentimes, the people who sell you the phone assemble the thing for you. That's a plus. Even so, it helps to know how to open your phone, access its guts, and reassemble it. Such knowledge comes in handy at a later time.

Opening the phone

Your cell phone isn't a refrigerator, and you don't need to open it all the time in the hope that the Sandwich Fairy will hand you a quick snack. But there are times when you may need to open the device, to replace the battery or access the MicroSD card.

If you've just received your phone, it might already be in an opened state. Skip to the next section for information on installing the battery.

The process of opening the phone involves removing its back cover. It happens in two general ways:

✔ Use your thumbs to slide the back cover up (or down) and lift it off the phone.

✔ Insert a thumbnail into the slot on the phone's top or edge, and pop off the back cover.

In either case, the phone is facing away from you when you pop off the back cover.

After the cover is removed, set it aside. You can then add or remove items from the phone's crammed interior.

- ✔ See the later section "Closing the phone" for information on replacing the back cover.

- ✔ If your new phone comes disassembled inside its box, the back cover may not be attached. Look for the cover and set it aside until after you've installed the battery and other components.

- ✔ Don't fret if you hear a clicking or popping sound when you pop off the back cover; this type of noise occurs normally when you remove a cover that doesn't slide off.

- ✔ Not every Android phone has a removable back cover. If yours doesn't, that's fine.

Installing the battery

The most common thing to install in a new Android phone is the battery. The battery is supplied separately inside the box, and unless the friendly folks at the Phone Store installed the battery for you, it's your job to stick it inside your new phone.

Before installing the battery, ensure that you don't first need to install other items in your phone. For example, some phones require installation of the MicroSD card before the battery is installed.

Obey these steps to stick the battery into your phone:

1. **If necessary, remove the battery from its plastic bag.**

2. **Remove the phone's back cover, as discussed in the preceding section.**

3. **Orient the battery.**

   The battery goes in only one way, but because of its shape, it can be inserted improperly.

   Look for an arrow or for written directions on the battery or inside the phone to find a hint to the proper orientation.

4. **Place the battery in the phone so that the contacts on the battery match the ones on the connector inside the phone.**

   Figure 1-1 illustrates an example of inserting the battery into an Android phone.

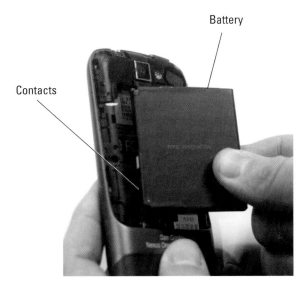

Figure 1-1: Sticking the battery in your phone.

5. Insert the battery the rest of the way, as though you're closing the lid on a tiny box.

When the battery is properly installed, it lies flush with the back of the phone.

After the battery is installed, your next step is to charge it. See the later section "Charge the Battery," and keep in mind that you may have additional items to install in your phone, as covered in the next several sections.

Removing the battery

It's not common, but you may need to remove the phone's battery. An example of a reason to replace the battery is to install a better model or access other items obscured by the battery inside the phone.

To remove the battery, follow these steps:

1. Remove the phone's back cover and set it aside.

2. Locate the "lift here" or "pull" tab on or around the battery.

3. Lift the battery out of the phone.

Just as you insert the battery, removing the battery works like opening the lid on a tiny box.

Set the battery aside.

If you're replacing the battery, store the original inside a nonmetallic box in a dark, dry location. If you need to dispose of the battery, do so properly; batteries are classified as hazardous waste and should not merely be placed in the trash can.

Installing the SIM card

A *SIM card* is used to identify a certain phone on a digital cellular network. Before you can use your phone, you must insert the SIM card into the phone's guts.

If the kind people at the Phone Store haven't installed the SIM card, you must do so yourself. Follow these steps:

1. **If necessary, remove the phone's back cover. Further, if required, remove the phone's battery.**

2. **Remove the SIM card from its container.**

   For a 4G LTE SIM card, pop the card out of the credit-card-size holder.

3. **Insert the SIM card into the SIM card slot inside your phone.**

   The SIM slot on some phones and mobile devices is on the device's outer edge. If so, open the tiny SIM slot cover and insert the SIM card into the slot.

   The SIM card is shaped in such a way that it's impossible to insert improperly. If the card doesn't slide into the slot, reorient the card and try again.

4. **Replace the battery and the phone's back cover.**

   You're done.

Well, you might want to skip Step 4, especially if you need to install a MicroSD card inside your phone. Keep reading in the next section.

- SIM stands for Subscriber Identity Module.

- You rarely, if ever, need to remove the SIM card.

- The SIM card can be used to store information, such as electronic messages and names and addresses, though you probably won't use this feature. See Chapter 8 for information on storing names and addresses on your Android phone.

- A typical way to use a SIM is to replace a broken phone with a new one: You plug the SIM from the old phone into the new phone, and instantly

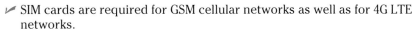

the phone is recognized as your own. Of course, the two phones need to use similar cellular networks for the transplant operation to be successful.

✔ SIM cards are required for GSM cellular networks as well as for 4G LTE networks.

Installing the MicroSD card

Many Android phones feature two forms of storage: internal and removable. Removable storage comes in the form of a memory card called the MicroSD card.

Not every phone uses the MicroSD card for storage. If yours does, you may have to install one. Further, if your phone didn't come supplied with a MicroSD card, either preinstalled or loose in the phone's box, you have to purchase one. In either case, you must install the card to get the most from your phone. Heed these directions:

1. **If necessary, remove the phone's back cover.**

2. **Locate the slot into which you stick the MicroSD card.**

   In some cases, you must remove the battery to access the MicroSD card slot.

3. **Insert the MicroSD card into the slot.**

   The card goes in only one way. If you're fortunate, a little outline of the card inside the phone illustrates the proper orientation.

   You may hear a faint clicking sound when the card is fully inserted.

4. **Reinstall the battery (if necessary), and reassemble the phone.**

To remove the card, open the phone and, if necessary, remove the battery. Push in the MicroSD card a tad, and a spring then releases the card and nudges it out a few fractions of an inch. Use your fingernail to help grab the card and pull it out the rest of the way.

✔ MicroSD cards are teensy! Keep them in a safe place where you won't lose them.

✔ Some MicroSD card adapters you can buy allow their data to be read by a computer, via either a standard Secure Digital (SD) memory slot or the USB port.

✔ If you're upgrading to a new Android phone, simply remove the MicroSD card from the old phone and install it on the new one. By doing so, you instantly transfer your pictures, music, and videos.

✔ MicroSD cards come in capacities rated in gigabytes (GB), just like most media storage or memory cards. Common MicroSD card capacities are 8GB, 16GB, and 32GB. The maximum size allowed on your phone depends on its design; some older phones cannot read higher-capacity MicroSD cards.

Closing the phone

When you're done with phone surgery, you need to close up the patient. Specifically, you must reinstall anything you removed — battery, SIM card, MicroSD card — and reattach the back cover.

The back cover affixes itself to the phone in the reverse manner in which it was removed:

✔ Position the cover over any slots or tab holes, and then use your thumbs to slide the back cover up (or down) to secure it on the phone.

✔ Position the cover directly over the back of the phone, and then press it gently on all sides to seal it shut.

When the back cover is on properly, you should see no gaps or raised edges. If the cover doesn't seem to go on all the way, try again. Never force it!

Charge the Battery

The phone's battery may have enough oomph in it to run the setup-and-configuration process at the Phone Store. If so, count yourself lucky. Otherwise, you need to charge the phone's battery. Don't worry about flying a kite and waiting for a lightning storm. Instead, follow these steps:

1. **If necessary, assemble the charging cord.**

   Connect the charger head (the plug thing) to the USB cable that comes with the phone. They connect in only one way.

2. **Plug the charger head and cable into a wall socket.**

3. **Plug the phone into the USB cable.**

   The charger cord plugs into the micro-USB connector, found at the phone's side or bottom. The connector plugs in only one way.

As the phone charges, a notification light on the phone's front side may glow. Some phones may use lights in different colors to show that the phone is charging, such as orange yellow or blinking green.

The phone may turn on when you plug it in for a charge. That's okay, but read Chapter 2 to find out what to do the first time the phone turns on. You also may need to contact your cellular provider for additional setup instructions before you turn on the phone.

- I recommend fully charging the phone before you use it.

- An Android phone's notification light commonly glows a steady green when it's fully charged.

- Not every Android phone has a notification light. In this case, you hear notification sounds to alert you to the battery's state.

- I've seen notification lights that use three colors: amber for charging, green for fully charged, and scary red for warning that the battery is low. Not every Android phone uses these colors.

- You can use the phone while it's charging.

- You can charge the phone in your car, using what was once called a cigarette lighter. Simply ensure that your car cell phone charger features the proper connector for your phone or that it's specifically designed for use with your cell phone brand.

- The phone also charges itself whenever it's plugged into a computer by way of a USB cable. The computer must be on for charging to work.

- Cell phones charge more quickly when plugged into the wall than to a computer's USB port or a car adapter.

- Many Android phones use the micro-USB connector. This connector has a flat, trapezoid shape, which makes it different from the mini-USB connector, which is squat and slightly larger and used primarily on evil cell phones.

Generic Android Phone Orientation

First impressions are everlasting. Your Android phone is, no doubt, a new thing. It's also an important thing that will grow to become an important part of your life. Now is not the time to botch your introduction!

It helps to know what's what on your new phone. Rather than fumble to find things later and never learn the names of its doodads, take a few seconds to examine your phone and locate important features and points of interest.

Recognizing things on your phone

I think it's cute when people refer to things they don't know as a doodad or thingamabob. Cute, but inaccurate. Take a gander at Figure 1-2, which illustrates common things found on the front and back of a typical Android cell phone.

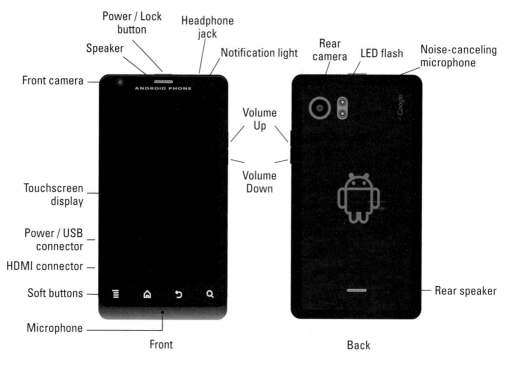

Power / Lock button
Headphone jack
Speaker
Notification light
Rear camera
LED flash
Noise-canceling microphone
Front camera
Volume Up
Volume Down
Touchscreen display
Power / USB connector
HDMI connector
Soft buttons
Rear speaker
Microphone

Front   Back

Figure 1-2: Your phone's face and rump.

The terms referenced in Figure 1-2 are the same as the terms used elsewhere in this book and in whatever scant Android phone documentation exists.

Not shown in Figure 1-2 is a physical keyboard, found on several Android phone models. The keyboard might be found below the touchscreen, or it might be hidden behind the touchscreen. See Chapter 4 for additional information on your phone's keyboard.

   ✔ The phone's Power Lock button, which turns the phone off or on, is found atop the phone, as shown in Figure 1-2, or it may be on the side.

   ✔ The main part of the phone is its *touchscreen* display. You use the touchscreen with one or more of your fingers to control the phone, which is where it gets the name *touch*screen.

- Not every Android phone features a front-facing camera.

- Some Android phones feature a pointing device, a trackball or keypad, that can be used to move a cursor to edit text, select links on a web page, or manipulate the phone in an interesting and useful manner. See Chapter 4 for details.

- The *soft buttons* appear below the touchscreen. Your phone may have two, three, or four of them, and they may sport different symbols depending on your phone's manufacturer. See Chapter 3 for more information.

- The *Power / USB connector* is the spot on the phone where you connect a USB cable. You use this cable to charge the phone or to communicate with a computer. See Chapter 20 for information on using the cable to connect to a computer and share files.

- Not every Android phone has an HDMI connector (refer to Figure 1-2). This connector allows the phone to use an external HDMI monitor or TV set to show movies, watch slide shows, or do other interesting things. See Chapter 20.

- The main microphone is found on the bottom of the phone. Even so, it picks up your voice loud and clear. You don't need to hold the phone at an angle for the microphone to work.

- The phone's volume can be adjusted by using the Volume button found on the phone's left or right side (refer to Figure 1-2).

- The Volume button might also be used as the Zoom function when using the phone's camera. See Chapter 15 for more information.

Using earphones

You don't need to use earphones to get the most from your Android phone, but it helps! If the nice folks who sold you the phone tossed in a pair earphones, that's wonderful! If they didn't, well then, they weren't so nice, were they?

The most common type of cell phone earphones are the *earbud* style: The buds are set into your ears. The sharp, pointy end of the earphones, which you don't want to stick into your ear, plugs into the top of the phone.

Between the earbuds and the sharp, pointy thing is often found a doodle on which a button sits. The button can be used to mute the phone or to start or stop the playback of music when the phone is in its music-playing mode.

You can also use the Doodle button to answer the phone when it rings.

A teensy hole that's usually on the back side of the doodle serves as the phone's microphone. The mic allows you to wear the earphones and talk on the phone while keeping your hands free. If you gesture while you speak, you'll find this feature invaluable.

✔ You can purchase any standard cell phone headset for use with your phone. Ensure that the headset features a microphone; you need to talk and listen on a phone.

✔ Some headsets feature extra doodle buttons. These headsets work fine with your phone, though the extra buttons may not do anything specific.

✔ The earbuds are labeled R for right and L for left.

✔ See Chapter 16 for more information on using your Android phone as a portable music player.

✔ Be sure to fully insert the earphone connector into the phone. The person you're talking with can't hear you well when the earphones are plugged in only part of the way.

✔ You can also use a Bluetooth headset with your phone, to listen to a call or some music. See Chapter 19 for more information on Bluetooth.

✔ Fold the earphones when you don't need them, as opposed to wrapping them in a loop. Put the earbuds and connector in one hand, and then pull the wire straight out with the other hand. Fold the wire in half and then in half again. You can then put the earphones in your pocket or on a tabletop. By folding the wires, you avoid creating one of those wire balls made of Christmas tree lights.

Adding accessories

Beyond earphones, you can find an entire Phone Store full of accessories and baubles you can obtain for your Android phone. The variety is seemingly endless, and the prices, well, they ain't cheap.

Docking station

A *docking station* is a heavy base into which you can set your phone. The most basic model simply props up the phone so that you can easily see it. I use the basic docking station on my nightstand, where my Android phone serves as my alarm clock. (See Chapter 17.)

More advanced docking stations offer HDMI output, USB connections, and perhaps even a laptop-size screen and keyboard.

Car mount

If you plan to use the phone while driving, a car mount is a must-have item. It provides a cradle into which you set your Android phone. It may also have a cable you can use to charge the phone while you drive. That way, the phone is handy and visible for making calls, listening to music, finding navigation instructions, or undertaking other interesting activities while you perilously navigate the roads.

Inductive charging coil

Though it sounds like a bogus technical term from the old *Star Trek* TV show, an inductive charging coil is a new technology you can really use. Basically, the coil replaces the battery and back cover so that you can wirelessly charge your phone. Not every Android phone manufacturer provides the inductive charging coil as an option.

HDMI cable

If your Android phone features an HDMI connector, you can obtain an HDMI cable. Using the cable, your phone can throw its sound and image onto a computer monitor or TV screen. It may sound like a silly thing at first, but I've used the HDMI cable on my Android phones so that the whole family can sit around our large-screen TV and enjoy rented movies. See Chapter 17 for more information about renting movies on your phone.

A Home for Your Phone

I've been in more than one older home that features a special vault in the wall, into which the phone was set. Later on, phones just sat on tables or were affixed to walls. Then came the cordless era, where phones were stored in couch cushions. Today's cell phones? They end up everywhere! Well, that is, unless you read my handy advice on where to store the phone, as described in this section.

Toting your Android phone

The compact design of the modern cell phone is perfect for a pocket or even the teensiest of party purses. It's well designed so that you can carry your phone in your pocket or handbag without fearing that something will accidentally turn it on, dial Mongolia, and run up a heck of a cell phone bill.

Your Android phone most likely features a proximity sensor, so you can even keep the phone in your pocket while you're on a call. The proximity sensor disables the touchscreen, which ensures that nothing accidentally gets touched when you don't want it to be touched.

✓ Though it's okay to place the phone somewhere when you're making a call, be careful not to touch the phone's Power Lock button (refer to Figure 1-2). Doing so may temporarily enable the touchscreen, which can hang up a call, mute the phone, or do any of a number of undesirable things.

✓ You can always store your phone in one of a variety of handsome carrying case accessories, some of which come in fine Naugahyde or leatherette.

✔ Don't forget that the phone is in your pocket, especially in your coat or jacket. You might accidentally sit on the phone, or it can fly out when you take off your coat. The worst fate for any cell phone is to take a trip through the wash. I'm sure the phone has nightmares about it.

Storing the phone

I recommend that you find a place for your phone when you're not taking it with you. Make the spot consistent: on top of your desk or workstation, in the kitchen, on the nightstand — you get the idea. Phones are as prone to being misplaced as are your car keys and glasses. Consistency is the key to finding your phone.

Then again, your phone rings, so when you lose it, you can always have someone else call your cell phone to help you locate it.

✔ Any of the various docking stations makes a handsome, permanent location for your Android phone.

✔ I store my phone on my desk, next to my computer. Conveniently, I have the charger plugged into the computer so that the phone remains plugged in, connected, and charging when I'm not using it.

✔ Phones on coffee tables get buried under magazines and are often squished when rude people put their feet on the furniture.

✔ Avoid putting your phone in direct sunlight; heat is bad news for any electronic gizmo.

✔ Do not put your phone in the laundry (see the preceding section). See Chapter 23 for information on properly cleaning the phone.

Setup and Configuration

As a sophisticated device, your Android phone doesn't just hop out of its box, introduce itself, and let you start making phone calls. Actually, come to think about it, popping out of the box in that manner *would* be quite sophisticated. Perhaps I meant to use the word *complicated* instead? Let me try again:

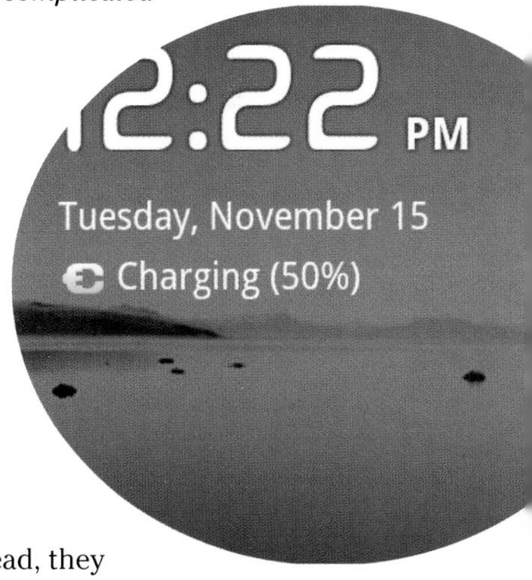

As a complicated device (yes, much better), your Android phone requires a bit of setup and configuration before you can get the most benefit from it. Sure, you can start making phone calls right away. But to get the most from your phone, you need to understand a few details, such as turning it on or off and getting the phone to work with your Google account on the Internet. This chapter describes all this madness in a calm and reassuring manner.

12:22 PM

Tuesday, November 15

Charging (50%)

Hello, Phone

Modern, technical gizmos lack an on–off switch. Instead, they feature power buttons. In the case of the typical Android phone, it's the *Power Lock* button, which might also be known as the *Power key*. This button can be used in several ways, which is why I had to write this section to explain things.

Turning on your phone for the first time

To turn on your phone for the first time, press its Power Lock button for a second or so. You may see the manufacturer's logo, the phone's brand name, or some fancy graphics and animation. What you're witnessing is the device's standard "I just woke up" start sequence.

Because this is the first time you've turned on your phone (reread the section heading), there are a few extra activities you must accomplish. Odds are good that the humans at the Phone Store completed these chores for you. If not, you can follow along with the instructions on the phone's touchscreen to activate your phone and set up your Google account.

Phone *activation* is what starts your new Android phone communicating with the cellular network. When the activation is complete, your phone can send and receive calls and access the Internet and other digital services.

To get the most from your Android phone, you need a Google account. If you have one, great. If not, refer to the later section "Google Account Setup" to get started.

By setting up your Google account, you coordinate whatever information you have on the Internet with your new Android phone. This information includes your e-mail messages and contacts on Gmail, appointments on Google Calendar, and information and data from other Google Internet applications.

The process for setting up the Google account involves typing your Gmail e-mail account name and password. Touch the Next button on the touchscreen to continue the steps. Here are some hints and suggestions to help you complete the setup process:

- Touch a text field to summon the onscreen keyboard. Use this keyboard to fill in the blanks. Chapter 4 covers using your phone's keyboard if you need tips or suggestions.

- You can also use your phone's physical keyboard, if it has one.

- Text typed into a password field appears briefly but is then replaced by black dots. The dots prevent prying eyes from purloining your password.

- You can touch the Done key to hide the onscreen keyboard, if it obscures part of the screen.

- If you're prompted for location services, ensure that you activate them all. You need these services in order to best use the phone's mapping and location abilities.

✔ After the initial setup, you're taken to the Home screen. Chapter 3 offers more Home screen information, which you should probably read right away, before the temptation to play with your new phone becomes unbearable.

Turning on the phone

Unlike turning on the phone for the first time, turning it on at any other time isn't that involved. In fact, under normal circumstances, you probably won't turn off your phone that much.

To turn on your Android phone, press and hold the Power Lock button for a moment. Eventually, you see a logo and perhaps some animation. You may hear sound effects, and the phone may even vibrate. Such drama.

Eventually, you're plopped onto an unlocking screen.

Figure 2-1 shows several different unlocking screens. The generic Android unlocking screen is the standard one, though your phone manufacturer may have conjured up a fancy one, as shown by the Motorola Droid 3 and HTC Thunderbolt unlocking screens, also illustrated in Figure 2-1.

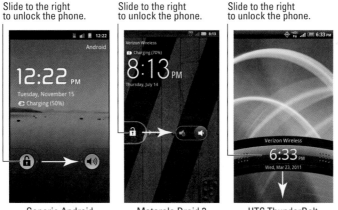

Slide to the right to unlock the phone. | Slide to the right to unlock the phone. | Slide to the right to unlock the phone.

Generic Android | Motorola Droid 3 | HTC ThunderBolt

Figure 2-1: Unlocking the phone.

To work the unlocking screen, touch your finger to the screen and move it in the direction indicated in Figure 2-1. Upon success, the phone is unlocked and you see the Home screen, which is where all the action takes place. Chapter 3 discusses the many things you can do at the Home screen.

✔ It isn't necessary to unlock the phone for an incoming call. For information on receiving phone calls, see Chapter 5.

✔ Additional locking screens are available on your Android phone, each of which is more sophisticated than the simple lock shown in Figure 2-1. See Chapter 22 for information about the Pattern, PIN, and Password lock screens.

✔ After unlocking the phone, you may hear alerts or see notifications. These messages inform you of various activities taking place in the phone, such as new e-mail, scheduled appointments, updated apps, and more. See Chapter 3 for information on notifications.

✔ Even if the phone has a security pattern, PIN, or password lock screen, you can still make emergency calls by touching the Emergency Call button.

✔ Android phones have different looks, and different unlocking screens, depending on their *skins*. That's the term used to describe the visual interface, effects, and animation a manufacturer uses to make its Android phone line look different from the generic Android phone.

Waking the phone

Most of the time, you don't turn off your phone. Instead, the phone does the electronic equivalent of falling asleep. Either it falls asleep on its own (after you ignore it for a while) or you put it to sleep by singing it a lullaby or following the information in the section "Snoozing the phone," later in this chapter.

In Sleep mode, the phone is still on and it can still receive calls (as well as e-mail and other notifications), but the touchscreen is turned off. See Chapter 5 for the specifics on how an incoming call wakes up the phone.

When the phone isn't ringing, you can wake it at any time by pressing the Power Lock button. A simple, short press is all that's needed. The phone awakens, yawns, and turns on the touchscreen display, and you can then unlock the phone as described in the preceding section.

✔ Touching the touchscreen when the screen is off doesn't wake up the phone.

✔ Loud noises don't wake up the phone.

✔ The phone doesn't snore while it's sleeping.

✔ See the later section "Snoozing the phone" for information on manually putting the phone to sleep.

  ✔ When your phone is playing music, which it can do while it's sleeping,
     information about the song appears on the lock screen (not shown in
     Figure 2-1). Touch the information to see controls to play and pause or
     to skip to the next or previous song. See Chapter 16 for more informa-
     tion on using an Android phone as a portable music player.

Google Account Setup

I'm serious: To get the most from your Android phone, you need a Google
account. Let me clarify: You need a *free* Google account. I hope that the *free*
part entices you.

You need a Google account because the Android operating system, which
your phone uses, was developed by Google — and because your phone and
the various Google services on the Internet work together to create an ideal,
21st century information resource.

If you don't believe me now, you'll definitely believe me after reading about
all the amazing things your phone can do — specifically, topics covered in
Parts III and IV of this book. Until then, don't doubt me further: If you don't
already have a Google account, set one up right now by following my advice
in this section.

Creating a Google account

If you don't already have a Google account, run — don't walk or trot — to a
computer and follow these steps to create your own Google account:

  1. **Open the computer's web browser program.**

  2. **Visit the main Google page at** www.google.com.

     Type **www.google.com** into the web browser's Address box.

  3. **Click the Sign In link.**

     Another page opens, where you can log in to your Google account, but
     you don't have a Google account, so:

  4. **Click the link to create a new account.**

     The link is typically found beneath the text boxes where you would log
     in to your Google account. As I write this chapter, the link is titled Sign
     Up for a New Google Account.

  5. **Continue heeding the onscreen directions until you've created your
     own Google account.**

Eventually, your account is set up and configured. I recommend that you log off and then log back on to Google, just to ensure that you did everything properly. Also create a bookmark for your account's Google page: Pressing Ctrl+D or Command+D does the job in just about any web browser.

Continue reading in the next section for information on synchronizing your new Google account with your Android phone.

✓ A Google account is free. Google makes zillions of dollars by selling Internet advertising, so it doesn't charge you for your Google account or any of the fine services it offers.

✓ The Google account gives you access to a wide array of free services and online programs. They include Gmail for electronic messaging, Calendar for scheduling and appointments, and an account on YouTube, along with Google Finance, blogs, Google Talk, and other features that are also instantly shared with your phone.

✓ Information on using the various Google programs on your phone is covered throughout this book — specifically, in Part IV.

Setting up a Google account on your phone

If you haven't yet configured a Google account, follow the steps in the preceding section and then continue with these steps:

1. Go to the Home screen.

The Home screen is the main screen on your phone. You can always get there by pressing the Home soft button, found at the bottom of the touchscreen.

2. Press the Menu soft button.

The Menu soft button is found at the bottom of the touchscreen. It may be labeled Menu or feature an icon. Refer to Table 3-1, in Chapter 3, to see the variety of icons that can adorn the Menu soft button.

3. Choose the Settings command.

The Settings command allows you to access internal options, controls, and settings for configuring your Android phone. It's a popular place to visit while you read this book.

4. Choose Accounts or Accounts & Sync.

The title for the Accounts option varies, depending on your phone and which version of the Android operating system it uses.

5. Choose Add Account.

A list of accounts that you can add appears.

6. **Choose Google.**

7. **Work through the steps on the screen to sign into your Google account.**

   You need to type your Google username and password.

   Wait while the phone contacts the Internet and synchronizes your Google account information.

8. **If prompted, ensure that check marks appear by the all the Data & Synchronization options.**

   By placing check marks by all items, you ensure that the phone completely synchronizes with all your Google account information.

9. **Touch the Finish button.**

10. **Touch the Finish Setup button.**

    You're done.

Press the Home soft button to return to the Home screen.

➳ If you change your Google password and forget to tell the phone about it, you see an alert notification, as shown in the margin. Pull down the notifications and choose Sign In Error for your Google account. Follow the directions on the screen to update your Google password.

➳ See Chapter 3 for more information about the Home screen and the App menu.

➳ Other accounts can be synchronized with your Android phone, such as Facebook, Twitter, and Yahoo! Mail. Various chapters throughout this book explain how to configure these accounts.

Goodbye, Phone

You can dismiss your Android phone in one of several ways. The most popular way is to put the phone to sleep, to *snooze* it. Another way is to turn off the phone. The most difficult way to dismiss the phone involves an unblemished goat and a full moon, but this book just doesn't have room enough to properly describe that method.

Snoozing the phone

To put your Android phone to sleep, press and release the Power Lock button. No matter what you're doing, the phone's touchscreen display turns off. The phone itself isn't off, but the touchscreen display goes dark and ignores your touches. The phone enters a low-power state to save battery life and also to relax.

✔ You can snooze the phone while you're making a call. Simply press and release the Power Lock button. The call stays connected, but the display is turned off.

✔ Snooze mode lets you continue talking on the phone while you put it in your pocket. When the phone is in Snooze mode, your pocket is in no danger of accidentally hanging up the call or muting it.

✔ Your Android phone will probably spend most of its time in Snooze mode.

✔ Snoozing does not turn off the phone; you can still receive calls while the phone is somnolent.

✔ Any timers or alarms you set are still activated when the phone is snoozing, and music continues to play. See Chapter 17 for information on setting timers and alarms; Chapter 16 covers playing music.

Controlling snooze options

There's no need to manually snooze your phone. That's because it has a built-in time-out: After a period of inactivity, or boredom, the phone snoozes itself automatically by using the same techniques honed by high school algebra teachers.

You have control over the snooze timeout value, which can be set anywhere from 15 seconds to 30 minutes. Obey these steps:

1. **At the Home screen, press the Menu soft button.**

2. **Choose Settings.**

3. **Choose Display.**

4. **Choose Screen Timeout.**

5. **Choose a time-out value from the list that's provided.**

   The standard value is 1 minute.

6. **Press the Home soft button to return to the Home screen.**

When you don't touch the screen or you aren't using the phone, the sleep timer starts ticking. About ten seconds before the time-out value you set (refer to Step 5), the touchscreen dims. Then the phone goes to sleep. If you touch the screen before then, the sleep timer is reset.

Hibernating the phone

Some Android phones feature Sleep mode. It's similar to the Hibernation feature found on Windows computers: The phone is placed into a very-low-power state, one notch above turning the thing off. Pressing the Power Lock button when the phone is hibernating turns it on more quickly than when you turn the phone all the way off.

Here's how to put your phone into Hibernation-Sleep mode:

1. **Press and hold the Power Lock button.**

   Eventually, you see the Phone Options menu, shown in Figure 2-2. Some Android phones may refer to the menu as Power Options instead of Phone Options.

2. **Choose the Sleep item.**

   The phone seemingly turns itself off, but it's hibernating.

Figure 2-2: The Phone Options menu.

If you change your mind and don't want to hibernate the phone, press the Back soft button to cancel.

Your phone cannot receive phone calls while it's in Hibernation-Sleep mode, but it can be turned on quickly: Press and hold the Power Lock button. The phone snaps back to life a lot faster than had you just turned off the phone. (See the next section.)

Hibernation-Sleep mode is ideal for "turning off the phone" when you're traveling by air. See Chapter 21.

Turning off the phone

To turn off your phone, press and hold the Power Lock button and choose the Power Off item from the Phone Options menu, shown earlier, in Figure 2-2. You see some animation as the phone shuts itself off. Eventually, the touchscreen goes dark.

The phone doesn't receive calls when it's turned off. Calls are routed instead to voice mail. See Chapter 7 for more information on voice mail.

3

The Android Tour

In This Chapter

▷ Understanding the soft buttons

▷ Using the touchscreen

▷ Changing the phone's volume

▷ Entering Vibration mode or Silent mode

▷ Using the phone horizontally

▷ Viewing Home screen panels

▷ Checking notifications

▷ Running applications and working widgets

▷ Reviewing recently used apps

Your Android phone gets its name from the Android operating system. Like Windows and the Macintosh OS X, the Android operating system is a computer program. It's designed for controlling the phone but also for important human-gizmo communications. As with Windows and the Mac OS X, those communications require a bit more instruction than what's obvious on the screen. Therefore, I've written this chapter to help you understand and use the Android operating system on your cell phone.

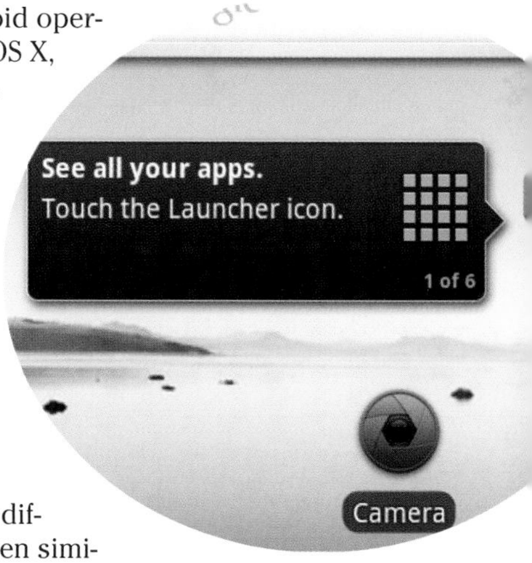

See all your apps.
Touch the Launcher icon.

1 of 6

Camera

Basic Operations

The way your Android phone does things is probably different from any other phone you've owned. It's not even similar to your computer. Rather than let you get frustrated or sit there befuddled by various new terms and jargon, I've crafted this section to orient you to basic operations and procedures for using the typical Android phone.

Using the soft buttons

Below the touchscreen on your Android phone dwell two to four buttons labeled with icons. They're *soft buttons,* and they perform specific functions no matter what you're doing on the phone. The most common buttons are Home, Menu, Back, and Search.

Home

Pressing the Home soft button displays the Home screen. It's kind of like the "quit" command in a computer program, and it works no matter what you're doing on your phone.

If you're already viewing the Home screen, pressing the Home soft button returns you to the main, center Home screen.

Pressing and holding the Home button displays a list of recently opened apps.

On some Android phones, you can press the Home soft button twice to activate the Double Tap Home Launch feature. It's a quick way to access common apps or phone features. See Chapter 22 for more information on this feature.

Menu

Pressing the Menu soft button displays a pop-up menu, from which you can choose commands to control whichever program you're using. You can press the Menu soft button again to hide the pop-up menu. If nothing happens when you press the Menu soft button, no pop-up menu is available.

On some phones, pressing and holding the Menu button summons the onscreen keyboard.

Every Android phone manufacturer tends to use its own symbol for the Menu soft button. Here are some varieties:

MENU

Believe it or not, the word *Menu* is the standard Android icon for the Menu soft button.

Back

The Back soft button serves several purposes, all of which fit neatly under the concept of "back." Press the soft button once to go back to a previous page, close a menu, close a window, dismiss the onscreen keyboard, and so on. I'm certain that the Back soft button is the one you'll press most often.

Search

The Search soft button is your direct connection to the phone's powerful Search command. It is, after all, a Google phone. Press the Search soft button once to summon the Phone-and-web search command. Or you can press the Search soft button in a specific app, such as Contacts (the phone's address book), to search within the app.

See Chapter 8 for more information on your phone's address book app.

On some Android phones, you press and hold the Search soft button to bring up the Voice Actions menu. You can then dictate a command into the phone. See Chapter 4 for more information on the Voice Command app.

Other phone buttons

Your phone may feature additional soft buttons, though they're not the traditional Android soft buttons. For example, many phones feature a green Answer button and a red Hang Up button. Though these buttons are useful for making and ending calls, they aren't part of the Amazon soft-button pantheon.

Manipulating the touchscreen

The touchscreen works in combination with one or two of your fingers. You can choose which fingers to use, or whether to be adventurous and try using the tip of your nose, but touch the touchscreen you must. Choose from several techniques:

Touch: In this simple operation, you touch the screen. Generally, you're touching an object such as a program icon or a control such as a gizmo that you use to slide something around. You might also see the term *press* or *tap*.

Double-tap: Touch the screen in the same location twice. A double-tap can be used to zoom in on an image or a map, but it can also zoom out. Because of the double-tap's dual nature, I recommend using the pinch and spread operations instead.

Long-press: Touch and hold part of the screen. Some operations, such as moving an icon on the Home screen, begin with the long-press.

Swipe: When you swipe, you start with your finger in one spot and then drag it to another spot. Usually, a swipe is up, down, left, or right, which moves displayed material in the direction you swipe your finger. A swipe can be fast or slow. It's also called a *flick*.

Pinch: A pinch involves two fingers, which start out separated and then are brought together. The pinch is used to zoom out on an image or a map.

Common Android icons

Beyond the soft buttons are certain symbols that commonly appear in many Android apps. Here's a sample:

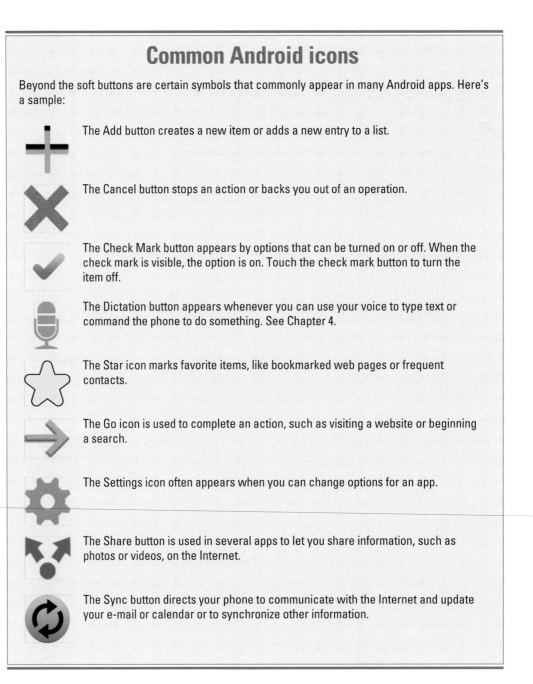

The Add button creates a new item or adds a new entry to a list.

The Cancel button stops an action or backs you out of an operation.

The Check Mark button appears by options that can be turned on or off. When the check mark is visible, the option is on. Touch the check mark button to turn the item off.

The Dictation button appears whenever you can use your voice to type text or command the phone to do something. See Chapter 4.

The Star icon marks favorite items, like bookmarked web pages or frequent contacts.

The Go icon is used to complete an action, such as visiting a website or beginning a search.

The Settings icon often appears when you can change options for an app.

The Share button is used in several apps to let you share information, such as photos or videos, on the Internet.

The Sync button directs your phone to communicate with the Internet and update your e-mail or calendar or to synchronize other information.

Spread: In the opposite of a pinch, you start with your fingers together and then spread them. The spread is used to zoom in.

Rotate: Use two fingers to twist around a central point on the touchscreen, which has the effect of rotating an object on the screen. If you have trouble with this operation, pretend that you're turning the dial on a safe.

You cannot use the touchscreen while wearing gloves, unless they're gloves specially designed for using electronic touchscreens, such as the gloves that Batman wears.

Setting the volume

The phone's volume control is found on the side of the phone. Press the top part of the button to raise the volume. Press the bottom part of the button to lower the volume.

A volume control works for whatever noise the phone is making when you use it: When you're on a call, the volume controls set the level of the call. When you're listening to music or watching a video, the volume controls set the media volume.

The volume can be preset for the phone or its media, alarms, and notifications. See Chapter 22 for more information.

"Silence your phone!"

You cannot be a citizen of the 21st century and not have heard the admonition "Please silence your cell phones." The quick way to obey this command with your Android phone is to keep pressing the Volume Down button until the phone vibrates. What you're doing is setting the phone to a combination of Silent mode and Vibration mode.

The phone can also be silenced by a swipe of your finger. Obey these steps:

1. **Wake up the phone.**

   Obviously, if the phone is turned off, you have no need to turn it on just to make it silent. So, assuming that your phone is snoozing, press the Power Lock button to see the unlock screen (refer to Figure 2-1, in Chapter 2).

2. **Slide the Silencer button to the left.**

   You're good.

Finally, you can thrust the phone into Silent mode by pressing and holding the Power Lock button. From the Phone Options menu, choose Silent Mode.

- Some Android skins, such as the HTC Sense, lack a quick-and-dirty silencing method from the lock screen. For these phones, you have to rely on the Volume Down button method.

- When the phone is silenced, the Silenced icon appears on the status bar.

- When the phone is in Vibration mode, the Vibration icon appears on the status bar.

- The sample icons shown in the margin are only two examples of how the Silenced and Vibration icons might look.

- You make the phone noisy again by undoing the directions in this section.

- The phone doesn't vibrate if you've turned off that option. See Chapter 22.

Changing the orientation

Android phones feature an *accelerometer* gizmo. It's used by various apps to determine in which direction the phone is pointed or whether you've reoriented the phone from an upright to a horizontal position.

The easiest way to see how the vertical-horizontal orientation feature works is to view a web page on your phone. Obey these steps:

1. **Touch the Browser app on the Home screen.**

   On some phones, the web browser app may be named Internet, and it may not always be on the Home screen. Regardless, when the web browser app starts, it moseys on out to the Internet. Eventually, the browser's first page, the *home page,* appears on the touchscreen.

2. **Tilt the phone to the left.**

   As shown in Figure 3-1, the web page reorients itself to the new, horizontal way of looking at the web. For some applications, it's truly the best way to see things.

3. **Tilt the phone upright again.**

   The web page redisplays itself in its original, upright mode.

You can also tilt the phone to the right to view the touchscreen in Landscape mode. Either way, the phone displays a web page horizontally, though it's more difficult to use the sliding keyboard when the phone is tilted to the right.

Oh, and don't bother turning the phone upside down and expect the image to flip that way, though some applications may delight you by supporting this feature.

Portrait orientation   Landscape orientation

Figure 3-1: Vertical and horizontal orientations.

> ✔ See Chapter 11 for more information on using your phone to browse the web.

> ✔ Most apps switch the view from portrait to landscape orientation when you tilt the phone. A few apps, however, are fixed to portrait orientation. Other apps, mostly games, appear only in portrait or landscape orientation.

> ✔ A useful application for demonstrating the phone's accelerometer is the game _Labyrinth_. It can be purchased at the Google Play Store, or a free version, _Labyrinth Lite,_ can be downloaded. See Chapter 18 for more information on the Google Play Store.

Behold the Home Screen

The first thing you see after you unlock your Android phone is the _Home screen_. It's the place to go whenever you end a phone call or quit an app, or when you press the Home soft button. Knowing how to work the Home screen is the key to getting the most from your phone.

Looking at the Home screen

The generic Android Home screen is shown in Figure 3-2. The image shown in the figure is doubtless a lot more boring than your phone's Home screen. But the generic Home screen helps you identify some basic points of interest.

Status bar: The top of the Home screen is a thin, informative strip that I call the _status bar_. It contains notification icons and status icons plus the current time.

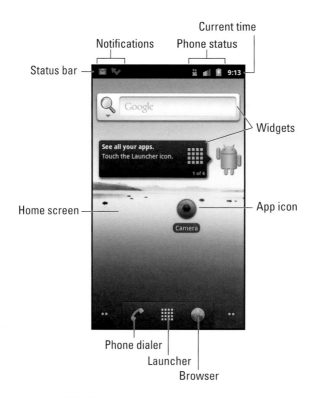

Figure 3-2: The Home screen.

Notifications: These icons come and go, depending on what happens in your digital life. For example, a new notification icon appears whenever you receive a new e-mail message or have a pending appointment. The section "Reviewing notifications," later in this chapter, describes how to deal with notifications.

Phone status: Icons on the right end of the status bar represent the phone's current condition, such as the type of network it's connected to, its signal strength and battery status, as well as whether the speaker has been muted or a Wi-Fi network connected, for example.

Widget: This teensy program can display information, let you control the phone, manipulate a phone feature, access a program, or do something purely amusing. You can read more about widgets in Chapter 22.

App icon: The meat of the meal on the Home screen plate is the App icon. Touching this icon runs its program, or *app.*

Phone Dialer: It's really an app icon, but you use the Phone Dialer to make calls. It's kind of a big deal.

Launcher: Touching the Launcher button displays the App menu, a paged list of all apps installed on your phone. The section "The App Menu," later in this chapter, describes how it works.

Other icons may dwell at the bottom of the Home screen. In Figure 3-2, the Browser icon appears. On some phones, the icons at the bottom of the screen form the *Dock*, which is a clutch of apps that remain at the bottom of every Home screen panel. See the next section for a discussion of Home screen panels.

The terms used in this section describe items on the Home screen. The terms are used throughout this book, as well as in whatever pitiful documentation exists for your phone. Specific directions for using individual Home screen gizmos are found throughout this chapter.

  ✔ The Home screen is entirely customizable. You can add and remove icons from the Home screen, add widgets and shortcuts, and even change wallpaper images. See Chapter 22 for more information.

  ✔ Touching part of the Home screen that doesn't feature an icon or a control does nothing — unless you're using the *live wallpaper* feature. In that case, touching the screen changes the wallpaper in some way, depending on the wallpaper that's selected. You can read more about live wallpaper in Chapter 22.

Viewing all Home screen panels

And now, the secret: The Home screen is several times wider than the one you see on the front of your Android phone. The Home screen has left and right wings. It could be three screens wide, it could be five, it could be seven. It could be more! The limit is set by your phone manufacturer and however it has modified the Android operating system.

Multiple Home screen panels give you more opportunities to place app icons and widgets on the Home screen. You switch between them by swiping your finger left or right across the touchscreen display. The Home screen slides over one panel in whichever direction you swipe.

  ✔ Some Home screens display panel indicators on the bottom of the screen, as shown earlier, in Figure 3-2. The indicators show you either which Home screen panel you're viewing or how many panels are to the left or right of the current Home screen.

  ✔ You might be able to see an overview of all Home screen panels: Press the Home soft button twice.

  ✔ You can touch a panel on the Home screen panel overview to instantly move to that panel.

✔ Some modifications to the Android operating system allow you to move the Home screen panels around while you're viewing the overview screen. You might also be able to add or remove panels; touch the Menu soft button to see whether any options appear while viewing the Home screen overview.

Using the Car Home

Your phone may also feature an alternative Home screen, provided for the scary proposition of using the phone while driving an automobile. The Car Home screen, designed to be easy to see at a glance, offers you access to the phone's more popular features without distracting you too much from the priority of piloting your car.

The Car Home screen appears automatically whenever your Android phone is nestled into a car mount phone holder accessory, discussed in Chapter 1. Touch the big buttons to access popular phone features. To return to the standard Home screen, press the Menu soft button and then the Exit command.

See Chapter 14 for information on using your Android phone for navigation, a handy feature available directly from the Car Home screen.

Home Screen Operations

I recommend getting to know three basic Home screen operations: reviewing notifications, starting programs, and using widgets.

Reviewing notifications

Notifications are represented by icons at the top of the Home screen, as illustrated earlier, in Figure 3-2. To see what the notifications say, peel down the top part of the screen, as shown in Figure 3-3.

The operation works like this:

1. **Touch the notification icons at the top of the touchscreen.**

2. **Swipe your finger all the way down the front of the touchscreen.**

   This action works like you're controlling a roll-down blind: Grab the top part of the touchscreen and drag it downward all the way. The notifications appear in a list, as shown in Figure 3-4.

   Drag the notification list all the way to the bottom of the touchscreen, to prevent it from rolling up again. Use the notification panel control to pull the list all the way down, as shown in Figure 3-4.

3. **Touch a notification to see what's up.**

Notification icon

Touch here.

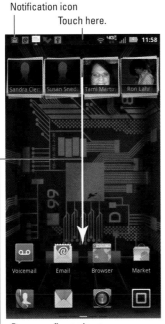

Drag your finger down
to display the notifications.

Figure 3-3: Accessing notifications
on the Droid Bionic.

Touching a notification opens the app that generated the alert. For example, touching the Gmail notification displays a new message in the inbox.

If you choose not to touch a notification, you can "roll up" the notification list by sliding the panel control back to the top of the touchscreen or by pressing the Back soft button.

✔ A notification icon doesn't disappear after you look with it — and those icons can stack up!

✔ Some Android phones allow you to dismiss individual notifications by touching the red Delete button (refer to Figure 3-4). There's no confirmation after you touch the Delete button.

✔ To dismiss all notification icons, touch the Clear button, shown in Figure 3-4.

✔ When more notifications are present than can be shown on the status bar, you see the More Notifications icon displayed, as shown in the margin. The number on the icon indicates how many additional notifications are available. (The More Notifications icon may not look exactly like the one shown in the margin.)

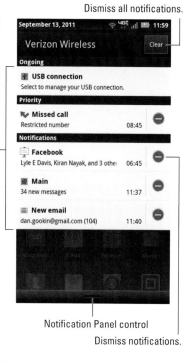

Touch a notification to
see more information
or deal with an issue.

Dismiss all notifications.

Notification Panel control

Dismiss notifications.

Figure 3-4: The notifications list for the
Droid Bionic.

✔ Dismissing notifications doesn't prevent them from appearing again
later. For example, notifications to update your programs continue to
appear, as do calendar reminders.

✔ Some programs, such as Facebook and Twitter, don't display notifications unless you're logged in. See Chapter 12.

✔ When new notifications are available, the phone's notification light flashes.
Refer to Chapter 1 for information on locating the notification light.

✔ Notification icons appear on the screen when the phone is locked. You
must unlock the phone before you can drag down the status bar to display notifications.

Starting an app

It's cinchy to run an app on the Home screen: Touch its icon. The app starts.

> ✔ Not all apps appear on the Home screen, but all of them appear when you display the App menu. See the section "The App Menu," a little later in this chapter.

> ✔ Whenever an app closes or you quit the app, you return to the Home screen.

> ✔ App is short for *application*.

Using a widget

A *widget* is a teensy program that "floats" over the Home screen, as shown earlier, in Figure 3-3. To use a widget, simply touch it. What happens after that depends on the widget.

For example, touching the Google Search widget displays the onscreen keyboard and lets you type, or dictate, something to search for on the Internet. For example, a weather widget may display information about the current weather, or a social networking widget may display status updates or tweets.

Information on these and other widgets appears elsewhere in this book. See Chapter 22 for information on working with widgets.

The App Menu

The place where you find all applications installed on your Android phone is on the *App menu*. It may be given other names in your phone's documentation, but I call it the App menu.

Even though you can find shortcut app icons on the Home screen, the App menu is where you need to go to find *everything*.

Starting an app from the Apps screen

The key to unlocking the App menu is to touch the Launcher icon on the Home screen. Though there's only one Launcher, your phone may have a different icon to represent it. Figure 3-5 illustrates the variety of available buttons, though more may still be out there.

Generic Android Original Droid Droid X2 AT&T Atrix Droid Bionic

Figure 3-5: Launcher button icon varieties.

After you touch the Launcher icon, you see the App menu screen. You can swipe through the icons by dragging your finger up or down — or left and right — across the touchscreen.

To run an app, touch its icon. The app starts, taking over the screen and doing whatever magical thing the app does.

> ✔ To help you locate a lost app, or one whose name you might have forgotten, press the Search soft button while viewing the App menu. Type all or part of the app's name. As you type, items whose names match the letters you've typed appear in the list. The word *Application* appears beneath the program name of any application in the list.

> ✔ Some versions of the Android operating system feature a Group menu on the App screen. You can use this menu to view different groups of apps, from all apps to recently opened apps or from downloaded apps to groups you create yourself.

> ✔ Creating app groups is covered in Chapter 18, along with information on downloading apps from the Google Play Store.

> ✔ The terms *program*, *application,* and *app* all mean the same thing.

Reviewing recently used apps

If you're like me, you probably use the same apps over and over, on both your computer and your phone. You can easily access the list of recent programs on your Android phone by pressing and holding the Home soft button. When you do, you see a list of the most recently accessed programs.

Choose a recent app from the list to open that app again or to return to the app if it's already open and running.

To exit the list of recently used apps, press the Back soft button.

You can press and hold the Home soft button in any application at any time to see the recently used apps list.

For programs you use all the time, consider creating shortcuts on the Home screen. Chapter 22 describes how to create shortcuts to apps, as well as shortcuts to people and shortcuts to instant messaging and all sorts of fun stuff.

4

Text to Type, Text to Edit

Typing on a phone. It sounds like a joke. At least my grandmother would have thought it was a joke. Today it's not only a reality, it's a necessity: There's a lot of stuff you can type and edit on your Android phone, including text messages, e-mail, web page addresses, social networking updates, and maybe even that novel you have rumbling about in the back of your brain.

Okay, well, maybe you won't use your phone to write a novel.

Your Android phone may be one of the few that features a physical keyboard. If so, great: You can use this keyboard for typing. Otherwise, you'll use an onscreen keyboard, which is essentially a computer keyboard that is shrunk and made flat to fit on the touchscreen. You can type. You can edit. You can read this chapter to see how it's done. No joke.

Keyboard Mania

Unless you're two feet tall or have hands like a Barbie doll, typing on your cell phone takes some getting used to. Fortunately, the learning curve is low: The keyboard you use looks similar to the standard QWERTY keyboard found on your everyday computer. And typing works similarly as well: Touch a key to produce a character on the screen. Sounds simple enough.

The basic keyboard on all Android phones is, logically, the *Android keyboard*. I prefer to call it the *onscreen keyboard* because it appears on the touchscreen. Variations of the keyboard come from different phone manufacturers, but the basic keyboard and its operation are similar on all Android phones.

Your phone may also sport a real keyboard (albeit real tiny as well). This built-in keyboard may be located right below the touchscreen or is often hidden behind it. This hidden keyboard either slides out from under the touchscreen or becomes visible by flipping up the touchscreen.

Many folks find a real keyboard preferable over the touchscreen keyboard on their phones. Me? My fingers are too fat for built-in keyboards. Then again, they're too fat for the onscreen keyboard. Regardless, both keyboard types are covered in this section.

- *QWERTY* refers to the keyboard layout currently popular in English-speaking countries. The letters in QWERTY are the first six letters in the top row on the keyboard.

- Android phones also let you dictate text as opposed to or in addition to typing. See the section "Voice Input," later in this chapter.

Displaying the onscreen keyboard

The onscreen keyboard shows up any time your phone demands text as input, such as when you type an e-mail, write something on the web, or compose an inappropriate text message to your boss's wife.

Normally, the keyboard pops up immediately — for example, when you touch a text field or an input box on a web page. Then you start typing with your finger or — if you're good — your thumbs.

The alphabetic version of the onscreen keyboard is shown in Figure 4-1. The onscreen keyboard on your phone may feature a subtly different layout, though all the same (or similar) keys should be there.

Some special keys change their appearance and function depending on what you're typing. For example, when you're typing an e-mail address, the Microphone key may change to the @ key. Likewise, the Enter/Return key has its variations, as shown in Figure 4-1. Here's what those special keys do:

Enter/Return: Just like the Enter or Return key on a computer keyboard, touching this key ends a paragraph of text. It's used mostly when filling in long stretches of text or when multiline input is available.

Next: This key appears whenever you're typing information into multiple fields. Touching the key switches from one field to the next, such as when typing a username and password.

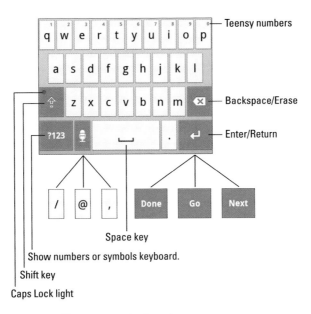

Teensy numbers

Backspace/Erase

Enter/Return

Space key

Show numbers or symbols keyboard.

Shift key

Caps Lock light

Figure 4-1: The onscreen keyboard.

Done: Use this key to dismiss the onscreen keyboard. Normally, this key appears whenever you finish typing text in the final field on a screen with several fields.

Go: This action key directs the app to proceed with a search, accept input, or perform another action.

The top row on the keyboard features teensy numbers (refer to Figure 4-1). To access these numbers, press and hold a key. For example, press and hold the P key to produce the 0 (zero) character.

The onscreen keyboard doesn't show all the characters you can type. To access those non-alphabetic characters, you need to display the symbols version of the onscreen keyboard. That's done by touching a special key, such as the ?123 key shown in Figure 4-1, though the key may be labeled differently on your phone. For example, the HTC Thunderbolt uses the 12# key to switch to the symbols keyboard(s).

To return to the QWERTY (alphabetic) keyboard layout from the symbols versions of the onscreen keyboard, touch the ABC key. Again, the key may be labeled something other than ABC on your phone; generally speaking, the key is in the same location as the key you touched to display the symbols keyboard layout(s).

Take a Swype at the old hunt-and-peck

You may be lucky and your phone manufacturer or cellular provider has blessed your Android phone with the Swype typing utility. It's designed to drastically improve your typing speed on a touchscreen phone. The secret to Swype is that you can type without lifting your finger; you literally swipe your finger over the touchscreen to rapidly type words.

Activate Swype by long-pressing any text box or location where you can type on the touchscreen. From the Edit Text menu, choose the Input Method item. Choose Swype. (If the Swype command isn't available, your phone probably lacks the Swype utility.)

To best understand Swype, use its onscreen Help system: Long-press the Swype key, illustrated nearby, to see the Swype Help menu. You can review the techniques for typing types of words, such as those with capital letters or double letters, and other tips. You can also touch the Tutorial button to learn how Swype works and pick up some typing tricks.

 ✔ Some keyboards feature even more teensy characters than the teensy numbers shown in Figure 4-1. Those teensy characters are accessed the same way: Press and hold the key. Also see the later section "Accessing special characters."

 ✔ Some applications show the keyboard when the phone is in landscape orientation. If so, the keyboard shows the same keys but offers more room for your stump-like fingers to type.

 ✔ Another type of onscreen keyboard is the Swype keyboard. See the following sidebar "Take a Swype at the old hunt-and-peck."

 ✔ See Chapter 22 for information on how to adjust the onscreen keyboard.

Choosing other keyboard variations

There are two variations on the Android keyboard: The first is the Compact QWERTY keyboard, and the second is the Phone Keypad keyboard. Both variations are shown in Figure 4-2.

The advantage of the Compact QWERTY keyboard is that you can type on it rather quickly by using your thumbs. The Phone Keypad keyboard is designed for those ancient cell phone users who grew accustomed to typing text using the standard phone dialpad.

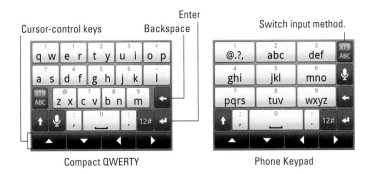

Figure 4-2: The Compact QWERTY and Phone Keypad keyboards.

To see whether these keyboard variations are available for your phone, heed these steps:

1. **At the Home screen, press the Menu soft button.**

2. **Choose Settings.**

3. **Choose Language & Keyboard.**

4. **Choose the command that controls the onscreen keyboard's settings.**

   The command is named after whatever term your phone manufacturer uses to refer to the onscreen keyboard: Touch Input or Multi-Touch, for example. The generic command name is Android Keyboard or Android Keyboard Settings.

5. **Choose Keyboard Types.**

   If you don't see a Keyboard Types command, the option for displaying the keyboard variations isn't available.

6. **Select a keyboard from the list.**

The way you type on the alternative keyboards depends on whether you choose the XT9 or ABC typing method, as illustrated in Figure 4-2. Here's how these methods work:

XT9: In this mode, the phone interprets your typing, matching words based on what you type on the keypad. For example, you type **43556** and the phone interprets it as *hello*.

ABC: In this mode, you must press the key button a number of times to display the proper letter. So you have to type **44** to get an *H* and then **33** to get an *E*. Typing *hello* is **44 33 555 555 666**. This method may seem awkward, but lots of folks are used to typing this way on a phone keypad.

A superscripted character, as shown in Figure 4-2, is accessed by pressing and holding a key. In most cases, the pop-up palette of characters appears, from which you can choose which character you want to type.

- Figure 4-2 shows the alternative keyboards as they appear on the HTC Thunderbolt. The keyboard variations available on your phone will doubtless look different.

- Other keyboards are available from the Google Play Store. Some of the good ones, such as Thumb Keyboard, cost money. Others are merely *skins*, which simply change the look of the standard QWERTY keyboard. See Chapter 18 for more information on the Google Play Store.

Using the built-in keyboard

A handful of Android phones feature a real keyboard, either right below the touchscreen or somehow hidden behind it. You can use the physical keyboard to perform your cell phone typing duties.

Generally speaking, the physical keyboard looks like a mini-version of the standard QWERTY keyboard. The keys are color-coded, with one color for standard keys and a second color for alternative (ALT or SYM) keys. See the later section "Typing on your phone" for information on how to access and use alternative keys.

A bonus to having the physical keyboard is that it often comes with direction keys: up, down, right, and left, plus maybe even an Activate or OK key. Using these keys is covered later in this chapter, in the section "Text Editing."

The Hunt-and-Peck

Trust me: No one touch-types on a cell phone. No one. Not even the most lithe and swift preteen texting fiend manages to spew forth cryptic prose without keeping one or more eyes on the phone. So don't feel bad if you can't type on your Android phone as fast as you can on a computer. On the phone, everything is hunt-and-peck.

Typing on your phone

Using your phone's keyboard works just as you expect: Touch the key you want, and that character appears in the program you're using. It's magic!

Typing can be quirky, depending on which keyboard you use, as covered in the sections that follow. For both the onscreen and physical keyboards, here are some helpful suggestions and thoughts:

✔ A blinking cursor on the touchscreen shows where new text appears, which is similar to how typing works on a computer.

✔ When you make a mistake, touch the Del key to back up and erase. This key may have the characters *DEL* on it, or it may be a backward-pointing arrow (à la Backspace key on the keyboard), or it may be a hollow, backward-pointing arrow with an X in it.

✔ See the later section "Text Editing" for more details on editing your text.

✔ Above all, *type slowly* until you get used to the keyboard.

✔ People generally accept the concept that composing text on a phone isn't perfect. Don't sweat it if you make a few mistakes as you type text messages or e-mail, though you should expect some curious replies about unintended typos.

✔ One way to gain forgiveness for your typos is to include the signature *Sent from my cell phone* in your e-mail messages. See Chapter 10.

✔ When you type a password, the character you type appears briefly but is then replaced, for security reasons, by a black dot.

✔ When you tire of typing, you can always touch the Microphone key on the keyboard and enter Dictation mode. See the section "Voice Input," later in this chapter.

Onscreen keyboard typing

As you type on the onscreen keyboard, the button you touch appears enlarged on the screen. That's how you can confirm that your fingers are typing what you intend to type.

✔ To set the Caps Lock feature, press the Shift key twice. The Shift key may appear highlighted, the shift symbol may change color, or a colored dot may appear on the key, all of which indicates that Caps Lock is on.

✔ Press the Shift key again to turn off Caps Lock.

✔ See the later section "Choosing a word as you type" to find out how to deal with automatic typo and spelling corrections.

Built-in keyboard typing

Whether the physical keyboard features all capital or all lowercase letters, you switch between them by using the Shift key. Press the Shift key once to type a single letter in uppercase, or press it twice to enter Caps Lock mode and type everything in uppercase.

The keyboard itself may indicate when the keys are shifted or in Caps Lock. A light may turn on when the keys are shifted. Otherwise, you might see a clue on the touchscreen when the keys are shifted. On some Android phones, the blinking cursor changes to show the shift and Caps Lock states.

Typing symbol keys on the physical keyboard is done by touching the SYM or ALT key. This key is color-coded to match the symbols on the keyboard. Touch the key once to type a single symbol character; touch the key twice to enter Symbol Lock mode and type all symbols. Touch the key again to deactivate Symbol Lock mode.

As with the shift key, entering Symbols mode may activate a light on the keyboard, or the touchscreen's cursor may change to indicate that you're typing alternative characters.

Accessing special characters

You can type more characters on your phone than are shown on either the onscreen or built-in keyboard. So don't think you're getting gypped when you don't see the key you want.

Onscreen keyboard special characters

On the onscreen keyboard, you access special characters by long-pressing a specific key. When you do, a pop-up palette of options appears, from which you choose a special character, such as optional characters for the O key, as shown in Figure 4-3.

- ✔ Extra characters are available in uppercase as well; press the Shift key before you long-press on the onscreen keyboard.

- ✔ Certain symbol keys on the onscreen keyboard may also sport extra characters. For example, various currency symbols might be available when you long-press the $ key.

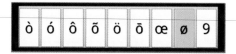

Figure 4-3: Optional characters on the O key.

Built-in keyboard special characters

Accessing special characters on the physical keyboard can be done in a number of ways. Generally speaking, look for a colored key that you access by pressing the SYM or ALT key. On the Motorola Droid 3, the key combination is ALT and then the Space key. Activating this combination displays a palette of symbols on the touchscreen, similar to the one shown in Figure 4-4.

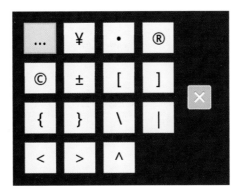

Figure 4-4: Special symbols available for the physical keyboard.

You might also be able to use the long-press technique on the physical keyboard: Press and hold a key to see a pop-up palette of alternative characters. For example, to type the ñ character, try long-pressing the N key.

Choosing a word as you type

Many Android phones sport the predictive-text feature, which displays words the phone thinks you're about to type before you type them. For example, you may type **abo** and a pop-up menu of words starting with *abo* appears: *above*, *about*, *abode*, and so on. Touch a word to choose it, or in many cases you can touch the Space key to select whichever word is highlighted.

To ensure that the word suggestions appear, or to turn them off, follow these steps:

1. **At the Home screen, press the Menu soft button.**

2. **Choose the Settings command.**

3. **Choose Language & Keyboard.**

4. **Choose the keyboard settings command.**

   The command might be named Touch Input, Multi-Touch, Android Keyboard, or something similar.

5. **Ensure that a check mark appears by the Show Suggestions option.**

   The option might also be named Predictive Text.

6. **If you see other options for self-correcting text or auto-complete, enable them as well.**

    Touch the Home soft button when you're done.

To disable the word-suggestion feature, remove the check mark in Step 5.

When you type a word that the phone doesn't recognize, you might be prompted to add the word to the phone's dictionary. (Yes, the phone has a dictionary.) Choose that option. Also see Chapter 24 for more information about the phone's dictionary.

Text Editing

You probably won't do a lot of text editing on your Android phone. Well, no major editing, such as for a term paper or ransom note. From time to time, however, you may find yourself wanting to fix a word. It's usually a sign that you're over 25; kids no longer seem to care about editing text.

Moving the cursor

The first task in editing text is to move the *cursor* — that blinking, vertical line where text appears — to the correct spot. Then you can type, edit, or paste, or simply marvel that you were able to move the slender cursor using your big, stubby finger.

To move the cursor, touch the part of the text where you want the cursor to blink. If you're lucky, the cursor finds itself in the proper spot. If it doesn't, you have to do some adjusting.

- ✔ Some Android phones feature the cursor tab, or a graphic that appears whenever you touch text on the screen. You can drag the tab around using your finger to more precisely position the cursor. A sample of what the tab may look like appears in the margin.

- ✔ If your phone has a physical keyboard, check to see whether it has arrow keys or some sort of directional keypad. If so, you can use the arrow keys to position the cursor.

- ✔ Some Android phones feature a pointing device, such as a trackball. You can use this gizmo to move the cursor as well.

Selecting text

If you're familiar with selecting text in a word processor, rest assured that selecting text on your Android phone works the same way. Well, *theoretically* it works the same way: Selected text appears highlighted on the touchscreen. It's the method of selecting text on a phone that's screwed up.

Your phone has several methods for selecting text, as covered in the following sections.

After the text is selected, you can do four things with it: Delete it, replace it, copy it, or cut it. Delete the text by touching the Del key on the keyboard. Replace text by typing something new while the text is selected. The later section "Cutting, copying, and pasting text" describes how to cut or copy text.

Text selection with your finger on the touchscreen

You can try two techniques to quickly select a word. The first is to tap your finger twice on the touchscreen. If that doesn't work, long-press the word and choose the Select Word command from the menu that appears. The word becomes highlighted, as shown in Figure 4-5.

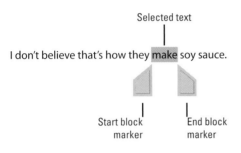

Selected text

I don't believe that's how they make soy sauce.

Start block marker

End block marker

Figure 4-5: Selecting a block of text.

The start block and end block markers, shown on either side of the selected word in Figure 4-5, are used to extend the selection. The markers may not look exactly like the ones shown in the figure, but they can be moved the same way.

  ✔ You may see a pop-up menu appear when a word is selected. The menu assists in selecting text or offers commands for cutting, copying, or sharing the text.

  ✔ Older versions of the Android operating system lack the start and end block markers.

Text selection with the built-in keyboard or pointing device

When your phone has the physical keyboard with cursor buttons or a control pad, you can select text by following these steps:

1. Move the cursor to the location where you want to start selecting text.

  You can use your finger, and then make fine adjustments, by using the direction keys on the built-in keyboard.

2. Press and hold the Shift key.

3. Use the direction keys to extend the selection up, down, left, or right.

The selected text appears highlighted on the screen.

If the phone features a pointing device, such as a trackball, you can use it to extend the selection: Start by selecting a word, and then move the cursor using the pointing device; the text is selected in the direction you move the cursor.

Text selection using the Edit Text menu

Start selecting text by pressing and holding — *long-pressing* — any part of the text screen or input box. Then the Edit Text menu appears, as shown in Figure 4-6.

Edit text

Select word

Select all

Paste

Input method

Figure 4-6: The Edit Text selection menu.

The first two options on the Edit Text menu (refer to Figure 4-6) deal with selecting text:

Select Word: Choose this option to select the word you long-pressed on the screen. You can then extend the selection as illustrated earlier, in Figure 4-5.

Select All: Choose this option to select all text, whether it's in the input box or you've been entering or editing it in the current application.

To back out of the Edit Text menu, press the Back soft button.

You can cancel the selection of text by pressing the Back soft button.

Text selection on a web page

When you're browsing the web on your phone, you select text by summoning a special menu item. Obey these steps:

1. **Press the Menu soft button to summon the web browser's menu.**

2. **Choose the Select Text command.**

   Sometimes, the Select Text command can be found by first choosing the More command.

3. **Drag your finger over the text on the web page you want to copy.**

   In some cases, you may see the start and end block markers, as shown earlier, in Figure 4-5. You might also see a rectangle appear, where you can drag the edges or corners to select large swaths of text.

4. **Touch the screen and choose the Copy command.**

   The text is instantly copied.

You can paste the text into any application on your phone that accepts text input. See the next section.

   ✔ On some phones, you may see a menu after you select the text. (Refer to Step 4.) The menu has options for copying the text, sharing the text, or looking up the text using Google, Wikipedia, a dictionary, or other options.

   ✔ If your phone has a pointing device (a trackball or direction pad), you can use it to extend the text selection on a web page.

   ✔ Refer to Chapter 11 for more information on surfing the web with your phone.

Cutting, copying, and pasting text

After selecting a chunk of text — or all text — on the screen, you can then cut or copy the text and paste it elsewhere. Copying or cutting and then pasting text works just like it does on your computer.

Follow these steps to cut or copy text on your phone:

1. **Select the text you want to cut or copy.**

   Selecting text is covered earlier in this chapter.

2. **Long-press the selected text.**

   Touch the highlighted text on the touchscreen, and keep your finger pressed down. You see the Edit Text menu with three items: Cut, Copy, and Paste.

3. **Choose Cut or Copy from the menu to cut or copy the text.**

   When you choose Cut, the text is removed; the cut-and-paste operation moves text.

4. **If necessary, start the app into which you want to paste text.**

5. **Touch the text box or text area where you want to paste the copied or cut text.**

6. **Position the cursor at the exact spot where the text will be pasted.**

7. **Long-press the text box or area.**

8. **Choose the Paste command or touch the Paste icon.**

   The text you cut or copied appears in the spot where the cursor was blinking.

The text you paste can be pasted again and again. Until you cut or copy additional text, you can use the Paste command to your heart's content.

You can paste text only into locations where text is allowed. Odds are good that if you can type, or whenever you see the onscreen keyboard, you can paste text.

Voice Input

One of the most amazing aspects of your Android phone is its uncanny ability to interpret your utterances. You can dictate text, you can dictate commands. You can even talk dirty to your phone, though you may not get the results you expect.

Dictating to your phone

Voice input is available whenever you see the Microphone icon, similar to the one shown in the margin. To begin voice input, touch its icon. The Voice Input screen appears, as shown in Figure 4-7.

Figure 4-7: The voice-input thing.

When you see the text *Speak Now,* speak directly at the phone.

As you speak, the Microphone icon (refer to Figure 4-7) flashes. The flashing doesn't mean that the phone is embarrassed by what you're saying. No, the flashing merely indicates that the phone is listening, detecting the volume of your voice.

After you stop talking, the phone digests what you said. You see your voice input appear as a wavelike pattern on the screen. Eventually, the text you spoke — or a close approximation of it — appears on the screen. It's magical, and sometimes comical.

> ✔ The first time you try to use Voice Input, you might see its description displayed. Touch the OK button to continue.

> ✔ The Dictation feature works only when voice input is allowed. Not every application features voice input as an option.

> ✔ The better your diction, the better the results. Try to speak only a sentence or less.

> ✔ You can edit your voice input just as you edit any text. See the section "Text Editing," earlier in this chapter.

> ✔ You have to "speak" punctuation to include it in your text. For example, you say, "I'm sorry comma Dave period" to have the phone produce the text *I'm sorry, Dave.*

> ✔ Common punctuation marks that you can dictate include the comma, period, exclamation point, question mark, and colon.

> ✔ Pause your speech before and after speaking punctuation.

> ✔ There's no way to dictate a capital letter, though you can say "Period" and then the first letter of the next word will be capitalized. (It's easier to edit your text and remove excess periods than to edit your text to capitalize.)

> ✔ Voice input may not function when no cellular data or Wi-Fi connection is available.

Controlling the phone with your voice

Some Android phones ship with the Voice Command app. It allows you to holler verbal orders to your phone.

Start the Voice Command app from the App menu. The opening screen may list suggestions for commands you can utter. For example, the Call command, in which you say "Call" followed by the number to call or the contact name. The phone may ask you for more detailed information, requiring you to reply "yes" or "no," similar to an annoying voice-mail menu at a Big Impersonal Company.

On some phones, the Voice Command app can be summoned by pressing the Search soft button twice.

Uttering f*** words

Android phones feature a voice censor. It replaces those naughty words you might utter, placing the word's first letter on the screen, followed by the appropriate number of asterisks or pound signs.

For example, if *shoot* were a blue word and you utter *shoot* when dictating text, the phone's Dictation feature would place s**** on the screen rather than the word *shoot*.

In some versions of the Android operating system, the entire word is replaced by asterisks or pound signs, like this: ####.

You may also find the offensive word autocorrected to a similar word, such as *shot*, *fake*, *darn*, *blech*, and others.

Your phone knows a lot of blue terms, including the infamous "Seven Words You Can Never Say on Television," but apparently the terms *crap* and *damn* are fine. Don't ask me how much time I spent researching this topic.

Part II
The Phone Part

The 5th Wave   By Rich Tennant

Cell Phone

"This model comes with a particularly useful function – a simulated static button for breaking out of long-winded conversations."

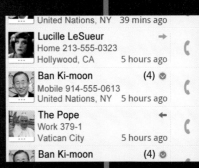

*T*he people who make and sell Android phones boast about everything the device does: mobile communications, e-mail, Internet, photos, video, social networking, maps and navigation, games, eBooks, movies, and more. Oh, and by the way, your phone can also be used as a phone. Yeah, it has that going for it as well.

This part of the book covers what your phone is at its core: a phone. It can send and receive phone calls, put people on hold, make conference calls, manage call waiting, record voice mail, and store information in a digital address book. I call it "the phone thing," but my editor dislikes the word thing in a title, so this part of the book is aptly titled "The Phone Part."

Incoming call

Sam Clemens
Mobile 1-314-555-1130

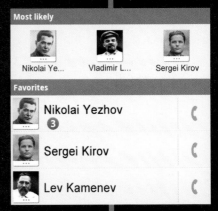

Most likely

Nikolai Ye... Vladimir L... Sergei Kirov

Favorites

Nikolai Yezhov
③

Sergei Kirov

Lev Kamenev

It's a Telephone

*T*he patent for the telephone was awarded to Alexander Graham Bell in 1876. Telephone-like devices existed before then, and a host of 19th century scientists worked on the concept. But Bell beat them all to the patent office, so he gets the credit. And it took many more years for people to patent other, ancillary inventions, including the busy signal (1878), the notion of a second line for teenage girls (1896), and the extension cord, which allowed for simultaneously talking and pacing (1902).

Making phone calls may seem simple enough, but if you've never used an Android phone, it may be an utterly new experience for you. Therefore, I wrote this chapter with some tips, suggestions, and worthy points, all covering that most basic of cell phone functions: making phone calls.

00:

Barack Obama
Home 202-456-1111

Reach Out and Touch Someone

Until they perfect teleportation, making a phone call is truly the next best thing to being there. Or, to copy another Phone Company slogan, you can use your Android phone to "reach out and touch someone." It all starts by punching in a number or choosing from the phone's address book a contact to call. This section explains how it works.

Making a phone call

To place a call on your phone, heed these steps:

1. **Touch the Dialer app or button on the Home screen.**

   Older versions of the Android operating system featured a phone button at the bottom of the Home screen. Newer versions use the Dialer app, which is often found at the bottom of the Home screen, though it also dwells on the App menu.

   Whether it's a button or an app, the Dialer sports the Phone Handset icon.

   The generic Android Dialer is shown in Figure 5-1. The one you see on your phone may be fancier or more colorful or entertaining. For example, some HTC phones may also show a list of recent calls just above the dialpad.

Figure 5-1: Dialing a phone number.

2. **Type the number to call.**

   Use the keys on the dialpad to type the number. If you make a mistake, touch the Delete button, shown in Figure 5-1, to back up and erase.

As you dial, you may hear the traditional touch-tone sound as you input the number. The phone may also vibrate as you touch the numbers.

Some Android phones may display matching contacts as you type a number. You can choose one of those contacts to complete the number for faster dialing.

3. **Touch the green Phone button to make the call.**

   The phone doesn't make the call until you touch the green button.

   As the phone attempts to make the connection, two things happen:

   • First, the Call in Progress notification icon appears on the status bar. The icon is a big clue that the phone is making a call or is actively connected.

   • Second, the screen changes to show the number you dialed, similar to the one shown in Figure 5-2 for the Nexus One phone on the T-Mobile network. When the recipient is in your Contacts list, the contact's name, photo, and social networking status (if available) may also appear, as shown in the figure.

   Even though the touchscreen is pretty, at this point you need to listen to the phone: Put it up to your ear, or listen using the earphones or a Bluetooth headset.

Call in progress

Place the call on hold.

Status bar

Phone number or contact information

Call duration

00:10

Barack Obama
Home 202-456-1111

Hang up.

Make a conference call.

Add call

End

Dialpad

Display the dialpad.

Activate Bluetooth headset.

Bluetooth

Mute

Speaker

Turn off the microphone.

Put the call on speaker.

Figure 5-2: A successful call on the Nexus One.

4. **When the person answers the phone, talk.**

What you say is up to you, though it's good not to just blurt out unexpected news: "I just ran over your cat" or "I think I just saw your daughter on the back of a motorcycle, leaving town at inappropriately high speeds."

Use the phone's Volume buttons (on the side of the device) to adjust the speaker volume during the call.

5. **To end the call, touch the red End Call button.**

The phone disconnects. You hear a soft *beep,* which is the phone's signal that the call has ended. The call-in-progress notification goes away.

 You can do other things while you're making a call: Press the Home button to run an application, read old e-mail, check an appointment, or do whatever. Activities such as these don't disconnect you, though your cellular carrier may not allow you to do other things with the phone while you're on a call.

To return to a call after doing something else, swipe down the notifications at the top of the screen and touch the notification for the current call. You return to the Connected screen, similar to the one shown in Figure 5-2. Continue yapping. (See Chapter 3 for information on reviewing notifications.)

✔ If you're using earphones, you can press the phone's Power Lock button during the call to turn off the display and lock the phone. I recommend turning off the display so that you don't accidentally touch the Mute button or End button during the call.

✔ You can connect or remove the earphones at any time during a call. The call is neither disconnected nor interrupted when you do so.

✔ You can't accidentally mute or end a call when the phone is placed against your face; a sensor in the phone detects when it's close to something, and the touchscreen is automatically disabled.

✔ Don't worry about the phone being too far away from your mouth; it picks up your voice just fine.

 ✔ To mute a call, touch the Mute button, shown in Figure 5-2. The Mute icon, similar to the one shown in the margin, appears as the phone's status (atop the touchscreen).

✔ Touch the Speaker button to be able to hold the phone at a distance to listen and talk, which allows you to let others listen and share in the conversation. The Speaker icon appears as the phone's status whenever the speaker is active.

Signal strength and network nonsense

Two technical-looking status icons appear to the left of the current time atop your Android phone's screen. These icons represent the network the phone is connected to and its signal strength.

The Signal Strength icon displays the familiar bars, rising from left to right. The more bars, the better the signal. An extremely low signal is indicated by zero bars. When there's no signal, you may see a red circle with a line through it (the International No symbol) over the bars.

When the phone is out of its service area but still receiving a signal, you see the Roaming icon, which typically includes an *R* near or over the bars. See Chapter 21 for more information on roaming.

To the left of the Signal Bar icon is the Network icon. No icon means that no digital cellular

network is available, which happens when the network is down or you're out of range. The icon may also disappear when you're making a call. Otherwise, you see an icon representing one of the different types of cellular data networks to which your phone can connect:

1X, **E**, **EDGE**, or **GSM:** This icon represents the original (slow) network.

3G: This icon is used for the second-fastest network.

4G, **4G LTE**, **H+**, or **HSPA:** This icon represents the fastest current-generation cellular data network.

Also see Chapter 19 for more information on the network connection and how it plays a role in your phone's Internet access.

- ✔ Don't hold the phone to your ear when the speaker is active.
- ✔ If you're wading through one of those nasty voice-mail systems, touch the Dialpad button, shown in Figure 5-2, so that you can "Press 1 for English" when necessary.
- ✔ See Chapter 6 for information on using the Add Call and Hold buttons.
- ✔ When using a Bluetooth headset, connect the headset *before* you make the call.
- ✔ If you need to dial an international number, press and hold the 0 (zero) key until the plus-sign (+) character appears. Then input the rest of the international number. Refer to Chapter 21 for more information on making international calls.
- ✔ You hear an audio alert whenever the call is dropped or the other party hangs up. The disconnection can be confirmed by looking at the phone, which shows that the call has ended.
- ✔ You cannot place a phone call when the phone has no service; check the signal strength, as shown earlier, in Figure 5-1. Also see the nearby sidebar, "Signal strength and network nonsense."

✔ You cannot place a phone call when the phone is in Airplane mode. See Chapter 21 for information.

✔ The Call in Progress notification icon (see Figure 5-2) is a useful thing. When you see this notification, the phone is connected to another party. To return to the phone screen, swipe down the status bar and touch the phone call's notification. You can then press the End Call button to disconnect or put the phone to your face to see who's on the line.

Dialing a contact

One of the less-talked-about features of your Android phone is its ability to serve as your personal address book. Of course, the address book doesn't merely list names and numbers — it's a complete database of your friends and contacts. This topic is covered in Chapter 8. For now, the trick is to use one of the contacts in your address book to dial the phone. Here's how it works:

1. **On the Home screen, touch the Dialer app icon, and then touch the Contacts tab at the top of the screen.**

   On some phones, you may have to start the specific Contacts app. The app may be named People on some Android phones.

   Figure 5-3 displays a sample of what the Contacts list might look like.

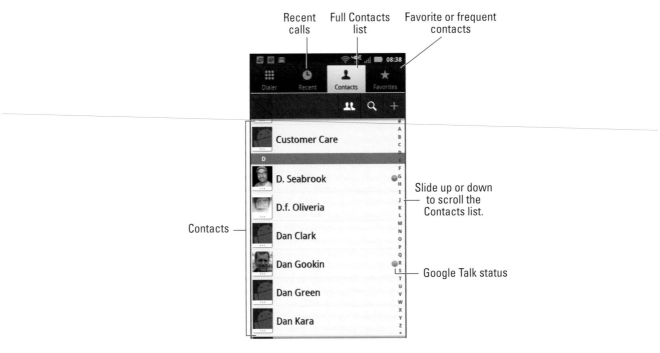

Figure 5-3: Perusing contacts on the Droid Bionic.

2. Scroll the list of contacts to find the person you want to call.

To rapidly scroll, you can swipe the list with your finger or use the index on the right side of the list, as shown in Figure 5-3. On some phones, the index may be on the left side of the list.

3. Touch the contact you want to call.

4. Touch the contact's phone number or the Phone icon by the phone number.

The contact is dialed immediately.

At this point, dialing proceeds as described earlier in this chapter.

Phoning someone you call often

Your Android phone is more computer than robot (thank goodness!). As such, it keeps track of your phone calls in a handy database that you can quickly review. Further, you can flag as favorites certain people whose numbers you want to keep handy. You can take advantage of these two features to quickly call the people you phone most often or to redial a number.

To use the call log to return a call, or to call someone right back, follow these steps:

1. Touch the Phone icon or Dialer app on the Home screen.

2. Touch the Recent tab, found at the top of the window, as shown in Figure 5-3.

The Recent tab displays a list of calls you've made and calls received. Though you can choose an item to see more information, to call someone back, it's just quicker to follow Step 3:

3. Touch the green Phone icon next to the entry.

The phone dials the contact.

People you call frequently, or contacts you've added to the Favorites list, can be accessed by touching the Favorites tab (refer to Figure 5-3). Scroll the list to find a favorite contact, and then touch the green Phone icon to dial.

✓ Some phones keep a list of recent calls above the dial pad. You can choose any of those recent calls to easily redial that number.

✓ Recent calls might also be found in the People app on some HTC phones. Touch the Call History button at the bottom of the People app's window to review the call log.

✓ Refer to Chapter 8 for information on how to make one of your contacts a favorite.

It's the Phone!

Who doesn't enjoy getting a phone call? It's an event! Never mind that it's the company that keeps calling you about lowering the interest rate on your credit cards. The point is that someone cares enough to call. Truly, the cell phone ringing can be good news, bad news, or mediocre news, but it always has a little drama to spice up an otherwise mundane day.

Receiving a call

Several things can happen when you receive a phone call on your Android phone:

- ✔ The phone rings or makes a noise signaling you to an incoming call.
- ✔ The phone vibrates.
- ✔ The touchscreen reveals information about the call, as shown in Figure 5-4.
- ✔ The emergency worker you're speaking with opens his eyes wide and runs away as an out-of-control jet bursts into a fireball just behind you.

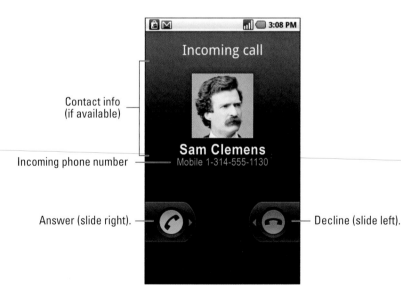

Figure 5-4: You have an incoming call.

The last item in the list happens in a certain Nicolas Cage movie. The other three possibilities, or a combination thereof, are your signals that you have an incoming call. A simple look at the touchscreen tells you more information, as illustrated in Figure 5-4.

To answer the incoming call, slide the green Answer button to the right (refer to Figure 5-4). Then place the phone to your ear or, if a headset is attached, use it. Say "Hello," or, if you're in a grouchy mood, say "What?" loudly.

To dispense with the incoming call, slide the red Ignore button to the left. The phone stops ringing, and the call is banished to voice mail.

On some Android phones, you may have to slide the answer bar *down* rather than to the right, as shown in Figure 5-5. For this visual design (or *skin*), you drag the bar *up* to dismiss the call, as illustrated in the figure.

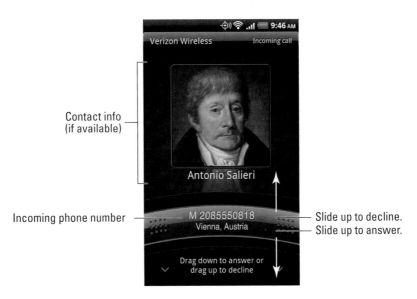

Figure 5-5: Dealing with an incoming call on an HTC phone.

Finally, you can simply silence the phone's ringer by pressing the Volume button up or down.

If you're already using the phone when a call comes in, such as browsing the web or playing *Fruit Ninja,* the incoming call screen looks subtly different from the one shown in Figure 5-4. Your choices for what to do with the call, however, are the same: Touch the green Answer button to accept the call or touch the red Ignore button to send the caller to voice mail.

When you're already on the phone and a call comes in, you can touch the green Answer button to accept the call and place the current call on hold. See Chapter 6 for additional information on juggling multiple calls.

> ✔ The contact's picture, such as the photos of Mr. Clemens in Figure 5-4 and Signore Salieri in Figure 5-5, appears only when you've assigned a picture to the contact. Otherwise, the generic Android icon shows up. The contact's social networking information may also appear, depending on whether the contact is one of your social networking pals.

> ✔ If you're using a Bluetooth headset, you touch the control on the headset to answer your phone. See Chapter 19 for more information on using Bluetooth gizmos.

> ✔ The sound you hear when the phone rings is known as the *ringtone*. You can configure your phone to play a number of ringtones, depending on who is calling, or you can set a universal ringtone. Ringtones are covered in Chapter 6.

Setting incoming call volume

Whether the phone rings, vibrates, or explodes depends on how you've configured it to signal you for an incoming call. Abide by these steps to set the various options (but not explosions) for your phone:

1. **At the Home screen, press the Menu soft button.**

2. **Choose Settings to display the phone's Settings screen.**

3. **Choose Sound.**

4. **Set the phone's ringer volume by touching Volume.**

5. **Manipulate the Ringtone slider left or right to specify how loud the phone rings for an incoming call.**

   After you release the slider, you hear an example of how loudly the phone rings.

6. **Touch OK to set the ringer volume.**

   If you'd rather mute the phone, touch the Silent Mode option on the main Sound Settings screen.

7. **To activate vibration when the phone rings, touch Vibrate.**

8. **Choose a vibration option from the Vibrate menu.**

   For example, choose Always to always vibrate the phone, or choose Only in Silent Mode to make the phone vibrate only after you mute the volume.

9. **Touch the Home button when you're done.**

When the next call comes in, the phone alerts you using the volume setting or vibration options you've just set.

   ✔ See Chapter 3 for information on temporarily silencing the phone.

   ✔ Turning on vibration puts an extra drain on the battery. See Chapter 23 for more information on power management for your phone.

   ✔ Also refer to Chapter 22 for additional sound options on your Android phone.

Who Called Who When?

One of the rare delightful things your phone does for you is to remember all your phone calls. It remembers calls you've made, incoming calls, even missed calls. Such a feature is far better than relying on teenagers, your pets, or indentured robots to keep track of your calls.

Dealing with a missed call

The notification icon for a missed call looming at the top of the screen means that someone called and you didn't pick up. Fortunately, all the details are remembered for you.

To deal with a missed call, follow these steps:

1. **Display the notifications.**

   See Chapter 3 for details on how to deal with notifications.

2. **Touch the Missed Call notification.**

   A list of missed calls is displayed. The list shows who called, with more information displayed when the phone number matches someone in your Contacts list. Also shown is how long ago they called.

3. **Touch an entry in the call log to return the call.**

Also see the next section for more information on the call log.

The phone doesn't consider a call you've dismissed as being missed. To review all your calls — incoming, outgoing, dismissed, and missed — see the next section.

Reviewing recent calls

Your Android phone keeps a record of all calls you make, incoming calls, and missed calls. The standard place to look for the call log is on the Recent tab in the Dialer app, as shown in Figure 5-6. Your call history might also be available in the People app: Touch the Call History button at the bottom of the screen.

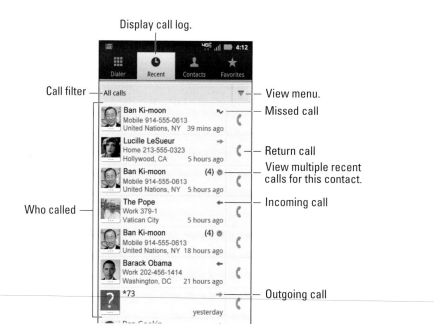

Figure 5-6: The call log.

Figure 5-6 displays a sample of what the call history may look like. You see a list of people who have phoned you or whom you have called, starting with the most recent call at the top of the list. An icon next to every entry describes whether the call was incoming, outgoing, or missed, as illustrated in the figure.

Touching an item in the call log displays contact information for the person who called, if that contact information exists. When no contact information exists, you see a pop-up menu of options for returning the call or sending a text message, for example.

To call someone back, touch the green Phone icon, shown in Figure 5-6. Not every Android phone's recent-call list features this icon. In those cases, you need to touch the entry to display the contact's information and then choose the option to call the contact from that screen.

You can filter the list of recent calls, directing the phone to show only missed calls, only received calls, or only outgoing calls. To do so, touch the View menu triangle, illustrated in Figure 5-6. Choose from the View menu which types of calls you want to see, or choose All Calls to display all recent calls.

✔ Using the call log is a quick way to add a recent caller as a contact: Simply touch an item in the list, and choose Add to Contacts from the Call Details screen. See Chapter 8 for more information about contacts.

✔ When you long-press an entry in the log, you see a pop-up menu. Choose the Remove from List item to banish the entry.

✔ To clear the call log, press the Menu soft button. Choose either the Clear List or Delete All command to wipe clean the call log.

More Telephone Things

A phone call was a phone call, and that's pretty much all that phones did until the 1980s. Around that time, the government started breaking up the old Bell System. Coincidentally, new features began to appear on the commonplace, mortal telephone: call waiting, speed dial, three-way calling, and eventually caller ID. Such things were breathtaking improvements to the old telephone, but for today's cell phone they're commonly included — and at no extra charge.

aximus Interrup

Mobile 812-555-1879

Rome, IN

Your Android phone is capable of a great many feats, all of which were once considered extras — *expensive* extras — for the once standard telephone. This chapter describes the potential. Whether your phone sports all the fancy features depends on how willing your cellular provider is to supply them.

Speed Dial

When I was a wee tot, I visited my dad's office. It amazed me how quickly he could dial our old home phone number. Yes, that was *dial*, as in turn the dial on the phone. With the dawn of the push-button phone, you could punch in numbers as fast as your fingers could dance. The fastest way to dial a number? Why, it's *speed dial.*

Not every Android phone features speed dial. To see whether yours does, heed these steps:

1. **At the Home screen, touch the Dialer app or Phone icon to reach the standard phone-dialing screen.**

   Ensure that you can see the dialpad on the screen. If necessary, touch the Dialer tab.

2. **Press the Menu soft button.**

   If no menu pops up at the bottom of the screen, your phone has no speed dial feature.

3. **Choose Speed Dial Setup.**

   Most carriers configure number 1 as the voice mail system's number. The remaining numbers, 2 through 9, are available to program.

4. **Touch a blank item in the list.**

5. **Choose a contact to speed-dial.**

6. **Repeat Steps 4 and 5 to add more speed dial contacts.**

When you're done adding numbers, press either the Back or Home button to exit the Speed Dial Setup screen.

Using speed dial is simple: Summon the phone dialer (refer to Figure 5-1, in Chapter 5) and then long-press a number on the dialpad. When you release your finger, the speed dial number is dialed.

Also see Chapter 8 for information on creating Favorite contacts.

Multiple Call Mania

As a human being, you're limited by your brain to hold only one conversation at a time. Even then, the ability to hold that conversation proves difficult for a lot of people. Like my Aunt Zelma. Man. Her mind wandered like a blind holy man in the desert. . . .

Sorry.

Your phone is probably capable of handling more than one call at a time. Managing these multiple calls is this section's topic.

Putting someone on hold

It's easy to place a call on hold using your Android phone — as long as your cellular provider hasn't disabled that feature: Simply touch the Hold button. Refer to Figure 5-2 in Chapter 5 for its location on the Call in Progress screen.

To "unhold" the call, touch the Unhold button that replaces the Hold button.

✓ The Hold button features the Pause icon, as shown in the margin.

✓ The Unhold button features the Play icon, as shown in the margin.

✓ Fret not if your phone lacks the Hold button. Rather than hold the call, mute it: Touch the Mute button on the Call in Progress screen. That way, you can sneeze or scream at the wall and the other person will never know.

Receiving a new call when you're on the phone

You're on the phone, chatting it up. Suddenly, someone else calls you. What happens next?

Your phone alerts you to the new call. The phone may vibrate or make a sound. Look at the front of the phone to see what's up with the incoming call, as shown in Figure 6-1.

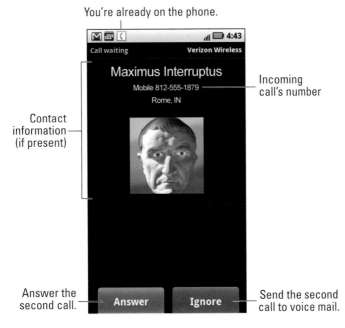

Figure 6-1: Suddenly, there's an incoming call!

You have three options:

Answer the call. Touch the green Answer button to answer the incoming call. The call you're on is placed on hold.

Send the call directly to voice mail. Touch the Ignore button. The incoming call is sent directly to voice mail.

Do nothing. The call eventually goes into voice mail.

When you choose to answer the call and the call you're on is placed on hold, you return to the first call when you end the second call. Or you can manage the multiple calls, as described in the next section.

Juggling two calls

After you answer a second call, as described in the preceding section, your phone is working with two calls at a time. In this particular situation, you can speak with only one person at a time; juggling two calls isn't the same thing as participating in a conference call.

There are a few options you can choose from while the phone is handling two calls:

Swap / Switch Calls: To switch between callers, touch the Swap button or Switch Calls button that appears on the touchscreen. Every time you touch that button, the conversation moves to the other caller. The current person is then put on hold.

Merge Calls: To combine all calls so that everyone is talking with everyone else (three people), touch the Merge Calls button. This button may not be available, or the merge feature may be suppressed by your cellular provider.

End Call: To end a call, touch the End Call button, just as you normally do.

After one call ends, the conversation returns to the other caller. You can then proceed to talk — discuss the weather, the local sports team, whatever — until you hang up or another call interrupts you.

- ✔ The number of different calls your phone can handle depends on your carrier. For most of us, it's only two calls at a time. In that case, a third person who calls you either hears a busy signal or is sent directly into voice mail.

- ✔ If the person on hold hangs up, you may hear a sound or feel the phone vibrate when the call is dropped.

- Your Android phone may feature a special multicall screen. It lists the calls you're working on and lets you easily switch between them, mute one, and otherwise control the multiple calls in a visual manner.

- When you touch the End button using an Android phone on the Verizon network, both calls may appear to have been disconnected. That's not the case: In a few moments, the call you didn't disconnect "rings" as though the person is calling you back. No one is calling you back, though: The phone is simply returning you to that ongoing conversation.

Making a conference call

Unlike someone interrupting a conversation by making an incoming call, a *conference call* is one you set out to make intentionally: You make one call and then *add* a second call. Touch a button on the phone's touchscreen and then everyone is talking. Here's how it works:

1. **Phone the first person.**

   Refer to Chapter 5 if you need to bone up on your Android phone-calling skills.

2. **After your phone connects and you complete a few pleasantries, touch the Add Call button.**

   The first person is put on hold.

3. **Dial the second person.**

   You can use the dialpad or choose the second person from the phone's address book or a recent call from the call log.

   Say your pleasantries and inform the party that the call is about to be merged.

4. **Touch the Merge or Merge Calls button.**

   The two calls are now joined: The touchscreen says *Conference Call,* and the End Last Call button appears. Everyone you've dialed can talk to and hear everyone else.

5. **Touch the End Call button to end the conference call.**

   All calls are disconnected.

When several people are in a room and want to participate in a call, you can always put the phone in Speaker mode: Touch the Speaker button.

Your Android phone may feature the Manage button while you're in a conference call. Touch this button to list the various calls, to mute one, or to select a call to disconnect.

Send a Call Elsewhere

Banishing an unwanted call is relatively easy on your Android phone. You can forbid the phone from ringing by touching the Volume button. Or you can send the call scurrying off into voice mail by using the red Ignore button, as described in the section in Chapter 5 about receiving a call.

Other options exist for the special handling of incoming calls. They're the forwarding options, described in this main section.

Forwarding phone calls

Call forwarding is the process by which you reroute an incoming call. For example, you can send to your office all calls you receive while you're on vacation. Then you have the luxury of having your cell phone and still making calls but freely ignoring anyone who calls you.

The options for call forwarding on your phone can be set by using either the Android operating system itself or the controls set up by your cellular provider.

Call forwarding affects Google Voice voice mail. Unanswered calls that you forward are handled by the forwarding number, not by Google Voice. Further, when you cancel call forwarding, you need to reenable Google Voice on your phone. See Chapter 7 for details.

Forward calls using Android settings

To confirm that call-forwarding options can be set by using the Android operating system, follow these steps:

1. **At the Home screen, press the Menu soft button.**
2. **Choose Settings.**
3. **Choose Call Settings.**
4. **Choose Call Forwarding.**

   If the option isn't available, use your cellular carrier to forward calls. See the next section.

You have several forwarding options:

Always Forward: All incoming calls are sent to the number you specify; your phone doesn't even ring. This option overrides all other forwarding options.

Forward When Busy: Calls are forwarded when you're on the phone and choose not to answer. This option is normally used to send a missed call to voice mail, though you can forward to any number.

Forward When Unanswered: Calls are forwarded when you choose not to answer the phone. Normally, the call is forwarded to your voice mail.

Forward When Unreached: Calls are forwarded when the phone is turned off, out of range, or in Airplane mode. As with the two preceding settings, this option normally forwards calls to voice mail.

5. Choose an option.

6. Set the forwarding number.

Or you can edit the number that already appears. For example, you can type your home number for the Forward When Unreached option so that your cell calls are redirected to your home number when you're out of range.

7. Touch OK.

The Call Forwarding Status icon appears atop the touchscreen whenever you've activated an Android operating system forwarding option.

To disable call forwarding, touch the Disable button when you're given the opportunity to type a forwarded phone number (refer to Step 6).

Forward calls using your cellular provider

Some Android phones are forced to use the forwarding methods provided by the cellular provider rather than by the Android operating system. For example, in the United States, using Verizon as your cellular provider, the call forwarding options work as described in Table 6-1.

Table 6-1	Verizon Call Forwarding Commands	
To Do This	*Input First Number*	*Input Second Number*
Forward unanswered incoming calls	*71	Forwarding number
Forward all incoming calls	*72	Forwarding number
Cancel call forwarding	*73	None

So, to forward all calls to (714) 555-4565, you input ***727145554565** and touch the green Phone button on your Android phone. You hear only a brief tone after dialing, and then the call ends. After that, any call coming into your phone rings at the other number.

You must disable call forwarding to return to normal cell phone operations: Dial *73.

Sending a contact directly to voice mail

You can configure your phone to forward any of your cell phone contacts directly to voice mail. It's a great way to deal with a pest! Follow these steps:

1. **Touch the Launcher icon on the Home screen.**

2. **Open the Contacts or People app.**

   You need to access the phone's address book.

3. **Choose a contact.**

   Use your finger to scroll the list of contacts until you find the annoying person you want to eternally banish to voice mail.

4. **Press the Menu soft button.**

5. **Choose Options.**

6. **Touch the square next to the Incoming Calls option.**

   A green check mark appears in the square, indicating that all calls from the contact (no matter which of their phone numbers is used) are sent directly into voice mail.

To "unbanish" the contact, repeat these steps, but in Step 6, touch the square to remove the green check mark.

> ✔ This feature is one reason you might want to retain contact information for someone with whom you never want to have contact.
>
> ✔ See Chapter 8 for more information on contacts.
>
> ✔ Also see Chapter 7, on voice mail.

Fun with Ringtones

I confess: Ringtones can be lots of fun. They uniquely identify your phone's jingle, especially when you forget to mute your phone and you're hustling to turn the thing off because everyone in the room is annoyed by your ringtone choice of *We Will Rock You.*

On your Android phone, you can choose which ringtone you want. You can create your own ringtones or use snippets from your favorite tunes. You can also assign ringtones for individual contacts. This section explains how it's done.

Choosing the phone's ringtone

To select a new ringtone for your phone, or to simply confirm which ringtone you're using already, follow these steps:

1. **At the Home screen, press the Menu soft button.**

2. **Choose Settings and then choose Sound.**

3. **Choose Phone Ringtone.**

   If you have a ringtone application, you may see a menu that asks you which source to use for the phone's ringtone. Choose Android System.

4. **Choose a ringtone from the list that's displayed.**

   Scroll the list. Tap a ringtone to hear its preview.

5. **Touch OK to accept the new ringtone, or touch Cancel to keep the phone's ringtone as is.**

You can also set the ringtone used for notifications: In Step 3, choose Notification Ringtone rather than Phone Ringtone.

Text messaging ringtones are set from within the Text Messaging app. See Chapter 9.

Setting a contact's ringtone

Ringtones can be assigned by contact so that when your annoying friend Larry calls, you can have your phone yelp like a whiny puppy. Here's how to set a ringtone for a contact:

1. **Choose the Contacts or People app from the App Menu screen.**

   Touch the Launcher button on the Home screen to see the App menu.

2. **From the list, choose the contact to which you want to assign a ringtone.**

3. **Touch the Menu soft button and choose Options, or scroll the contact's information until you see the Options area (near the bottom).**

4. **Choose Ringtone.**

5. **If prompted, choose Android System as the source of the ringtone.**

   Or, if you're using an app such as Zedge, choose it to use that app as the source of the ringtone.

6. **Choose a ringtone from the list.**

   It's the same list that's displayed for the phone's ringtones.

7. **Touch OK to assign the ringtone to the contact.**

Whenever the contact calls, the phone rings using the ringtone you've specified.

To remove a specific ringtone for a contact, repeat the steps in this section but choose the ringtone named Default Ringtone. (It's found at the top of the list of ringtones.) This choice sets the contact's ringtone to be the same as the phone's ringtone.

Using music as a ringtone

You can use any tune from your phone's music library as the phone's ringtone. The first part of the process is finding a good tune to use. Follow along with these steps:

1. **Touch the Launcher button on the Home screen to display all apps on the phone.**

2. **Touch Music to open the music player.**

3. **Choose a tune to play.**

   See Chapter 16 for specific information on how to use the Music app and use your Android phone as a portable music player.

   To be able to select a song as a ringtone, it must either appear on the screen or be playing.

4. **Press the Menu soft button.**

5. **Choose Use As Ringtone.**

   The song — the entire tune — is set as the phone's ringtone. Whenever you receive a call, that song plays.

If these steps don't work, try this approach:

1. **At the Home screen, press the Menu soft button.**
2. **Choose Settings and then Sound.**
3. **Choose Phone Ringtone.**
4. **Touch the New Ringtone button atop the list of ringtones.**

   You see the list of songs stored in the phone's music library.

5. **Choose a song.**

   The song plays; touch the song again to stop.

6. **Touch the OK button to add that song to the list of ringtones.**
7. **Touch the Apply button.**

   The new musical ringtone is set.

The song you've chosen is added to the list of ringtones. It plays — from the start of the song — when you have an incoming call and until you answer the phone, send the call to voice mail, or choose to ignore the call and eventually the caller goes away and the music stops.

You can add as many songs as you like by repeating the steps in this section. Follow the steps in the earlier section "Fun with Ringtones" for information on switching among different song ringtones. Refer to the steps in the earlier section "Setting a contact's ringtone" to assign a specific song to a contact.

A free app at the Google Play Store, Zedge, has oodles of free ringtones available for preview and download, all shared by Android users around the world. See Chapter 18 for information about the Google Play Store and how to download and install apps such as Zedge on your phone.

Creating your own ringtones

You can use any MP3 or WAV audio file as a ringtone for your phone, such as a personalized message, a sound you record on your computer, or an audio file you stole from the Internet. As long as the sound is in either the MP3 or WAV format, it can work as a ringtone on your phone.

The secret to creating your own ringtone is to transfer the audio file from your computer to the phone. This topic is covered in Chapter 20, on synchronizing files. After the audio file is in the phone's music library, you can choose the file as a ringtone in the same way you can assign any music on the phone as a ringtone, as described in the preceding section.

7

Leave Your Message at the Tone

In This Chapter

▶ Configuring basic voice mail

▶ Retrieving messages

▶ Getting a Google Voice account

▶ Setting up Google Voice for voice mail

▶ Reading a Google Voice message

*V*oice mail is nothing new. Way back when, it was called "Can you take a message?" The person taking the message was only as reliable as such persons can be. Teenagers? They didn't take the best messages. Therefore, concerned telephone scientists developed answering machines. Those gizmos eventually morphed into the voice mail system, which is merely a fancier term for *answering machine* or *an electronic gizmo that takes a message*. See? Nothing is new.

Your phone doesn't really have a voice mail system. Nope, that's the job of your cellular provider. It's the same, boring voice mail system they offer to all their cell phone customers, even customers who have non-Android phones and even those dreaded non-smartphones, or dumb-phones. That choice isn't the end of your voice mail options, however, as this chapter cleverly describes.

Marie Antoinette
(211) 555-1793
Received: 3:12pm (7 secs)

Hey Dan for. Did you get a chance give me a c thanks bye.

Boring Carrier Voice Mail

The most basic, and most stupid, form of voice mail is the free voice-mail service provided by your cell phone company. This standard feature has few frills and nothing that stands out differently, especially for your nifty Android phone.

Carrier voice mail picks up missed calls as well as calls you thrust into voice mail. A notification icon, looking similar to the one shown in the margin, appears whenever someone leaves you a voice mail message. You can use the notification to dial into your carrier's voice mail system, listen to your calls, and use the phone's dialpad to delete messages or repeat messages or use other features you probably don't know about because no one ever pays attention.

Setting up carrier voice mail

If you haven't yet done it, set up voice mail on your phone. I recommend doing so even if you plan on using another voice mail service, such as Google Voice. That's because carrier voice mail remains a valid and worthy fallback option for when those other services don't work.

Even if you believe your voice mail to be set up and configured, consider churning through these steps, just to be sure:

1. **At the Home screen, press the Menu soft button.**

2. **Choose Settings.**

   The Settings screen appears.

3. **Choose Call Settings and then Voicemail Service.**

4. **Choose My Carrier, if it isn't chosen already.**

   Or, if it's the only option, you're set.

You can use the Voicemail Settings command to confirm or change the voice mail phone number. (Check with your cell phone carrier for the number, though the proper number is most likely already in use.)

After performing the steps in this section, call the carrier voice mail service to finish the setup: Set your name, a voice mail password, a greeting, and various other steps as guided by your cellular provider's cheerful robot.

✔ If your Android phone features speed dial, long-pressing the 1 key on the dialpad connects you with your carrier's voice mail service.

✔ You can also use the Voice Mail button on the dialpad to quickly connect to your voice mail. Refer to Figure 5-1, in Chapter 5.

✔ Some Android phones come with the Voicemail app, though the ones I've seen aren't that fancy.

✔ Complete your voice mailbox setup by creating a customized greeting. If you don't, you may not receive voice mail messages, or people may believe that they've dialed the wrong number.

Retrieving your messages

 When you have a voice mail message looming, the New Voicemail notification icon appears on the status bar, similar to the one shown in the margin. You can either pull down this notification to connect to the voice mail service or dial into the voice mail service by using the Voicemail button on the dialpad.

What happens next depends on how your carrier has configured its voice mail service. Typically, you have to input your PIN or password, and then new messages play or you hear a menu of options. My advice: Look at the phone so that you can see the dialpad, and touch the Speaker button so that you can hear the prompts.

In case you need to remember the prompts, you can write them down here:

Press _____ to listen to the first message.

Press _____ to delete the message.

Press _____ to skip a message.

Press _____ to hear the menu options.

Press _____ to hang up.

While you're at it, in case you ever forget your voice mail password, write it down here:

_____

The Wonders of Google Voice

Perhaps the best option I've found for working your voice mail is something called Google Voice. It's more than just a voice mail system: You can use *Google Voice* to make phone calls in the United States, place cheap international calls, and perform other amazing feats. For the purposes of this section, the topic is using Google Voice as the voice mail system on your Android phone.

✔ Even when you choose to use Google Voice, I still recommend setting up and configuring the boring carrier voice mail, as covered earlier in this chapter.

✔ You may need to reset Google Voice after using call forwarding. See Chapter 6 for more information on call forwarding, and see the section "Adding your phone to Google Voice," later in this chapter, for information on reestablishing Google Voice as your phone's voice mail service.

Configuring Google Voice

You need to create a Google Voice account on the Internet before you configure your Android phone for use with Google Voice. Start your adventure by visiting the Google Voice home page on the Internet: `http://voice.google.com`.

If necessary, sign in to your Google account. You use the same account name and password you use to access your Gmail.

Your next task is to configure a Google Voice number to be used for your phone, as covered in the next section. Or, if you've just signed up for a Google Voice number, choose the options to use your existing cell phone number and select the "Lite" version of Google Voice. It sets you up with voice mail for your phone, which is the ultimate goal.

- ✔ If all you want is to use Google Voice as your voice mail service, choose the option that says Just Want Voicemail for Your Cell.

- ✔ Google Voice offers a host of features: international dialing, call forwarding, and other stuff I am not aware of and, honestly, am quite afraid of.

Adding your phone to Google Voice

After you have a Google Voice account, you add your phone number to the list of phone numbers registered for Google Voice. As in the preceding section, I recommend that you complete these steps on a computer connected to the Internet, but keep your phone handy:

1. **Click the Gear icon in the upper-right corner of the Google Voice home page, and choose the Voice Settings command from the menu.**

   The Voice Settings command may change its location in a future update to the Google Voice web page. If so, the purpose of this step is to access the Settings screen, where you register phone numbers for use with Google Voice.

2. **Click the Add Another Phone link.**

3. **Work the steps to verify your phone for use with Google Voice.**

   Eventually, Google Voice needs to phone your cell phone. When it does, use the dialpad on your phone to type the code number you see on your computer's screen. After confirming the code number, you see your Android phone listed as a registered phone — but you're not done yet:

4. **Click the Activate Voicemail link.**

   You must activate your phone for it to work with Google Voice. This step is the most important one in adding your number to Google Voice!

5. **On your phone, dial the number you see on your computer screen, or otherwise obey the instructions to forward your busy, unanswered, or unreachable calls to the Google Voice number.**

   Refer to Chapter 6 for more information on call forwarding options.

6. **On your computer screen, click the Done button.**

Your Android phone is now registered for use with Google Voice.

Getting your Google Voice messages

Google Voice transcribes your voice mail messages, turning the audio from the voice mail into a text message you can read. The messages all show up eventually in your Gmail inbox, just as though someone sent you an e-mail rather than left you voice mail. It's a good way to deal with your messages, but not the best way.

The best way to handle Google Voice is to use the Google Voice app, available from the Google Play Store. Use the QR code in the margin, or visit the Google Play Store to search for and install the app. (See Chapter 18 for details on the Google Play Store; refer to this book's introduction for information on QR codes.)

After the Google Voice app is installed, you have to work through the setup, which isn't difficult. Eventually, you see the app's main interface, which looks and works similarly to an e-mail program. You can review your messages or touch a message to read or play it, as illustrated in Figure 7-1.

When new Google Voice messages come in, you see the Google Voice notification icon appear, as shown in the margin. To read or listen to the message, pull down the notifications and choose the item labeled Voicemail from *whomever.*

   ✓ With Google Voice installed, you see two notices for every voice mail message: one from Google Voice and another for the Gmail message.

   ✓ The Google Voice app works only after you activate Google Voice on your phone, as described in the preceding section.

Incoming phone
number

Contact info
(if available)

Message text
translation

Play message.

Turn on speaker.

Figure 7-1: Voice mail with the Google Voice app.

- ✓ You can best listen to the message when using the Google Voice app. In Gmail, you see a transcript of the message, but you must touch the Play Message link to visit a web page and then listen to the message.

- ✓ The text translation feature in Google Voice is at times astonishingly accurate and at other times not so good.

- ✓ The text *Transcript Not Available* appears whenever Google Voice is unable to create a text message from your voice mail or whenever the Google Voice service is temporarily unavailable.

8

The Address Book

*F*riends may come and go, but enemies tend to accumulate. Of course, not everyone is a politician, so for most people, friends accumulate in great abundance. Your Android phone deftly stores information about the people you know in its own electronic address book. Therein you'll find e-mail addresses, physical addresses, random information such as birthdates, plus the obvious phone number. It's indispensible, and it's this chapter's topic.

The People You Know

Your phone's address book is stored in an app traditionally named Contacts. That's its original Android name. Your cell phone may use a different app, such as the People app found on HTC phones, but the idea is the same: It's the app you use to see information about the people you know.

Accessing the address book

To peruse your phone's address book, open the Contacts or People app. You may find a shortcut for it on the Home screen, but you'll certainly find the app on the App Menu screen. You can also view your contacts by touching the Contacts tab in the Dialer app.

Figure 8-1 shows the Contacts app on a typical Android phone. The address book on your phone may look subtly different, but most of the items illustrated in the figure should be there.

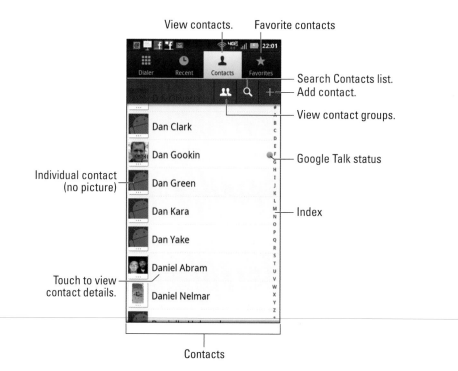

Figure 8-1: The Contacts list.

Scroll the list by swiping your finger. You can use the index on the right side of the screen (refer to Figure 8-1) to quickly scroll your contacts up and down.

Viewing a contact's information

To do anything with a contact, you first have to choose it: Touch a contact name, and you see more information, similar to what's shown in Figure 8-2.

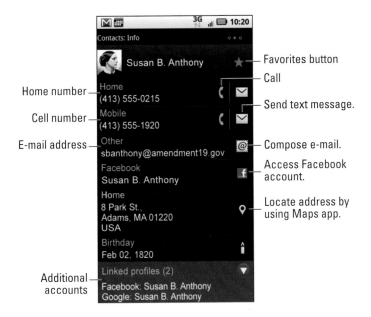

Figure 8-2: More details about a contact.

You can do a multitude of things with the contact after it's displayed, as illustrated in Figure 8-2:

Make a phone call. To call the contact, touch one of the contact's phone entries, such as Home or Mobile. You touch either the entry itself or the Phone icon by the entry.

Send a text message. Touch the Text Message icon (refer to Figure 8-2) to open the Text Messaging app and send the contact a message. See Chapter 9 for information about text messaging.

Compose an e-mail message. Touch the Email link to compose an e-mail message to the contact. When the contact has more than one e-mail address, you can choose to which one you want to send the message. Chapter 10 covers using e-mail on your phone.

View social networking info. Visit the contact's Facebook, Twitter, or another social networking account by touching the appropriate item. See Chapter 12 for additional information about social networking on your Android phone.

Locate your contact on a map. When the contact has a home or business address, you can touch the little doohickey next to the address, shown in Figure 8-2, to summon the Maps application. Refer to Chapter 14 to see all the fun stuff you can do with Maps.

Oh, and if you entered birthday information for a contact, you can view it as well. Singing "Happy Birthday" is something you have to do on your own.

- ✔ When you're done viewing the contact, press the Back soft button.

- ✔ In the People app, information about a contact is divided into areas: Action, Information, and Options. Use the Actions area to place calls, send text messages, compose e-mail, and do other action-like things.

- ✔ Information about your contacts is pulled from multiple sources: your Google account, the phone's storage, and your social networking sites. When you see duplicated information for a contact, it's probably because the information comes from two or more of those sources.

- ✔ Many Android phones feature an account named Me. That's your own information as known by the phone. The Me account may be in addition to your other accounts shown in the address book.

- ✔ A weird contact named BAL, MIN, or Warranty Center isn't a real person, but instead is a shortcut to one of the various services offered by your cellular provider. For example, the BAL contact is used on Verizon phones to get a text message listing your current account balance.

Sorting the address book

Your contacts are displayed in a certain order. On my phone, it's alphabetically by first name and first name first. You can change the order to whatever you like by following these steps:

1. **Start the Contacts app.**

2. **Press the Menu soft button and choose Display Options.**

3. **Choose Sort List By.**

4. **Select First Name or Last Name to sort the list accordingly.**

    I prefer sorting by last name, which is how most Rolodex products are organized.

5. **Choose View Contact Names As.**

6. **Choose either First Name First or Last Name First, which specifies how contacts are displayed in the list.**

    The way the name is displayed doesn't affect the sort order. So, if you choose First Name First (as I do) as well as Last Name for the sort order (as I do), you still see the list sorted by last name.

7. **Press the Back soft button when you're done.**

The Contacts list is updated, displayed per your preferences.

If you're using an HTC Android phone with the People app, the steps for sorting the phone's address book are subtly different: In the People app, press the Menu soft button, and choose View and then Sort Contact List. You can then choose how to sort and display the list. Further, you can choose the View Contact Name As option to choose first-name-first or last-name-first.

Searching contacts

Rather than scroll your phone's address book with angst-riddled desperation, press the Search soft button. The Search Contacts text box appears. Type a few letters of the contact's name, and you see the list of contacts narrowed to the few who match the letters you type. Touch a name from the search list to view the contact's information.

There's no correlation between the number of contacts you have and the number of bestest friends you have — none at all.

Making New Friends

There are many ways to put contact information into your phone. You can build a Contacts list from scratch, but that's tedious. More likely, you collect contacts as you use your phone. Or you can borrow contacts from your Gmail contacts. In no time, you'll have a phone full of contact information.

Your social networking friends are automatically merged into the address book whenever you add social networking sites to your Android phone. See Chapter 12 for details.

Adding a contact from the call log

One of the quickest ways to build up your Contacts list is to add people as they phone you — assuming that you've told them about your new phone number. After someone calls, you can use the call log to add the person to your phone's address book. Obey these steps:

1. **Open the Dialer app.**
2. **Touch the Call Log or Recent tab at the top of the screen.**
3. **Choose the phone number from the list of recent calls.**
4. **Choose Add to Contacts.**
5. **Choose Create a New Contact.**

6. **Choose your Google account for the location to store the new contact.**

   By choosing your Google account, you ensure that the contact's information is duplicated from your phone to your Google account on the Internet.

   Other options may also present themselves for storing contact information. For example, if you use Yahoo! Mail more than Google (and Yahoo! Mail is available as a choice), you can choose that option instead.

   You can, optionally, place a green check mark by the setting Remember This Choice so that you're not prompted again.

7. **Touch OK.**

8. **Fill in the contact's information.**

   Fill in the blanks, as many as you know about the caller: given name and family name, for example, and other information, if you know it. If you don't know any additional information, that's fine; just filling in the name helps clue you in to who is calling the next time that person calls (using the same number).

   Touch the Next button on the onscreen keyboard to hop between the various text fields for the contact.

   I recommend that you add the area code prefix to the phone number, if it's not automatically added for you.

9. **Touch the Save button to create the new contact.**

You can also follow these steps to add a new phone number to an existing contact. In Step 5, choose the contact from your phone's address book. The new phone number is added to the existing contact's information.

For HTC Android phones, you find the call log in the People app. Long-press a recent entry and choose the command Save to People to create a new address book item for that phone number.

Creating a new contact from scratch

Sometimes it's necessary to create a contact when you meet another human being in the real world. In that case, you have more information to input, and it starts like this:

1. **Open the Contacts or People app.**

2. **Press the Menu soft button and choose the New Contact command.**

   You may also find the Add Contact button near the top of the screen.

3. **If prompted, choose an account as the place to store the contact, and then touch the OK button.**

   I recommend choosing Google, unless you use another account listed as your main Internet mail account, such as Yahoo!.

4. **Fill in the information on the Add Contact screen as the contact begrudgingly gives you information.**

   Fill in the text fields with the information you know: the Given Name and Family Name fields, for example.

   To expand a field, touch the green Plus button on the touchscreen and then press the OK button.

   Touch the gray button to the left of the phone number or the e-mail address to choose the location for that item, such as Home, Work, or Mobile.

   Touch the More button at the bottom of the list to expand that area and add *even more* information!

5. **Touch the Done or Save button to complete editing and add the new contact.**

You can also create new contacts by using your Gmail account on a computer. This option offers you the luxury of using a full-size keyboard and computer screen, though whenever you meet a contact face-to-face, creating the contact using your phone will have to suffice.

Importing contacts from your computer

Your computer's e-mail program is doubtless a useful repository of contacts you've built up over the years. You can export these contacts from your computer's e-mail program and then import them into your Android phone. It's not the simplest thing to do, but it's a quick way to build up your phone's address book.

The key is to save or export your computer e-mail program's records in the *vCard* (.vcf) file format. These records can then be imported into the phone and read by the address book app. The method for exporting contacts varies depending on the e-mail program:

- ✔ **In the Windows Live Mail program,** choose Go⇨Contacts, and then choose File⇨Export⇨Business Card (.VCF) to export the contacts.

- ✔ **In Windows Mail,** choose File⇨Export⇨Windows Contacts, and then choose vCards (Folder of .VCF Files) from the Export Windows Contacts dialog box. Click the Export button.

- ✔ **On the Mac,** open the Address Book program, and choose File⇨Export⇨ Export vCard.

After the vCard files are created, connect the phone to your computer and transfer the vCard files from your computer to the phone. Directions for making this type of transfer are found in Chapter 20.

After the vCard files have been copied to the phone, you import them into the phone's address book. The method varies from phone to phone.

For most Android phones, follow these steps:

1. **In the Contacts app or People app, press the Menu soft button.**
2. **Choose Import/Export.**
3. **Choose the command Import from SD Card.**
4. **Choose to save the contacts to your Google account.**
5. **If prompted, choose the option Import All vCard Files.**
6. **Touch the OK button.**

    Work any additional steps, such as choosing an account type or touching the OK button when prompted.

For phones running a variation of the Motoblur interface, try these steps in the Contacts app:

1. **Press the Menu soft button and choose the Manage Contacts option.**
2. **Choose the SD Card option beneath the heading Import Contacts From.**
3. **If prompted, choose your Google account from the list, and then touch the OK button.**
4. **If prompted, choose Import All vCard Files.**
5. **Touch the OK button.**

The imported contacts are also synchronized to your Gmail account, which instantly creates a backup copy.

Building up contacts from your social networking sites

Your phone's address book can easily pull in all your social networking friends and followers. The trick is to access your social networking accounts using your Android phone. The rest happens pretty much automatically.

If your phone came with a specific social networking app, you can use it to connect to your social networking sites and mix your people with the phone's address book. Even if your phone lacks such software, it's easy to add. See Chapter 12, which covers social networking on Android phones.

Finding a new contact using its location

When you use the Maps application to locate a restaurant, a cobbler, or an erotic boutique, you can quickly create a contact for that business based on its location. Here's how:

1. **After searching for your location by using the Maps app, touch the cartoon bubble that appears on the map.**

   For example, in Figure 8-3, a sushi bar has been found.

Touch here to see more information.

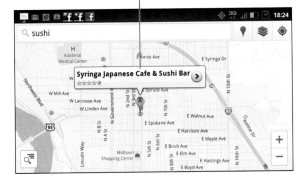

Figure 8-3: A business has been located.

2. **Press the Menu soft button and choose the command Add As a Contact.**

   If you don't see the Add As a Contact command, touch the More button on the screen, and then choose Add As a Contact.

3. **If prompted, choose in which account to store the contact.**

   The information from the Maps application is copied into the proper fields for the contact, including the address and phone number, plus other information (if available).

4. **Touch the Save button.**

   The new contact is created.

See Chapter 14 for detailed information on how to search for a location using the Maps application.

When things change for a contact, or perhaps your thumbs were a bit too big when you created the contact while you were jumping rope, you can edit the contact information. Aside from editing existing information or adding new items, you can do a smattering of other interesting things, as covered in this section.

Address Book Management

Sure, some folks just can't leave well enough alone. For example, some of your friends may change their phone numbers. They may move. They may finally get rid of their damned AOL e-mail addresses. When such things occur, you must undertake the task of address book management. It's not as boring as it sounds, and the topic isn't limited to updating information.

Making basic changes

To make minor touch-ups on any contact, start by locating and displaying the contact's information. Press the Menu soft button, and choose the Edit or Edit Contact command.

The contact's information is displayed, organized by source: Google contact information and information from social networking sites, plus information from other sources.

Change, add, or edit information by touching a field and typing on either the onscreen keyboard or your phone's physical keyboard, if it's blessed with one.

Some information cannot be edited. For example, fields pulled in from social networking sites can be edited only by that account holder on the social networking site.

When you're done editing, touch the Save button.

Adding a picture to a contact

The simplest way to add a picture to a contact is to have the image already stored in the phone. You can snap a picture and save it (covered in Chapter 15), grab a picture from the Internet (covered in Chapter 11), or use any image already stored in the phone's Gallery app (covered in Chapter 15). The image doesn't even have to be a picture of the contact — any image will do.

After the contact's photo, or any other suitable image, is stored on the phone, follow these steps to update the contact's information:

1. **Locate and display the contact's information.**

2. **Press the Menu soft button and choose the Edit or Edit Contact command.**

3. **Touch the icon where the contact's picture would go, or touch the existing picture assigned to the contact.**

   The icon shows a generic placeholder if no picture is assigned.

4. **Choose the option to select a photo from the Gallery.**

   The option could be titled Select Photo from Gallery or just Gallery.

   If you have other image management apps on your phone, you can instead choose the app's command from the list.

5. **Browse the gallery to look for a suitable image.**

   See Chapter 15 for more information on using the Gallery.

6. **Touch the image you want to use for the contact.**

7. **Optionally, crop the image.**

   You can use Figure 8-4 as a guide, though the cropping tool on your phone may look different from the one shown in the figure.

Drag cropping box.　　Resize cropping box.

Full image

Figure 8-4: Cropping a contact's image.

8. **Touch the Save button to set the contact's image.**

9. If necessary, touch the Save button again to finish editing the contact.

The image is now assigned, and it appears whenever the contact is referenced on your phone.

> **TIP**
>
> You can add pictures to contacts on your Google account by using any computer. Just visit your Gmail Contacts list to edit a contact. You can then add to that contact any picture stored on your computer. The picture is eventually synced with the same contact on your Android phone.

- ✔ Pictures can also be added by your Gmail friends and contacts when they add their own images to their accounts.

- ✔ You may also see pictures assigned to your contacts based on pictures supplied on Facebook or other social networking sites.

- ✔ Some images in the Gallery may not work for contact icons. For example, images synchronized with your online photo albums may be unavailable.

- ✔ To remove or change a contact's picture, follow Steps 1 through 3 in the preceding list. Choose Remove Icon to get rid of the existing image; choose Change Icon to set a new image.

Making a favorite

A *favorite* contact is someone you stay in touch with most often. The person doesn't have to be someone you like — just someone you (perhaps unfortunately) phone often, such as your bookie.

The list of favorite contacts is kept on the Dialer app's Favorites tab, as shown in Figure 8-5. The top part of the list shows favorite favorites, or those favorites you've contacted frequently. At the bottom of the list, you see people you contact frequently but who are not (yet) favorites. Below that is a list of people you frequently contact — ideal candidates for promotion to the Favorites list.

To add a contact to the Favorites list, display the contact's information and touch the Star button in the contact's upper-right corner, as shown earlier, in Figure 8-2. When the star is red, as shown in the figure, the contact is one of your favorites.

To remove a favorite, touch the contact's star again, and it loses its color. Removing a favorite doesn't delete the contact, but instead removes it from the Favorites list.

- ✔ The star's color may be, instead of red, green or yellow or another festive color.

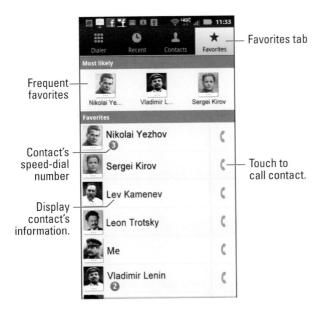

Favorites tab

Frequent favorites

Contact's speed-dial number

Display contact's information.

Touch to call contact.

Figure 8-5: Favorite contacts.

✔ Some Android phones may not feature the Favorites list.

✔ A contact has no idea whether they're one of your favorites, so don't believe that you're hurting anyone's feelings by not making them a favorite.

Removing a contact

Every so often, consider reviewing your phone's contacts. Purge the folks whom you no longer recognize or you've forgotten. It's simple:

1. **Locate the contact in your phone's address book, and display the contact's information.**

2. **Press the Menu soft button, and choose the command Delete or Delete Contact.**

   A warning may appear, depending on whether the contact has information linked from your social networking sites. If so, dismiss the warning by touching the OK button.

3. **Touch OK to remove the contact from your phone.**

Because the Contacts list is synchronized with your Gmail contacts in your Google account, the contact is also removed there.

Part III
Mobile Communications

Checking your Gmail inbox.

OpenCdA Wambooli Picasa Web

Wikipedia eBay Mobile Amazon

S ure, your Android phone is a phone. But it's really a mobile communications device. That's because there's more to communications than making traditional phone calls. For example, there's texting, which is perhaps the only way teenagers know how to communicate. Add e-mail, the web, social networking, and even video calls and you not only have 21st century digital communications, you also have every topic covered in this part of the book.

9

When Your Thumbs Speak

*T*exting is the popular name for using your Android smartphone to send short, typed messages to another cell phone. Doing so basically turns your sophisticated, 21st century mobile communications device into something roughly the equivalent of a 19th century telegraph. Still, texting has its place; teenagers find texting preferable for their communications needs. It's useful, and often best, to send a short burst of text to someone rather than to hold a phone call. In fact, I often text a friend to say "Are you available?" before I call, just to ensure that they have time to talk. And I'm definitely not a teenager.

Msg 4U

There are several reasons to use your Android phone's texting abilities. First, texting is short and quick. It's to-the-point communications. Second, it's quiet. You can send and receive texts where phone calls would be disruptive. Third, it's probably the only way you'll get your children and grandchildren to communicate with you.

Texting on your phone is handled by a specific app. On all the Android phones I've surveyed, never once was the app named Texting. This name would be logical, but no. Instead, the app is likely named Messages, Messaging, Text Messaging, or a name that's close but not quite the same as Texting.

- If you're over 25, the translation of this section's title is "Message for You."

- A shortcut to your phone's texting app might be found on the Home screen.

- Don't text while you're driving or in a movie theater or in any other situation where it's awkward and inappropriate to pay more attention to your phone than to your surroundings.

- Your cellular service plan may charge you per message for every text message you send. Some plans feature a given number of free (included) messages per month. Other plans, favored by teenagers (and their parents), feature unlimited texting.

- The nerdy term for text messaging is *SMS*, which stands for Short Message Service.

Composing a new text message to a contact

Because most cell phones sport a text messaging feature, you can send a text message to just about any mobile number. It works like this:

1. **Open the Contacts app or People app, or somehow finagle the Contacts list.**

2. **Choose a contact, someone to whom you want to send a text message.**

3. **Touch the Message icon next to the contact's mobile number.**

   The Message icon may look similar to the one shown in the margin.

   On some Android phones, you may see a specific command on a contact's information screen to compose a text message. For example, the Send Message command appears in the Actions area in the People app on certain HTC phones.

   After selecting the option to compose a new text message, you see the conversation window, similar to the one shown in Figure 9-1. If you've already texted with the contact, your existing conversation appears, as shown in the figure.

4. **Type the message text.**

   Be brief. A text message has a 160-character limit. You can check the screen to see whether you're nearing the limit (refer to Figure 9-1). To help you stay under the limit, see the later sidebar "Common text-message abbreviations," for useful text-message shortcuts and acronyms.

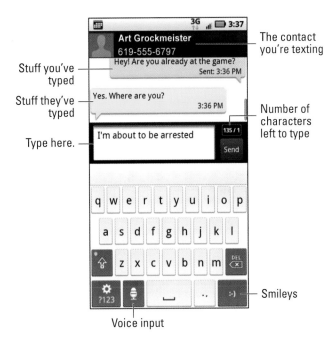

Stuff you've typed

Stuff they've typed

Type here.

The contact you're texting

Number of characters left to type

Smileys

Voice input

Figure 9-1: Typing a text message.

5. Touch the Send button.

The message is sent instantly. Whether the contact replies instantly depends. When the person replies, you see the message displayed (refer to Figure 9-1).

6. Read the reply.

7. Repeat Steps 4 through 6 as needed — or eternally, whichever comes first.

You don't need to continually look at your phone while waiting for a text message. Whenever your contact chooses to reply, you see the message recorded as part of an ongoing conversation. See the later section "Receiving a text message."

 ✔ You can send text messages only to cell phones. Aunt Ida cannot receive text messages on her landline that she's had since the 1960s.

 ✔ Add a subject to your message by touching the Menu soft button and choosing Add Subject.

 ✔ You can dictate text messages by using the keyboard's Microphone button. See Chapter 4 for more information on voice input.

Common text-message abbreviations

Texting isn't about proper English. Indeed, many of the abbreviations and shortcuts used in texting are slowly becoming part of the English language, such as LOL and BRB.

The weird news is that these acronyms weren't invented by teenagers. Sure, the kids use them, but the acronyms find their roots in the Internet chat rooms of yesteryear. Regardless of a shortcut's source, you might find it handy for typing messages quickly. Or, maybe you can use this reference for deciphering an acronym's meaning. You can type acronyms in either upper- or lowercase letters.

2	To, also		NRN	No reply needed (necessary)
411	Information		OMG	Oh my goodness!
BRB	Be right back		PIR	People in room (watching)
BTW	By the way		POS	Person over shoulder (watching)
CYA	See you		QT	Cutie
FWIW	For what it's worth		ROFL	Rolling on the floor, laughing
FYI	For your information		SOS	Someone over shoulder (watching)
GB	Goodbye		TC	Take care
GJ	Good job		THX	Thanks
GR8	Great		TIA	Thanks in advance
GTG	Got to go		TMI	Too much information
HOAS	Hold on a second		TTFN	Ta-ta for now (goodbye)
IC	I see		TTYL	Talk to you later
IDK	I don't know		TY	Thank you
IMO	In my opinion		U2	You too
JK	Just kidding		UR	You're, you are
K	Okay		VM	Voice mail
L8R	Later		W8	Wait
LMAO	Laughing my [rear] off		XOXO	Hugs and kisses
LMK	Let me know		Y	Why?
LOL	Laugh out loud		YW	You're welcome
NC	No comment		ZZZ	Sleeping
NP	No problem			

✓ You can send a single text message to multiple recipients: Just type additional phone numbers or contact names in the To field when you're composing a new message.

✓ Some cell phones allow you to reply to everyone in a text message that has multiple recipients. When this feature is available, you see both the Reply and Reply All buttons when composing your reply to the message.

✓ Phone numbers and e-mail addresses sent in text messages become links. You can touch a link to call that number or visit the web page.

✓ Continue a conversation at any time: Open the phone's texting app, peruse the list of existing conversations, and touch one to review what has been said or to pick up the conversation.

✓ Do not text and drive. Do not text and drive. Do not text and drive.

Sending a text message to a phone number

The situation is rare, but it can come up: You have a cell phone number, and you need to send a text. Follow these steps:

1. **Open the phone's texting app.**

   You see a list of current conversations (if any), organized by contact name or phone number. If not, press the Back soft button to get to that main screen.

2. **Touch the button that says New Message or Compose Message or looks like a plus sign.**

   The plus button is commonly used on Android phones to mean "create a new something" or "add something," so you may see it used instead of the more specific New Message or Compose Message buttons.

3. **Type a cell phone number in the To field.**

   When the number you type matches one or more existing contacts, you see those contacts displayed. Choose one to send a message to that person; otherwise, continue typing the phone number.

4. **Touch the Compose Message text box.**

   The text box might be named Add Text instead of Compose Message.

5. **Type your text message.**

6. **Touch the Send button to send the message.**

Whether to send a text message or an e-mail

Sending a text message is similar to sending an e-mail message. Both involve the instant electronic delivery of a message to someone else. And both methods of communication have their advantages and disadvantages.

Above all, you can only send a text message to another cell phone. E-mail is available to anyone who has an e-mail address, whether or not the persons use a mobile communications device.

Text messages are pithy; short and to the point. They're informal, more like quick chats. Indeed, the speed of reply is often what makes text messaging useful. But, like sending e-mail,

sending a text message doesn't guarantee a reply.

An e-mail message can be longer than a text message. You can receive e-mail on any computer or device that can access the Internet, such as your Android phone. E-mail message attachments (pictures, documents) are handled better, and more consistently, than text message (MMS) media.

Finally, though e-mail isn't considered formal communication, not like a physical letter or a phone call, it's considered more formal than a text message.

After you send the message, I recommend that you create a new contact for the number: Long-press the phone number you sent the text to (found atop the screen). Choose the commands from the menu to create a new contact, such as View Contact and then Create New Contact. Fill in the blanks, using the good information in Chapter 8 to help guide you.

Receiving a text message

Whenever a new text message comes in, you see the message appear briefly at the top of the phone's touchscreen. Then you see the New Text Message notification, similar to the one shown in the margin.

To view the message, pull down the notifications, as described in Chapter 3. Touch the messaging notification, and that conversation window immediately opens.

Forwarding a text message

It's possible to forward a text message, but it's not the same as forwarding e-mail. In fact, when it comes to forwarding information, e-mail has text messaging beat by well over 160 characters.

TIP

Opt out of text messaging

You don't have to be a part of the text messaging craze. Indeed, it's entirely possible to opt out of text messaging altogether. Simply contact your cellular provider and have them disable text messaging on your phone. They will happily comply, and you'll never again be able to send or receive a text message.

People opt out of text messaging for a number of reasons. A big one is cost: If the kids keep running up the text messaging bill, simply disabling the feature is often easier than continuing to pay all the usage surcharges. Another reason is security: Viruses and spam can be sent via text message. If you opt out, you don't have to worry about receiving these unwanted text messages.

When forwarding works as an option, your phone lets you forward only the information in a text messaging cartoon bubble, not the entire conversation. Here's how it works:

1. **If necessary, open a conversation in the phone's texting app.**

2. **Long-press the text entry (the cartoon bubble) you want to forward.**

3. **From the menu that appears, choose the command Forward or Forward Message.**

   From this point on, forwarding the message works like sending a new message from scratch:

4. **Type the recipient's name (if the person is a contact), or type a phone number.**

   The text you're forwarding appears, already written, in the text field.

5. **Touch the Send button to forward the message.**

Multimedia Messages

Even though the term *texting* sticks around, this cell phone feature has for some time had the ability to send media along with text. You can attach a picture, a video, an audio attachment, or a number of other interesting things to your text message. When you do, the message ceases to be a text message and becomes a *multimedia message*.

✔ There's no need to run a separate program or do anything fancy to send media in a text message; the same text app is used on your phone for sending both text and media messages. Just follow the advice in this section.

✔ The official name for a multimedia text message is Multimedia Messaging Service, which is abbreviated MMS.

✔ Not every mobile phone can receive MMS messages. Rather than receive the media item, the recipient may be directed to a web page where the item can be viewed on the Internet.

Attaching media to a text message

The most consistent way to compose a multimedia message is to attach existing media — something you've already saved on your phone — to the outgoing message. Obey these steps:

1. **Compose a text message as you normally do.**

2. **Press the Menu soft button, and choose the Insert or Attach command.**

   You may also see the Paperclip button on the message composition screen, which you can also use for attaching media.

   A pop-up menu appears, listing various media items you can attach to a text message. The items may look something like this:

   Appointment: Invite someone to attend an event you've scheduled using the Calendar app.

   Audio: Attach a song or an audio clip from the music library, or record a new audio clip, such as your voice.

   Contact: Attach contact information in the form of a vCard.

   Location: Send a URL of your current, or another, location.

   Picture: Take a picture and attach it to the text message, or choose an image stored in the phone's Gallery.

   Slideshow: Create a collection of photos to send together.

   Video: Shoot a new video to attach, or choose a video you've taken with the phone and stored in the Gallery.

   More options may appear on the menu, depending on which apps you have installed on your Android phone.

Text messaging alternatives

Life doesn't turn totally dismal when you find yourself unduly bound by text message limitations on your cell phone contract. Just because you're limited to sending (and receiving) only 250 messages a month doesn't mean that you and your friends must stay horribly out of touch or that your thumbs will atrophy from the lack of typing. A smattering of free alternatives to text messaging are available, all of which use the Internet and some of which may come preinstalled on your phone.

Mobile IM: The Mobile IM app found on some Android phones hooks you into a slew of instant messaging (IM) services, such as Windows Live!, Yahoo!, and even the venerable old AOL Instant Messaging (AIM).

Talk: The Talk app connects you with the Google Talk service on the Internet. It's not really a texting app; it's a chat app. You can summon a list of friends, all configured from your Google account, and chat it up — as long

as they're available. My advice is to configure Google Talk on your computer first, and then you can find the same friends available on your phone. (Also see Chapter 13 for more information on the Talk app.)

Skype: The Skype app can be used to chat as well, if you've set up a slew of friends and they also have Skype or the full-fledged Skype program on their desktop computers. Chatting on Skype is easy and free. See Chapter 13 for more details.

Of course, these apps use the Internet, so if your phone has a data restriction, you face, theoretically, a surcharge for using more Internet than your cell phone plan allows. Even so, text messaging applications tend not to eat up much in terms of Internet usage. So type away!

See Chapter 18 for information on obtaining these apps for your phone, if they aren't preinstalled.

3. Choose a media attachment from the pop-up menu.

What happens next depends on the attachment you've selected. You're taken to the appropriate app on your phone, where you can choose an existing media item or create a new one.

4. If you like, compose a message to accompany the media attachment.

5. Touch the Send button to send your media text message.

In just a few, short, cellular moments, the receiving party will enjoy your multimedia text message.

✔ Not every phone is capable of receiving multimedia messages.

✔ Be aware of the size limit on the amount of media you can send; try to keep your video and audio attachments brief.

✔ An easier way to send a multimedia message is to start with the source, such as a picture or video stored on your phone. Use the Share command or button (refer to the icon in the margin), and choose MMS to share the media item. Information about the various Share commands on your phone is covered throughout this book.

✔ Some video attachments can be too large for multimedia messages. The phone warns you when it happens, but more importantly, review the special options in Chapter 15 for creating multimedia message video attachments.

Receiving a multimedia message

A multimedia attachment comes into your phone just like any other text message does, but you see a thumbnail preview of whichever media was sent, such as an image, a still from a video, or the Play button to listen to audio. To preview the attachment, touch it. To do more with the multimedia attachment, long-press it. Choose how to deal with the attachment by selecting an option from the menu that's displayed.

For example, to save an image attachment, long-press the image thumbnail and choose the Save Picture command.

Some types of attachments, such as audio, cannot be saved.

Text Message Management

You don't have to manage your messages. I certainly don't. But the potential exists: If you ever want to destroy evidence of a conversation, or even do something as mild as change the text messaging ringtone, it's possible. Heed my advice in this section.

Removing messages

Though I'm a stickler for deleting e-mail after I read it, I don't bother deleting my text message threads. That's probably because I have no pending divorce litigation. Well, even then, I have nothing to hide in my text messaging conversations. If I did, I would follow these steps to delete a conversation:

1. **Open the conversation you want to remove.**

   Choose the conversation from the main screen in your phone's text messaging app.

2. **Touch the Menu soft button and choose the Delete command.**

3. **Touch the Delete button to confirm.**

   The conversation is gone.

If these steps don't work, an alternative is to open the main screen in the text messaging app and long-press the conversation you want to zap. Choose the Delete command from the pop-up menu, and then touch the OK button to confirm.

Setting the text message ringtone

The sound you hear when a new text message floats in is the text message ringtone. It might be the same sound you hear for all notifications, though on some Android phones it can be changed to something unique. If so, follow these steps to set your Android phone's text message ringtone:

1. **Open the texting app.**

2. **Ensure that you're viewing the main screen, which lists all your conversations.**

   If you're not viewing that screen, press the Back soft button.

3. **Press the Menu soft button.**

4. **Choose the Settings command or Messaging Settings command.**

5. **Choose Select Ringtone.**

6. **Pluck a ringtone from the list.**

7. **Touch the OK button.**

If these steps don't seem to work, refer to Chapter 6, which covers setting ringtones for incoming calls.

10

E-Mail This and That

In This Chapter

▷ Understanding e-mail on your phone

▷ Configuring your e-mail accounts

▷ Receiving a new message

▷ Using the universal inbox

▷ Creating and sending e-mail

▷ Working with e-mail attachments

▷ Making an e-mail signature

▷ Changing the manual delete setting

The art of writing a letter is ancient, probably dating back well before the 1940s. No one knows what that first letter said, though I'd venture to guess it probably wasn't a thank-you note. Fast-forward to the dawn of the telegraph: The first message was supposedly, "What hath God wrought?" The first telephone call was supposedly, "Mr. Watson. Come here. I want you." And in the 1960s, the first e-mail message was sent between two computer scientists, one asking the other whether he wanted to buy some cheap Viagra.

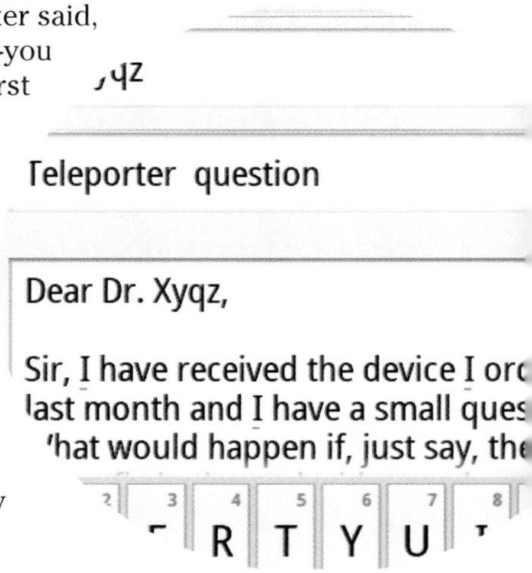

One of the many delightful things your phone can do for you, specifically in the realm of mobile communications, is send and receive e-mail. You can use your phone as a supplement to your computer for your e-mail chores, or your phone can be your only e-mail gizmo.

Teleporter question

Dear Dr. Xyqz,

Sir, I have received the device I ord
last month and I have a small ques
'hat would happen if, just say, the

R T Y U

E-Mail on Your Android Phone

Two apps on your Android phone handle e-mail: Gmail and Email.

The Gmail app hooks directly into your Google Gmail account. In fact, they're exact echoes of each other: The Gmail you receive on your computer is also received on your phone.

The Email app, which might be called Mail, is used to connect to non-Gmail electronic mail, such as the standard mail service provided by your Internet service provider (ISP) or a web-based e-mail system such as Yahoo! Mail or Microsoft Live mail.

Regardless of the app, electronic mail on your phone works identically on your computer: You can receive mail, create new messages, forward mail, send messages to a group of contacts, and work with attachments, for example. As long as your phone has a data connection, e-mail works just peachy.

- The generic Android name for the non-Gmail e-mail app is Email. That's how I refer to the app throughout this chapter.

- The Email app can be configured to handle multiple e-mail accounts, as discussed later in this section.

- Your phone may also feature the generic Messaging app, which can be used to handle all e-mail, text messaging, and other forms of communications. See the section "Visiting the universal inbox," later in this chapter.

- Although you can use your phone's web browser to visit the Gmail website, you should use the Gmail app to pick up your Gmail.

- If you forget your Gmail password, visit this web address:

  `www.google.com/accounts/ForgotPasswd`

Setting up a web-based e-mail account

To access any non-Gmail e-mail account, you need to configure your Android phone. The process is easy for web-based e-mail accounts such as Yahoo! Mail or Hotmail; follow these general steps to set things up:

1. **Open an app to add a new account to your phone.**

   You can add a new account in several ways:

   Start the My Accounts app. It may be found on the App menu. The app might also be named Accounts.

   Choose the Accounts or Accounts & Sync item in the Settings app. You can start the Settings app from the App menu; or at the Home screen, press the Menu soft button and choose Settings.

   Open the Mail app. When the app is open, press the Menu soft button and choose the New Account command. (You may need to choose the More command first and then New Account.)

2. **Touch the Add Account button.**

3. **If your account type is shown in the list, such as Yahoo! Mail, choose it. Otherwise, choose the Email icon.**

4. **Type your account's e-mail address.**

5. **Type the password for the account.**

6. **If you see the option Automatically Configure Account, ensure that a green check mark appears next to it.**

7. **Touch the Next button.**

   In a few magical moments, the e-mail account is configured and added to the account list.

   If you goofed up the account name or password, you're warned: Try again.

8. **Touch the Done button.**

   The account is added to the list on the My Accounts screen.

You can repeat the steps in this section to add more web-based e-mail accounts. To add other types of accounts, read the next section.

Setting up an ISP e-mail account

For e-mail provided by your Internet service provider (ISP) or office, or another large, intimidating organization, you have to work the manual setup. The steps are involved, but as long as you have the details from your ISP, things should work smoothly. Heed these general steps:

1. **Follow Steps 1 and 2 in the preceding section.**

   Get to the place in your phone where you add new accounts, and then touch the Add Account button.

2. **Choose the Email icon to add your Internet e-mail account.**

   In some cases, the option that's presented may be titled Manual Setup.

3. **Type the e-mail address you use for the account.**

4. **Type the password for that account.**

5. **If the green check mark by the option Automatically Configure Account is present, remove it.**

   In some cases, your non-web-based e-mail account can be configured automatically. Count yourself blessed in that case because Step 6 is likely your last step. Otherwise, you need to supply more information.

6. **Touch the Next button.**

   If the account is configured automatically, great. Otherwise, continue: You see a list of options for configuring an e-mail account. The information supplied from your ISP or another large, intimidating organization is necessary to complete the steps and set up your e-mail account.

7. **Choose General Settings.**

8. **Fill in the information for account name, real name, and e-mail address.**

   In the Account Name field, type a name to recognize the account, such as Comcast Email or whatever name helps you recognize the account. For my main e-mail account, I used the name Main.

   In the Real Name field, type your name or screen name or whatever name you want to appear in the From field of your outgoing e-mail messages.

   The Email Address field is the address your recipients use when replying to your messages.

9. **Touch the OK button.**

   If necessary, press the Back soft button to dismiss the onscreen keyboard so that you can see the OK button.

10. **Choose Incoming Server.**

11. **Fill in the fields per the information provided by your ISP.**

    For most ISP e-mail, the server type is the POP mail server, shown at the top of the screen.

    The Server field contains the name of the ISP's POP server. The phone may guess at the name; confirm that it's correct. If not, type the correct server name.

    The *username* is the name you use to log in to your ISP to retrieve e-mail. The *password* is your ISP e-mail password. Both fields should be preset for you.

12. **Touch the OK button.**

13. **Choose Outgoing Server.**

14. **Fill in the fields.**

    Fill in the SMTP server name as provided by your ISP.

    If your username and password aren't already filled in for you, type them now.

15. **Touch the OK button.**

16. **Touch OK one more time to create the e-mail account.**

You can set up a ton of e-mail accounts on your Android phone, one for every e-mail account you have.

You've Got Mail

All Android phones work flawlessly with Gmail. In fact, if Gmail is already set up to be your main e-mail address, you'll enjoy having access to your messages all the time from your phone.

Non-Gmail e-mail, handled by the Email program, must be set up before it can be used, as covered earlier in this chapter. After completing the quick and occasionally painless setup, you can receive e-mail on your phone just as you can on a computer.

Getting a new message

You're alerted to the arrival of a new e-mail message in your phone by a notification icon. The icon differs depending on the e-mail's source.

For a new Gmail message, you see the New Gmail notification, similar to the one shown in the margin, appear at the top of the touchscreen.

For a new e-mail message, you see the New Email notification.

Yahoo! Mail also features its own New Mail notification icon, though your phone may not use this specific icon.

To deal with the new-message notification, drag down the notifications and choose the appropriate one. You're taken directly to your inbox to read the new message.

Checking the inbox

To peruse your Gmail, start the Gmail app. It can be found on the App menu. The Gmail inbox is shown in Figure 10-1.

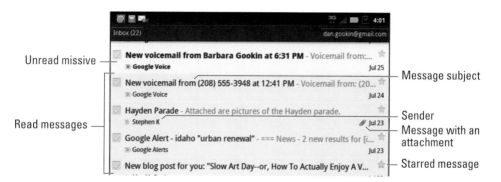

Figure 10-1: The Gmail inbox.

To open the inbox screen when you're reading a message, press the Back soft button.

To check your Email inbox, open the Email app. You're taken to the inbox in your primary e-mail account. To view other e-mail accounts, you may be able to choose them from a menu, or you can opt to view the universal inbox, which is covered in the next section.

✔ Search your Gmail messages by pressing the Search soft key when you're viewing the Gmail inbox.

✔ Gmail is organized using *labels*, not folders. To see your Gmail labels from the inbox, touch the Menu soft button and choose Go to Labels.

Visiting the universal inbox

Many Android phones feature an app that gives you access to your messages from multiple sources. For example, the Messaging app can be used to access not only e-mail messages but also messages from social networking sites, text messaging, and other sources. Figure 10-2 shows an example of what a universal inbox might look like.

Figure 10-2: All your messages, in one place.

If your phone lacks the Messaging app, you might be able to view all your messages using the Email (or Mail) program: Choose the option to view all accounts, which may be accessed from a button or toolbar or by pressing the Menu soft button.

✔ New messages in an account are denoted by a number shown in a blue bubble (refer to Figure 10-2).

- ✔ The universal inbox app doesn't normally list your Gmail account. Because Gmail is part of the Google pantheon of apps, it's treated separately on Android phones.

Reading an e-mail message

As mail comes in, you can read it by choosing a new e-mail notification, such as the Gmail notification, described earlier in this chapter. You can also choose new e-mail by viewing the universal inbox, as covered in the preceding section. Reading and working with messages operate much the same as in any e-mail program you've used.

The way the message looks in the inbox depends on whether you're using the Gmail, Email, or Messaging app. Figure 10-3 shows the Gmail interface; Figure 10-4 shows the Email and Messaging apps' message-reading interface.

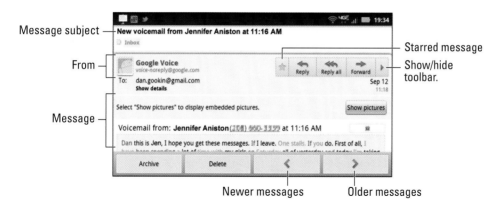

Figure 10-3: Reading a Gmail message on your phone.

Browse messages by touching the arrow buttons at the bottom of the message screen. The buttons may point left and right, as shown in Figure 10-3, or they can point up and down instead. The difference was created merely to confuse you.

Replying to a message works similarly to composing a new message in the Gmail or Email program. Refer to the appropriate section later in this chapter.

- ✔ To access additional e-mail commands, touch the Menu soft button. For example, commands in the Email app shuffle messages between folders, flag messages, and print e-mail.

- ✔ Use Reply All only when everyone else *must* get a copy of your reply. Because most people find endless Reply All e-mail threads annoying, use the Reply All option judiciously.

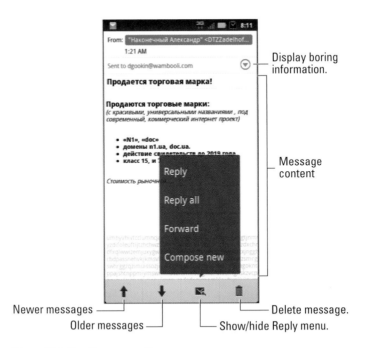

Figure 10-4: Reading an e-mail message.

✔ To forward a Gmail message, touch the Forward button. In the Email program, the Forward command appears on the same menu as the Reply command, shown earlier, in Figure 10-4.

✔ When you touch the Star icon in a Gmail message, you're flagging the message. These starred messages can be viewed or searched separately, making them easier to locate later.

✔ If you've properly configured the Email program, you don't need to delete messages you've read. See the section "Configuring the manual delete option," later in this chapter.

✔ I find it easier to delete (and manage) Gmail using a computer.

Make Your Own E-Mail

Though I use my phone often to check e-mail, I don't often use it to compose new messages. That's because most e-mail messages don't demand an immediate reply. When they do, or when the mood hits me and I feel the desperation that only an immediate e-mail message can quench, I compose a new e-mail message on my Android phone using the methods presented in this section.

Composing a new electronic message

Crafting an e-mail epistle on your Android phone works exactly the same as creating one on your computer. Well, it's *exactly* the same if your computer has a teensy screen and keyboard, but you get the idea. Figure 10-5 shows the basic setup.

Figure 10-5: Writing a new e-mail message.

Here's how to create an e-mail message by using your phone:

1. **Start an e-mail app, either Gmail or Email.**

   You may also be able to compose a new message from the universal inbox app, if your phone has one. In the Messaging app (refer to Figure 10-2), you touch the green Plus button and then choose an account.

2. **Press the Menu soft button and choose Compose.**

   You must view the inbox, not a specific message, for the Compose command to be available.

   The new-message screen appears, looking similar to the one shown in Figure 10-5 but with none of the fields filled in.

3. **If necessary, touch the To field to select it.**

4. **Type the first few letters of a contact name, and then choose a matching contact from the list that's displayed.**

   You can also send to any valid e-mail address not found in your Contacts list, by typing that address.

5. **Type a subject.**

6. **Type the message.**

7. **Touch the Send button to whisk your missive to the Internet for immediate delivery.**

   In Gmail, you can touch the Save Draft button to store the message in the Drafts folder. You can open this folder to reedit the message; touch Send to send it.

Copies of the messages you send in the Email app are stored in the Sent mailbox. If you're using Gmail, copies are saved in your Gmail account, which is accessed from your phone or from any computer connected to the Internet.

- ✒ To cancel a message, press the Menu soft button and choose the Discard command. Touch either the OK or Discard button to confirm.

- ✒ To summon the CC field in Gmail, press the Menu soft button and choose the command Add Cc/Bcc; in the Email app, press the Menu soft button and choose the button Add CC.

- ✒ The formatting toolbar (refer to Figure 10-5) may not be available in your phone's Email app.

- ✒ Refer to Chapter 8 for more information on the phone's address book.

- ✒ Chapter 4 covers typing, voice input, and text editing.

Sending a new message to a contact

A quick and easy way to compose a new message is to find a contact and then create a message using that contact's information. Heed these steps:

1. **Open the phone's address book app.**

   The app is traditionally named Contacts, though the name People is also popular.

2. **Locate the contact to whom you want to send an electronic message.**

   Review Chapter 8 for ways to hunt down contacts in a long list.

3. **Touch the contact's e-mail address.**

4. Choose Email to send an e-mail message using your main e-mail account, or choose Gmail to send the message using Gmail.

Other options may be available for composing the message. For example, a custom e-mail app you've downloaded may show up there as well.

At this point, creating the message works as described in the preceding sections; refer to them for additional information.

When using the Email app, you may be required to choose a specific account for sending the message. If not, the phone chooses your main, or *default,* account.

Message Attachments

Your Android phone lets you view most e-mail attachments, depending on what type of information is attached. You can also send attachments, though it's more of a computer activity, not one that's completely useful on a cell phone. That's because cell phones, unlike computers, aren't designed for creating or manipulating information.

Messages with attachments are flagged in the inbox with the Paperclip icon, which seems to be the standard I-have-an-attachment icon in most e-mail programs. When you open one of these messages, you may see the attachment right away, especially when it's a picture. Otherwise, you see the Attachment button, similar to the one shown in Figure 10-6.

Figure 10-6: E-mail attachment options.

Touch the Preview button to witness the attachment on your phone; touch the Download or Save button to save the attachment to your phone's storage.

What happens after you touch the Preview or View button depends on the type of attachment. Sometimes, you see a list of apps from which you can choose one to open the attachment. Many Microsoft Office documents are opened by the QuickOffice app.

Some attachments cannot be opened. In these cases, use a computer to fetch the message and attempt to open the attachment. Or you can reply to the message and inform the sender that you cannot open the attachment on your phone.

> ✔ Sometimes, pictures included in an e-mail message aren't displayed. Find the Show Pictures button in the message, and touch it to display the pictures.

> ✔ The View Attachment button in the Email app (refer to Figure 10-6) shows thumbnail previews for some image attachments.

> ✔ You can add an attachment to an e-mail message you create: Touch the Menu soft button, and choose either the Attach or Attach Files command. You can then choose what to attach.

> ✔ See Chapter 15 for more information on the Gallery app and to see how image and video sharing work on your phone.

E-Mail Configuration

You can have oodles of fun and waste oceans of time confirming and customizing the e-mail experience on your Android phone. The most interesting things you can do are to modify or create an e-mail signature, specify how mail you retrieve on the phone is deleted from the server, and assign a default e-mail account for the Email app.

Creating a signature

I highly recommend that you create a custom e-mail signature for sending messages from your phone. Here's my signature:

```
DAN

This was sent from my Android phone.
Typos, no matter how hilarious, are unintentional.
```

To create a signature in Gmail, obey these directions:

1. **Start Gmail.**

2. **Press the Menu soft button.**

3. **Choose More and then Settings.**

   If you see no settings, choose Back to Inbox and repeat Steps 2 and 3.

4. **Choose Signature.**

5. **Type or dictate your signature.**

6. **Touch OK.**

You can obey these same steps to change your signature; the existing signature shows up after Step 4.

To set a signature for the Email app, heed these steps:

1. **Start a new message.**

2. **Press the Menu soft button.**

3. **Choose More and then Email Settings.**

   In some cases, the command might be General Settings.

4. **Choose Compose Options.**

   Or you may be lucky and find the Signature command.

5. **If prompted, choose your e-mail account.**

   You create a separate signature for each e-mail account, so when you have multiple accounts, repeat these steps.

6. **Edit the Email Signature area to reflect your new signature.**

   The preset signature was probably set by your cellular provider, something like "Sent from my Verizon Wireless phone because Verizon has the fastest network available in the most places and you should switch to Verizon right now no matter which phone you have or, if you already have a Verizon phone, buy a second one on the Family plan."

   Feel free to edit the preset signature at your whim.

7. **Touch the Done button.**

When you have multiple e-mail accounts, repeat these steps to configure a signature for each one. Choose the e-mail account first before you follow the second set of steps to create a signature.

Configuring the manual delete option

Non-Gmail e-mail that you fetch on your phone typically remains on the e-mail server. That's because, unlike your computer's e-mail program, the phone's Email app doesn't delete messages after it picks them up. The advantage is that you can retrieve the same messages later using your computer. The disadvantage is that you can end up retrieving mail you've already read and replied to.

You can control whether the Email app removes messages after they're picked up. Follow these steps:

1. **Open the app or find the location on your phone where your e-mail accounts are listed.**

   Refer to the earlier section "Setting up a web-based e-mail account," which describes the various account locations. On the standard Android phone, at the Home screen, press the Menu soft button, choose Settings, and then choose Accounts or Accounts & Sync.

2. **From the list of accounts, choose the e-mail account you want to configure.**

3. **Choose the Other Settings command.**

4. **Place a green check mark by the option Remove Manually Deleted Emails from the Server.**

5. **Touch the OK button to confirm the new setting.**

6. **Press the Home soft button to return to the Home screen.**

When you delete a message by using the Email app, the message is also deleted from the mail server. It isn't picked up again, not by the phone, another mobile device, or any computer that fetches e-mail from that same account.

- Mail you retrieve using your computer's mail program is deleted from the mail server after it's picked up. That's normal behavior. Your phone cannot pick up mail from the server if your computer has already deleted it.

- Deleting mail on the server isn't a problem for Gmail. No matter how you access your Gmail account, from your phone or from a computer, the inbox lists the same messages.

11

Out on the Web

In This Chapter

▸ Looking at a web page on your phone

▸ Browsing around the web

▸ Bookmarking pages

▸ Working with multiple browser windows

▸ Searching the web

▸ Sharing a link

▸ Downloading stuff from the web

▸ Changing the home page

I'm certain that when Tim Berners-Lee developed the World Wide Web back in 1990, he had no idea that people would one day use it on their cell phones. Nope, the web was designed to be viewed on a computer, specifically one with a nice, roomy, high-resolution monitor and full-size keyboard. Cell phones? They had teensy LED screens. Browsing the web on a cell phone would have been like viewing the *Mona Lisa* through a keyhole.

Well, okay; viewing the web on your cell phone *is* kind of like viewing the *Mona Lisa* through a keyhole. The amazing thing is that you can do it in the first place. For some web pages, it's workable. For others, you have my handy advice in this chapter for making the web useful — nay, enjoyable — on your Android phone.

▸ Your phone has apps for Gmail, social networking (Facebook, Twitter, and others), YouTube, and potentially other popular locations or activities on the web. I highly recommend using these applications on the phone over visiting their websites using the phone's browser.

▸ If possible, activate the phone's Wi-Fi connection before you venture out on the web. See Chapter 19 for more information on Wi-Fi.

✔ If you have a fast 4G phone, be aware that browsing the web by using that cellular data signal quickly uses up your monthly download quota. At top speeds, it's easy to rack up data surcharges.

Behold the Web

Your World Wide Web cell phone adventure is brought to you by the Browser app. It's found on the App menu, like all apps on your Android phone. You may also find a copy of the Browser app on the main Home screen panel. Using the Browser app works similarly to using a web browser on a computer. Even so, I've written this section to give you a quick orientation.

On some Android phones, the Browser app is named Internet. It's still basically the same Browser app, though it has a different name. In this chapter (and elsewhere in this book), I refer to the app as *Browser*.

Surfing the web on your phone

When you first open the Browser app, you're taken to the home page. Figure 11-1 shows the Google website, which is the preconfigured home screen for all Android phones (though your cellular provider may have hijacked the page to its own home page). You can reset the home page to a different one, as described later in this chapter.

Because your cell phone screen isn't a full desktop screen, not every web page looks good on it. Here are a few tricks you can use:

✔ Pan the web page by dragging your finger across the touchscreen. You can pan up, down, left, and right.

✔ Double-tap the screen to zoom in or zoom out.

✔ Pinch the screen to zoom out, or spread two fingers to zoom in.

✔ Tilt the phone to its side to read a web page in Landscape mode. Then you can spread or double-tap the touchscreen to make teensy text more readable.

Visiting a web page

To visit a web page, type its address in the Address box (refer to Figure 11-1). You can also type a search word, if you don't know the exact address of a web page. Touch the Go button by the Address bar to search the web or visit a specific web page.

If you don't see the Address box, swipe your finger so that you can see the top of the window, where the Address box lurks.

Share.

Bookmark page.

Address box

Go.   Stop.

Dictate
address.

Web page

Figure 11-1: The Browser app beholds the Google home page.

You click links on a page by using your finger on the touchscreen: Touch a link to "click" it and visit another page on the web.

✔ To reload a web page, press the Menu soft button and choose the Refresh command. Refreshing updates a website that changes often, and the command can also be used to reload a web page that may not have completely loaded the first time.

✔ For phones with the Internet app, the Refresh button is found to the right of the Address text box.

✔ To stop a web page from loading, touch the Stop (X) button that appears to the right of the Address box. (Refer to Figure 11-1.)

✔ If your phone features a pointing device, such as a trackball, you can use it to hop between links on a web page. Press the trackball to "click" a link. The same trick applies to arrow keys on the physical keyboard, which can also be used to hop between links.

Browsing back and forth

To return to a previous web page, press the Back soft button. It works just like clicking the Back button on a computer's web browser.

The Forward button also exists in the Browser app: Press the Menu soft button and choose the Forward command.

To review the long-term history of your web browsing adventures, follow these steps:

1. **Press the Menu soft button.**

2. **Choose Bookmarks.**

3. **At the top of the Bookmarks page, choose History.**

   If your phone uses the Internet app, touch the History button in the lower-right corner of the screen.

To view a page you visited weeks or months ago, you can choose a web page from the History list.

To clear the History list, press the Menu soft button while viewing the list, and choose the Clear History command.

Using bookmarks

Bookmarks are those electronic breadcrumbs you can drop as you wander the web. Need to revisit a website? Just look up its bookmark. This advice assumes, of course, that you bother to create (I prefer *drop*) a bookmark when you first visit the site. Here's how it works:

1. **Visit the web page you want to bookmark.**

2. **Touch the Bookmark button, found at the top of the Browser screen.**

   Refer to Figure 11-1 to see the location of the Bookmark button. After pressing the button, you see the Bookmarks screen, looking similar to the one shown in Figure 11-2. The screen lists your bookmarks, showing website thumbnail previews.

3. **Touch the Add button.**

   The Add button appears in the upper-left square on the Bookmarks screen (refer to Figure 11-2). The button specifies, just below the square, the name of the site or page you're bookmarking.

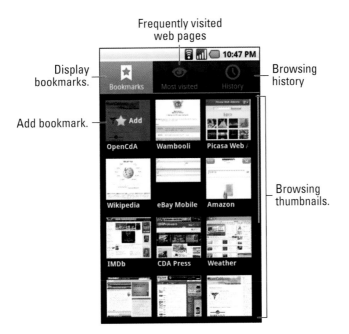

Figure 11-2: Adding a bookmark.

4. If necessary, edit the bookmark name.

The bookmark is given the web page name, which might be kind of long. I usually edit the name to fit beneath the thumbnail square.

5. Touch OK.

If your phone features the Internet app, add a bookmark by visiting the page you want to bookmark, pressing the Menu soft button, and choosing the Add Bookmark command.

After the bookmark is set, it appears on the list of bookmarks. You can swipe the list downward to see the bookmarks and all their fun thumbnails.

Another way to add a bookmark is to touch the Most Visited tab at the top of the Bookmarks screen (refer to Figure 11-2). This screen lists the web pages you frequent. To add one of these pages, long-press it and choose the Add Bookmark command.

✔ To visit a bookmark, press the Menu soft button and choose the Bookmarks command. Touch a bookmark thumbnail to visit that site.

✔ Remove a bookmark by long-pressing its thumbnail on the Bookmarks screen. Choose the command Delete Bookmark. Touch the OK button to confirm.

✔ Bookmarked websites can also be placed on the Home screen: Long-press the bookmark thumbnail, and choose the command Add Shortcut to Home.

✔ You can switch between Thumbnail and List views for your bookmarks: When viewing the Bookmarks screen, press the Menu soft button and choose the List View command to switch to List view. To return to Thumbnail view, press the Menu soft button and choose Thumbnail View.

✔ When held horizontally, the phone displays its bookmark thumbnails in a long list that you can swipe left or right.

 ✔ You can obtain the MyBookmarks app at the Google Play Store. The app can import your Internet Explorer, Firefox, and Chrome bookmarks from your Windows computer into your Android phone. See Chapter 18 for more information on the Play Store.

✔ Refer to Chapter 4 for information on editing text.

Managing multiple web page windows

The latest version of the Browser app sports more than one window, so you can have multiple web pages open at a time. You can summon another browser window in one of several ways:

✔ **To open a link in another window,** long-press the link and choose the command Open in New Window from the menu that appears.

✔ **To open a bookmark in a new window,** long-press the bookmark and choose the Open in New Window command.

✔ **To open a blank browser window,** press the Menu soft button and choose New Window.

You switch between windows by pressing the Menu soft button and choosing the Windows command. All open Browser windows are displayed on the screen; switch to a window by choosing it from the list. Or you can close a window by touching the Minus button to the right of the window's name.

New windows open using the home page that's set for the Browser application. See the section "Setting a home page," later in this chapter, for information.

Searching the web

The handiest way to find things on the web is to use the Google Search widget, often found floating on the Home screen and shown in Figure 11-3.

Use the Google Search widget to type something to search for; touch the Microphone button to dictate what you want to find on the Internet.

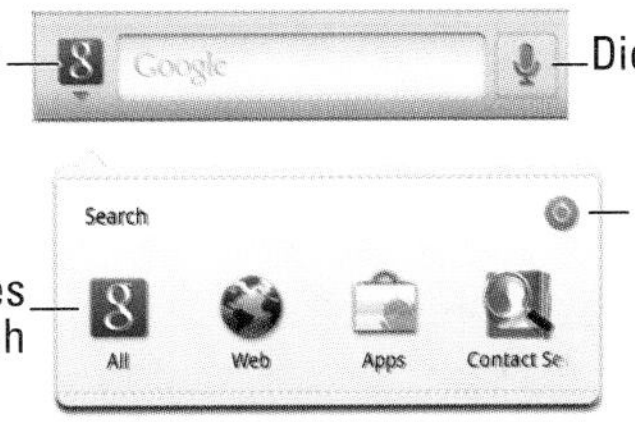

Figure 11-3: The Google Search widget.

To search for something anytime you're viewing a web page in the Browser app, press the Search soft button. Type the search term into the box. You can choose from a suggestions list or touch the Go button to complete the search using the Google search engine.

To find text on the web page you're looking at, rather than search the entire Internet, follow these steps:

1. **Visit the web page where you want to find a specific tidbit o' text.**

2. **Press the Menu soft button.**

3. **Choose the More command and then choose Find on Page.**

4. **Type the text you're searching for.**

5. **Use the left- or right-arrow button to locate that text on the page —
   backward or forward, respectively.**

   The found text appears highlighted in a hideous shade of green.

6. **Touch the X button when you're done searching.**

See Chapter 22 for more information on widgets, such as the Google Search widget.

The Perils and Joys of Downloading

One of the most abused words in all technology is *download*. People don't understand what it means. It's definitely not a synonym for *transfer* or *copy*, though that's how I most often hear it used.

For the sake of your Android phone, a *download* is a transfer of information from another location to your phone. When you send something from the phone, you *upload* it. There. Now the nerd in me feels much better.

You can download information from a web page into your phone. It doesn't work exactly like downloading does for a computer, which is why I wrote this section.

✔ There's no need to download new apps to your phone. All the apps you want can be obtained from the Android Market, covered in Chapter 18.

✔ When the phone is downloading information, you see the Downloading notification. It's an animated icon, though the icon shown in the margin isn't animated in this edition of the book. Completed downloads feature the Download Complete icon, which is not animated.

Grabbing an image from a web page

The simplest thing to download is an image from a web page. It's cinchy: Long-press the image. You see a pop-up menu appear, from which you choose the command Save Image.

✔ The image is copied and stored on your phone. You can view the image by using the Gallery app; refer to Chapter 15 for information on the Gallery.

✔ Your phone may have the Downloads app. (Check the App menu). You can use the Downloads app to peruse and review your web page downloads.

Downloading a file

When a link opens a document on a web page, such as a Microsoft Word document or an Adobe Acrobat (PDF) file, you can download that information to your phone. Simply long-press the download link, and choose the Save Link command from the menu that appears.

You can view the link by referring to the Downloads screen. See the next section.

Reviewing your downloads

You can view downloaded information by perusing the Downloads screen. Summon this screen while using the Browser app by pressing the Menu soft button and choosing the Downloads command. Sometimes you may need to first choose the More command and then choose Downloads.

The Downloads screen presents a list of downloaded items, organized by date. To view the download, you have to choose an item. The phone then starts the appropriate app to view the item so that you can see it displayed on the touchscreen.

Well, of course, some of the things you can download you cannot view. When this happens, you see an appropriately rude error message.

You can quickly review any download by choosing the Download notification.

Web Controls and Settings

More options and settings and controls exist for the Browser app than just about any other app I've used on any Android phone. It's complex. Rather than bore you with every dang doodle detail, I thought I'd present just a few of the options worthy of your attention.

Setting a home page

The *home page* is the first page you see when you start the Browser app, and it's the first page that's loaded when you fire up a new window. To set your home page, heed these directions in the Browser app:

1. **Browse to the page you want to set as the home page.**

2. **Press the Menu soft button.**

3. **Choose More and then Settings.**

    A massive list of options and settings appears.

4. **Choose Set Home Page.**

5. **Touch the Use Current Page button.**

    Because you obeyed Step 1, you don't need to type the web page's address.

6. **Touch OK.**

    The home page is set.

If you want your home page to be blank (not set to any particular web page), set the name of the home page (in Step 5) to `about:blank`. That's the word *about,* a colon, and then the word *blank,* with no period at the end and no spaces in the middle. I prefer a blank home page because it's the fastest web page to load. It's also the web page with the most accurate information.

Changing the way the web looks

You can do a few things to improve the way the web looks on your phone. First and foremost, don't forget that you can orient the phone horizontally to see the wide view on any web page.

From the Settings screen, you can also adjust the text size used to display a web page. Heed these steps:

1. **Press the Menu soft button.**

2. **Choose More and then Settings.**

3. **Choose Text Size.**

   The command might be titled Default Zoom.

4. **Select a better size from the menu.**

   For example, try Large or Huge.

5. **Press the Back soft button to return to the web.**

I don't make any age-related comments about text size at this time, and especially at this point in my life.

Setting privacy and security options

With regard to security, my advice is always to be smart and think before doing anything questionable or tempting on the web. Use common sense. One of the most effective ways that the Bad Guys win is by using *human engineering* to try to trick you into doing something you normally wouldn't do, such as click a link to see a cute animation or a racy picture of a celebrity or politician. As long as you use your noggin, you should be safe.

As far as the phone's settings go, most of the security options are already enabled for you, including the blocking of pop-up windows (which normally spew ads).

If web page cookies concern you, you can clear them from the Settings window. Follow Steps 1 and 2 in the preceding section, and choose the option Clear All Cookie Data. Touch the OK button to confirm.

You can also choose the command Clear Form Data to remove any memorized information you may have typed on a web page.

Remove the check mark from Remember Form Data. These two settings prevent any characters you've input into a text field from being summoned automatically by someone who may steal your phone.

You might be concerned about various warnings regarding location data. What they mean is that the phone can take advantage of your location on Planet Earth (using the phone's GPS, or global satellite positioning system) to help locate businesses and people near you. I see no security problem in leaving this feature on, though you can disable location services from the Browser's Settings screen: Remove the check mark by Enable Location. You can also choose the item Clear Location Access to wipe out any information that's saved in the phone and used by certain web pages.

See the earlier section "Browsing back and forth" for steps on clearing your web browsing history.

12

Social Networking

In This Chapter

▶ Accessing your social networking accounts

▶ Updating your status

▶ Sharing photos on Facebook

▶ Using the Facebook app

▶ Setting up a Twitter client

▶ Accessing other social networking sites

Social networking is that 21st century phenomenon that proves many odd beliefs about people. For example, it's possible to have hundreds of friends and never leave your house. You can jealously guard your privacy against the wicked intrusions of the government and Big Brother, all while letting everyone on the Internet know that you've just "checked in" to Starbucks and are having an iced mocha frappuccino. And you can share your most intimate moments with humanity, many of whom will "like" the fact that you've just broken up or that your cat was run over by the garbage collection service.

One of your Android phone's key duties is to keep you connected with your social networking universe. You can use specific apps for popular services such as Facebook and Twitter, or your phone may come with a general app that handles all your social networking duties in one spot.

Your Android Phone Gets Social

The point of social networking is to be social. The benefit to being on the Internet is that you don't have to wear proper social clothing. That's such a potent combination, but it doesn't benefit you until you start adding some social networking accounts to your life and to your phone.

Setting up social networking

The Internet is bursting with social networking opportunities. So is your phone. But before you can get anything started, you need to harbor a few accounts on some of the popular social networking sites.

I recommend first setting up your social networking accounts on the web — preferably, using a computer. That way, you have a full-size screen and keyboard to help you create the accounts and get things configured. Though you can add new accounts using your phone, I find it more convenient to first use a computer.

After your accounts are set up and you experience the thrill of social networking on a computer, you're ready to have the same, albeit more mobile, experience on your phone.

Adding social networking accounts

Before you become the mobile master of your digital social life, you need to let your phone know about your social networking accounts. The process works similarly to adding non-Gmail e-mail accounts, which is covered in Chapter 10. For social networking, you simply inform the phone of your existing social networking accounts, which the phone then adds to your account repertoire.

All accounts on your Android phone, mail or social networking, are kept in one specific location: the Accounts screen. Here is one way to get there and add a social networking account or three:

1. **At the Home screen, press the Menu soft button.**

2. **Choose Settings.**

3. **Choose either Accounts or Accounts and Sync.**

4. **Touch the Add Account button.**

5. **Choose your social networking site from the list of accounts.**

   Don't despair if no social networking accounts are listed. It simply means that your phone lacks an all-in-one social networking app. You can still use the individual social networking apps, as covered later in this chapter. See the section "Various Social Networking Apps."

6. **Type your social networking login (user ID or e-mail address), and then type your password.**

7. **Touch the Next button (if necessary), and then eventually touch the Done or Finish button.**

Repeat these steps as necessary to notify your phone of additional social networking accounts.

✔ Your Android phone may sport either an Accounts app or a My Accounts app on the App menu. You can use this app as a quick shortcut to get to the Accounts screen.

✔ The Accounts screen can also be used to manage your social networking accounts. Choose an account from this screen to update a password, for example. Or, when things become entirely dismal, you can use the Accounts screen to remove an account.

✔ To *change* the password for a social networking account, use the social networking site on the web — preferably, by using a computer. After making the change, you need to *update* the account information on your phone.

Your Digital Social Life

You may be lucky: Your Android phone may have come with an all-in-one social networking app. The app might be titled Social Networking or Friend Stream or another clever name. No matter what, this app is a good place to start for your cell phone social networking adventures.

✔ I refer to the generic social networking app as *the Social Networking app* in this section.

✔ Not all is lost if your phone lacks a general social networking app. Simply refer to the later section "Various Social Networking Apps" for information on obtaining specific social networking apps for popular services such as Facebook and Twitter and others.

Finding out what's going on

When you start the Social Networking app, you see a list of status updates, news, and tweets from your social networking pals, similar to the ones shown in Figure 12-1. Tiny icons flag the various social networking sites from which the information is pulled, as illustrated in the figure.

Notification icons

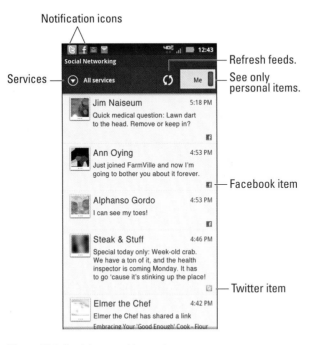

Services ———

Refresh feeds.

See only personal items.

Facebook item

Twitter item

Figure 12-1: Social networking updates.

Touching an entry displays more details, such as comments, links, or images. For example, if you want to "like" an item in Facebook, touch that item to see its details. Touch the Like button on the details screen to like the post, or touch the Add Comment button to express your opinion.

✏ Updates to your social networking sites are flagged by notification icons, as illustrated in Figure 12-1. Choose the notification icon, as described in Chapter 3, to see what's up.

• To see only information intended for you, touch the Me button at the top of the screen, as shown in Figure 12-1.

• Some social networking apps may list buttons along the bottom of the screen that let you customize the information you're viewing.

✏ You might also be able to filter which networking sites show up in the list. For example, in Figure 12-1 you can touch the Services button to choose the sites you want to view.

Setting your status

There's no point in doing the social networking thing if you aren't going to be social. When you use the Social Networking app, sharing the most intimate details of your life with the entire online universe is as simple as it can be potentially embarrassing.

Depending on the app, setting your status can be done in one of several ways.

For example, you can press the Menu soft button and choose the Set Status command. Or a text box might say "Status" or "What's on your mind?" Fill in that text box to create an update.

Figure 12-2 shows the status update portion of the Social Networking app on the Droid Bionic. You can fill in the fields, choose which networking sites to update, or attach media, as illustrated in the figure.

Type your status. ── What do robot vampires suck?

Sites to post to ── To: ── Post your new status.
── Attach location or website link.

Current Twitter tweet ── Imagine how much better the world would be if we all simply fixed our own backyards. *3 minutes ago*

Current Facebook status ── Sometimes you really need to take off your shoes and walk barefoot in the kitchen before you realize how badly the floor needs sweeping. *6 hours ago*

Figure 12-2: Sharing your status.

Updating your status is done by touching the Post button or Share button. Your social networking sites are updated immediately.

- ✓ When you post to Facebook, your status explains that you posted using a mobile device. This text is a clue to others that you used your phone to set your status.

- ✓ Your phone's social networking app may also have a widget, which you can use directly on the Home screen. Social networking widgets may merely display updates from your friends or followers, or they can be used to post updates. See Chapter 22 for information on installing widgets on the Home screen.

- ✓ You can use the Attach button (refer to Figure 12-2) to share websites, images already stored on the phone, and other information.

✔ It's also possible to share information with social networking sites by using the various Share buttons and commands found on many Android apps.

✔ There's no way to unpost a status using the Social Networking app. For that kind of magic, I recommend visiting the social networking site on a computer.

Uploading a picture

Sometimes, you may find a social networking app that features a camera button. If so, you can use the button to instantly snap a picture and upload it to the social networking site. Beyond that, the best way to upload a picture is to use the Camera app to take the picture and then use the Share command to send the picture to your social universe. Here are the general steps to follow:

1. **View the image you want to share.**

   You can view the image immediately after you take it or view it in the phone's Gallery app (see Chapter 15).

2. **Touch the Share button, found at the bottom of the screen.**

   You may need to touch the screen so that the onscreen menu appears and you can see the Share button. If there's no Share button, press the Menu soft button and look for a Share command.

3. **From the menu that opens, choose the command to share the image on your social networking site.**

   The command might be the same as the name of the site, such as Facebook or Twitter, or it might have a generic name, such as Photo Share.

4. **Replace the image's long, cryptic name with a more appropriate description.**

   The name that's shown is the image's filename as it's stored on your phone. Long-press the name to select it, and then type something new.

5. **Touch the Send button to upload the image and its description.**

In just a few Internet seconds, the image is uploaded, online, and available for viewing by your friends and followers.

Various Social Networking Apps

I've used a lot of phones that have general social networking apps. The apps are okay, but the best way to experience the thrill of social networking on your Android phone is to obtain a specific app for a specific social networking service.

Using the Facebook app

 The Facebook for Android app is the best way to enjoy the Facebook experience on your Android phone. You can scan the QR code shown in the margin or visit the Google Play Store to search for the Facebook app, as described in Chapter 18.

The News Feed screen for the Facebook app is shown in Figure 12-3. You can use this screen to do most of the Facebook things you can do on the web, including upload a photo or keep your status up-to-date wherever you go with your phone.

News feed and updates

Facebooky things to do

Notification

Comment/ Like

Figure 12-3: Facebook on your phone.

After installing the Facebook for Android app, accept the licensing agreement and sign in. You need to sign in even if you've already configured Facebook for any general social networking app you may have already installed on your phone. (They're two separate apps.)

Set your Facebook status by touching the Status button, illustrated in Figure 12-3.

To take a picture with the Facebook app, touch the Photo Button, which is shown in Figure 12-3, though there are picture-uploading options all over the Facebook app. You get to decide whether to upload a picture you've already taken from the Gallery or choose the Capture a Photo command to take a picture immediately.

After you take the picture, touch the Done button. Add a caption, and then touch the Upload button to send the picture to Facebook.

To sign out of Facebook on your phone, touch the Menu soft button when viewing the main Facebook screen, and choose the Logout command. Touch the Yes button to confirm.

Tweeting to other twits

The Twitter social networking site proves the hypothesis that everyone will be famous on the Internet for 140 characters or fewer.

Like Facebook, Twitter is used to share your existence with others or simply to follow what others are up to or thinking. It sates some people's craving for attention and provides the bricks that pave the road to fame — or so I believe. I'm not a big Twitter fan, but your phone is capable of letting you *tweet* from wherever you are.

The Twitter application provides an excellent interface to many Twitter tasks. You can search for it at the Google Play Store or use your phone to scan its QR code, shown in the margin. Chapter 18 offers more information on installing new apps on your phone.

After installing the app, sign in. You eventually see the Twitter app's main interface, where you can read tweets from the people you're following.

To tweet, touch the New Tweet icon, shown in the margin. Use the New Tweet screen to send text, upload an image from the Gallery, or take a new picture.

➤ Some HTC phones come with the Peep app, which is also used to access and share information with Twitter.

➤ They say that of all the people who have accounts on Twitter, only a small portion of them actively use the service.

➤ A message posted on Twitter is a *tweet*.

➤ You can post messages on Twitter or follow others who post messages.

Exploring other social networking opportunities

The web is brimming with new social networking phenomena. My guess is that each of them is trying to dethrone Facebook as the king of the social networking sites. Good luck with that.

Despite the fact that Facebook and Twitter capture a lot of media attention, other popular social networking sites are out there, such as

➤ LinkedIn

➤ Google+

➤ Meebo

➤ MySpace

These sites may have special Android apps you can install on your Android phone, such as the MySpace Mobile app for MySpace.

As with Facebook and Twitter, you should always configure an account by using a computer and then set up options on your phone.

After adding social networking apps, you may see them appear on the various Share menus found on several apps. Use the Share menus to help you share media files with your online social networking pals.

13

Veni, Vidi, Dixi (Video Chat)

In This Chapter

▷ Setting up Google Talk

▷ Adding friends to the Talk app

▷ Doing a video chat

▷ Working with the Skype app

▷ Getting Skype contacts

▷ Chatting on Skype

▷ Making a Skype voice or video call

The holy grail of telecommunications is video chat. It was something that everyone took for granted would happen in the future; various science fiction films and TV shows always showed people in the future (which was predicted to be sometime around 1980) as using video phones. Of course, that prophecy never came to pass . . . until now.

As long as your cell phone features a front-facing camera and has the proper app installed — and the app is permitted by your cellular provider to offer you the service — you can video-chat on your Android phone. Even if your phone is unable to perform the feat, you can still use the video chat apps to keep in touch, chat, or even place Internet phone calls. The future is here.

Google Can Talk . . . and See

Your phone may have shipped with a video chat app on board. A bunch of these apps are out there, including Qik, Tango, and a few others. The one that I consider the standard is Google Talk. It's not that Google Talk is any better than the others — it's just that Google Talk is from Google, and Android is the Google phone operating system. Therefore, this section covers using Google Talk, including its video chat feature.

✔ Google Talk should be preinstalled on your phone. If it isn't, you can try looking for it at the Google Play Store (see Chapter 18). If it doesn't show up there, you have to find other options for video chat on your Android phone.

✔ Google Talk is directly available on the Internet. It's found on the main Gmail page. If your computer has a camera, you can activate the video chat feature on your computer as well as on your phone.

✔ Google Talk started out as an extension of Gmail on the Internet, primarily as a way to instantly text-chat with your Google friends. Eventually, they added video chat and, lo, over all these years, video chat is now available on your Android phone and on other Android mobile devices.

Using Google Talk

Get started with Google Talk by starting the Talk app on your phone. Like all apps, it can be found on the App menu, though you may be lucky and find the Talk app shortcut right on the Home screen.

When you start the Talk app the first time, you're prompted to sign in using your Google account: Touch the Sign In button. I'm sure they could have made the setup more painful than that, but they didn't.

After signing in, you see the main Talk screen, shown in Figure 13-1. Your Google contacts who have activated Google Talk, either on a computer or on a mobile gizmo such as an Android phone, are shown along with whether they're available to chat.

You can do one of three things with your friends while using the Talk app: text-chat, voice-chat, or video-chat. But before you do any of these, you need to get some friends.

✔ Set your status by touching your account name at the top of the list (see Figure 13-1). You can also set a status message and determine whether you're available for voice or video chat.

✔ To sign out of Google Talk, press the Menu soft button and choose the Sign Out command.

Inviting a friend to Google Talk

Yeah, it happens: You have no friends. Well, at least you have no friends showing up on the Friends list in the Talk app. This problem can easily be fixed by heeding these steps in the Talk app:

1. **Press the Menu soft button.**

2. **Choose the Add Friend command.**

Touch to set your status.

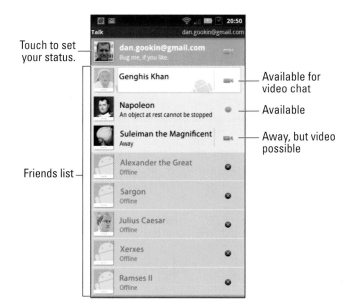

Available for video chat

Available

Away, but video possible

Friends list

Figure 13-1: Google Talk.

3. **Type your friend's name or e-mail address.**

   As you type, matches from your phone's address book appear in a list. Choose a friend from the list to instantly stuff their address into the text box.

4. **Touch the Send Invitation button.**

The best way for your pal to receive the invitation is for them to be using a mobile device that's running the Talk app or to be on a computer with the Gmail web page open. After receiving the invitation, the friend finds it listed in their Friends list; Google Talk initiations have the heading Chat Invitation.

Your friend can be on a computer or a mobile device to use Google Talk; it doesn't matter which. But they must have a camera available in order to video-chat.

Typing at your friends

The most basic form of communications with the Talk app is *text chatting*, or typing at another person, which is probably one of the oldest forms of communications on the Internet. It's also the most tedious, so I'll be brief.

Text chatting starts by touching a contact from the Friends list. Type your message, as shown in Figure 13-2. Touch the Send button to send your comment.

Current chat friend

Video chat

Type text message.

Send message.

Figure 13-2: Text chatting.

You type, they type, and so on until you grow tired or the phone runs out of battery juice.

When you're done talking, press the Menu soft button and choose the Friends List command to return to the main Talk screen (refer to Figure 13-1). You can choose another friend from the list to chat with or press the Home soft button to do something else with your phone.

Resume a conversation by choosing the same contact from the Friends list.

Talking and video chat

Take the conversation up a notch by touching either the Voice or Video button on the right side of the text chat window (refer to Figure 13-2). The Camera icon (shown in the figure) means that video chat is available; the Microphone icon indicates that voice (not video) chat is available; the round dot means text-only.

When you start a voice or video chat, your friend receives a pop-up invite and a Talk notification. Or, if a friend is asking you to voice- or video-chat, you see the pop-up. Touch the Accept button to begin talking.

Figure 13-3 shows a video chat. The person you're talking with appears in the big window, and you're in the smaller window. With the connection made and the invite accepted, you can begin enjoying video chat.

Mute the microphone.   Person you're calling

Enter text chat.   Switch cameras.   End video chat.   You

Figure 13-3: Video chat with Google Talk.

The controls atop the screen may vanish after a second; touch the screen to see the controls again.

To end the conversation, touch the X (Close) button. Well, say "Goodbye" first, and then touch the X button.

- ✔ When you're nude, or you simply don't want to video-chat, touch the Decline button for the video chat invite. Then choose that contact, and reply with a text message or voice chat instead.

- ✔ You can disable incoming voice and video chats by deselecting the Allow Video and Voice Chats item on your Talk account's status screen: At the main Talk screen, touch your account in the Friends list (refer to Figure 13-1).

- ✔ I highly recommend using a Wi-Fi network for video chat. Though you might be able to use the digital cellular network, the service may be limited.

- ✔ Your phone's front-facing camera is at the top, near the speaker. It can be left, right, or center. If you want to make eye contact, look directly into the camera, though when you do, you can't see the other person.

Skype the World

The popular Skype app is used the world over as a free way to make Internet phone calls and to video-chat. Plus, if you're willing to pony up some money, you can make inexpensive calls to phones around the world. So although Google Talk might be enough of a topic for this chapter, far more people are using Skype. Skype may end up being a better choice for text, video, and voice chat on your Android phone.

Obtaining a Skype account

Get started with Skype by creating an account. I recommend visiting www.skype.com on a computer, where you can enjoy the full screen and keyboard.

At the Skype website, click the Join Skype button or, if the page has been updated since this book went to press, find and click a similarly labeled button. Sign up according to the directions offered on the website.

After you have a Skype account, your next step is to obtain the Skype app for your Android phone, as covered in the next section.

✔ As with other web services, you create a Skype name to identify your user account. It's the name you use to identify yourself to others who use Skype.

✔ If you want to use Skype to place calls to real phones or to dial internationally, stuff some cash into your account. Log in to the Skype website, and follow the directions for getting Skype Credit.

✔ There's no charge for using Skype to chat with other Skype users. As long as you know the other party's Skype name, connecting and chatting are simple. See the later section "Chatting with another Skype user."

Getting Skype for your phone

Your Android phone may already come with the Skype app preinstalled. If not, you can visit the Google Play Store and download the app. If you have a bar-code-scanning app, you can also scan the icon in the margin, as described in this book's introduction.

After installing Skype, follow these steps to get started:

1. **Start the Skype app.**

2. **Read the initial, informational screens.**

   You can't make emergency calls using Skype.

3. **Type your Skype account name and password.**

4. **Touch the Sign In button.**

   You may be asked to accept the terms of agreement; do so. You may be offered a tour to preview how Skype works. Feel free to skip the tour.

One of the biggest questions you're asked when you first run the Skype app on your phone is whether you want to synchronize your contacts. I recommend choosing the preset option, Sync with Existing Contacts. Touch the Continue button.

The main Skype screen is shown in Figure 13-4. The Contacts button lists people and phone numbers you've connected with on Skype. The next section, about building your Skype Contacts list, describes how to get more contacts than just Skype Test Call.

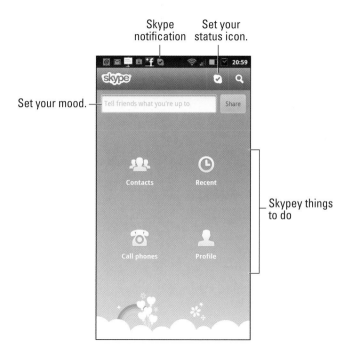

Figure 13-4: Skype's main screen.

The Skype app stays active the entire time your phone is on. If you desire to sign out of Skype, follow these steps:

1. **Touch the Profile button on the Skype app's main screen.**

   Refer to Figure 13-4.

2. **Press the Menu soft button.**

3. **Choose Sign Out.**

4. **Touch the Yes button.**

You're prompted to sign back in to Skype the next time you run the app.

To quickly access Skype, touch the Skype notification, shown in the margin.

Building your Skype Contacts list

Text, voice, and video chat on Skype over the Internet are free. If you can use a Wi-Fi connection, you can chat without incurring a loss of your cellular plan's data quota. Before you can talk, however, you need to connect with another Skype user.

Yes, the other person must have a Skype account. Further, the person must agree to your request to become a Skype contact.

The Skype app can scan your phone's address book for any potential Skype subscribers you may have missed. The operation can take some time — like, over an hour — though it's worth the time you spend waiting. To find your friends on Skype, follow these steps:

1. **Touch the Contacts button on the Skype app's main screen.**

2. **Press the Menu soft button.**

3. **Choose Search Address Book.**

   You most likely already have a gaggle of contacts in your phone. The Skype app can scour that list and discover which ones are already on Skype.

4. **Touch the Continue button.**

   This operation can take some time. (I'm serious — more than an hour). Be patient.

   You can snooze the phone while Skype is plowing through the address book.

   Eventually, you see a list of Skype contacts that the Skype app has found in your Contacts list.

5. **Touch the Continue button.**

6. **Remove the check marks by the contacts you do not want to add.**

   The Skype app lists all contacts it could find who have Skype accounts. If you add these contacts (see Step 7), a Skype request is sent to each one. If you don't want to send a request to someone in the list, remove the check mark by that contact's name.

   Be sure to check the list! Skype searches for matching text, not for individuals, so random and unusual Skype contacts will doubtlessly show up in the list, especially ones that list multiple Skype names; look for `Customer Care` and `noreply`, and be sure to remove them.

7. **Touch the Add button.**

8. **Type an introductory message.**

   The contact has to approve you as a Skype buddy, so make the message sound important but not urgent, wanting but not desperate.

9. **Touch the Add Contacts button.**

   The contacts are added to the Contacts tab, but they sport the question mark status until they agree to accept your Skype invitation.

If scanning the phone's address book doesn't do the job, you can try searching for a specific contact:

1. **Touch the Contacts button on the Skype app's main screen.**

2. **Press the Menu soft button.**

3. **Choose Add Contacts.**

4. **Type a name or phone number.**

5. **Touch the Search button to start the search.**

6. **Scroll the list of results to find the exact person you're looking for.**

   If your friend has a common name, the list is extensive. You can use city information to help narrow the list, but not every Skype user specifies a current city. The Skype username may also help you identify specific people.

7. **Touch an entry to add it to your Contacts list.**

   You see a full-page description for the contact, where you can choose to call them, chat on Skype, or add them to your Contacts list.

8. **Touch the Add button.**

No matter how you add someone to your list, you see the Question Mark icon as that person's status until they agree to accept your request.

✔ You can always e-mail people you know and ask whether they're on Skype.

✔ Some people may not use Skype often, so it takes a while for them to respond to your friend request.

✔ If you accidentally add unusual or odd Skype contacts, my advice is to delete them. To remove a contact, long-press the contact's name in the list and choose the Remove Contact command from the pop-up menu.

✔ You can block a contact by long-pressing the entry and choosing the Block Contact command from the pop-up menu.

✔ If the Skype app crashes during a contact-searching operation, you've probably collected some bogus Skype contacts. It happens. A good way to get out of this situation is to use the Skype program on a computer to clean up and remove unwanted contacts. You may also need to uninstall and then reinstall the Skype app. See Chapter 18 for information on uninstalling apps.

Chatting with another Skype user

You can text-chat with any Skype user, which works similarly to texting, though with no maximum-character limitations. The only restriction is that you can chat only with other Skype users.

To chat, choose a contact from the Contacts list (refer To Figure 13-4). You see a screen with more detailed information about the contact. Choose the option Send IM, where the IM stands for Instant Message. If your Skype friend is online and eager, you'll be chatting in no time, as shown in Figure 13-5.

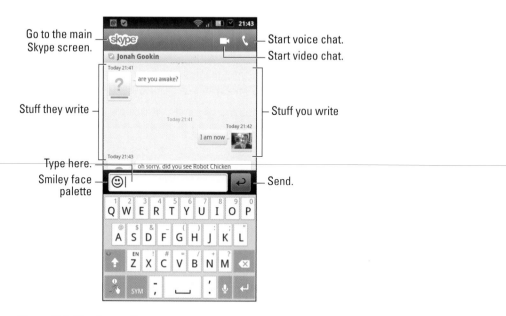

Figure 13-5: Chatting on Skype.

Type your text in the box illustrated in Figure 13-5. Touch the Send button to publish your comment. You can also use the Smiley button to insert a cute graphical image into your text. The conversation unfolds similarly to the one shown in Figure 13-5.

✏ The Skype Chat notification, shown in the margin, appears whenever someone wants to chat with you. It's handy to see, especially when you may have switched away from the Skype app to do something else on your phone. Simply touch the notification to get into the conversation.

✏ You can add more people to the conversation, if you like: Touch the bottom Menu soft button, and choose the Add command. Select the contacts that you want to join your chat session, and then touch the Add Selected button. It's a gang chat!

✏ To stop chatting, press the Back soft button. The conversation remains in the Skype app, even after the other person has disconnected.

✏ Old chats stored in the Skype app are accessed from the Recent icon button (refer to Figure 13-4).

✏ For the chat to work, the other user must be online and available.

Using Skype for voice and video chat

Typing is so 19th century, so why bother? When you tire of typing at your Skype buddies, you can have them "pick up the phone" and start a voice or video chat. Follow these steps:

1. **Touch the Contacts icon on the Skype app's main screen.**

2. **Choose a contact.**

   Chatting works best when the contact is available: Look for the green Check Mark icon by their name.

3. **Choose Skype Call from the Actions tab on the contact's information screen.**

   If prompted, choose the contact's Skype account, not their phone number. You can't place a Skype phone call unless you have Skype Credit. Even then, it's probably cheap (or free) to make a regular call using your phone instead of Skype.

   In a few Internet seconds, the other person picks up and you're speaking with each other.

4. **Talk.**

   Blah-blah-blah. There's no time limit, though Internet connection problems may inadvertently hang you up.

To disconnect the call, touch the red End Call button.

When someone calls you on Skype, you see the Skype incoming-call screen, similar to the one shown in Figure 13-6. Touch the Audio button to answer as a voice-only call; touch the Video button (if it's available) to answer using video. Touch Decline to dismiss the call, especially when it's someone who annoys you.

Figure 13-6: An incoming Skype voice call.

The incoming-call screen (see Figure 13-6) appears even when the phone is sleeping; the incoming call wakes up the phone, just as a real call would.

✔ Voice and video chat on Skype over the Internet are free. When you use a Wi-Fi connection, you can chat without incurring a loss of your cellular plan's data minutes.

✔ You can chat with any user in your Skype Contacts list, by using a mobile device, a computer, or any other gizmo on which Skype is installed.

✔ Video chat is available only on a handful of cell phones that have front-facing cameras but also are allowed to video chat. Not every Android phone with a front-facing camera has video chat available. (Blame the cellular provider.)

✔ Video chat may be available only over Wi-Fi or 4G connections.

✔ Calling a real phone — cellular, landline, or international — with Skype is possible only when you have Skype Credit. See Chapter 21.

✔ If you plan to use Skype a lot, get a good headset.

✔ It's impossible to tell whether someone has dismissed a Skype call or simply hasn't answered. And Skype has no voice mail so that you can leave a message.

Part IV
Amazing Android Phone Feats

*Y*our phone can do what? It's a question you'll enjoy hearing. That's because your mere cell phone is more than a cell phone. Beyond phone calls and Internet communications come a whole slew of interesting and useful features. Indeed, a single Android phone can replace about half a dozen fun and useful electronic gizmos you may already be toting around with you.

The typical Android phone can also be used as a GPS, or navigation, tool. It serves as both a still and video camera. You can use your phone to enjoy music, check your schedule, calculate the tip on your dinner check, wake you in the morning, play games, and use a host of other useful and interesting features, all covered in this part of the book.

Fun with Maps and Navigation

*W*here are you? More importantly, where is the nearest Mexican restaurant? Normally, these questions can be best answered when you're somewhere familiar or with someone who knows the territory or while standing at a brightly lit intersection and the restaurant nearby is wafting the aroma of chili peppers and tequila and the sign says *Roberto's*.

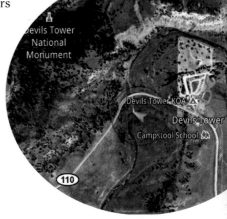

The answer to the questions "Where are you?" and "What's nearby?" are readily provided by the Maps app. This app uses your phone's global positioning system (GPS) abilities to gather information about your location. It also uses Google's vast database to locate interesting places nearby and even get you to those locations. The Maps app is truly amazing and useful — if you understand how it all works. This chapter can help.

Basic Map

Perhaps the best thing about using the Maps app is that there's no risk of improperly folding anything. Even better, the Maps app charts everything: freeways, highways, roads, streets, avenues, drives, bike paths, addresses, businesses, and points of interest.

Using the Maps app

Start the Maps app by choosing Maps from the App menu, or you may find a shortcut to the Maps app lurking on the Home screen. If you're starting the app for the first time or if it has recently been updated, you can read its What's New screen; touch the OK button to continue.

Your Android phone communicates with GPS satellites to hone in on your current location. (See the later sidebar "Activate your locations!") It's shown on the map, similar to Figure 14-1. The position is accurate to within a given range, as shown by a blue circle around your location on the map.

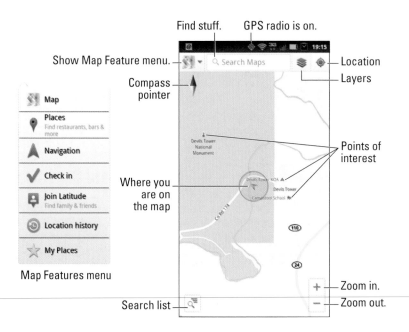

Figure 14-1: Your location on the map.

Here are some fun things you can do when viewing the basic street map:

Zoom in: To make the map larger (to move it closer), touch the Zoom In button, double-tap the screen, or spread your fingers on the touchscreen.

Zoom out: To make the map smaller (to see more), touch the Zoom Out button or pinch your fingers on the touchscreen.

Pan and scroll: To see what's to the left or right or at the top or bottom of the map, drag your finger on the touchscreen; the map scrolls in the direction you drag your finger.

Rotate: Using two fingers, rotate the map clockwise or counterclockwise. Touch the Compass Pointer (shown earlier, in Figure 14-1) to reorient the map with north at the top of the screen.

Perspective: Tap the Location button to switch to Perspective view, where the map is shown at an angle. Touch the Location button again (though now it's truly the Perspective button) to return to flat-map view or, if that doesn't work, touch the compass pointer.

The closer you zoom in to the map, the more detail you see, such as street names, address block numbers, and businesses and other sites — but no tiny people.

- ✔ Touching the Map Features button displays a menu full of interesting things you can do with the Maps app, as shown in Figure 14-1. Several of these items are covered elsewhere in this chapter.

- ✔ The blue triangle (refer to Figure 14-1) shows in which general direction the phone is pointing.

- ✔ When the phone's direction is unavailable, you see a blue dot as your location on the map.

- ✔ When all you want is a virtual compass, similar to the one you lost as a kid, you can get the Compass app from the Google Play Store. See Chapter 18 for more information about the Google Play Store.

- ✔ Perspective view can be entered only for your current location.

Adding layers

You add details from the Maps app by applying layers: A *layer* can enhance the map's visual appearance, provide more information, or add other fun features to the basic street map, such as in Satellite view, shown in Figure 14-2.

The key to accessing layers is to touch the Layers button, illustrated in Figure 14-2. Choose an option from the Layers menu to add that information to the Map app's display.

You can add another layer by choosing it from the Layers menu, but keep in mind that some layers obscure others. For example, the terrain layer overlays the satellite layer so that you see only the terrain layer.

Activate your locations!

The Maps app works best when you activate all the phone's location technology. I recommend that you turn on three location settings: From the Home screen, press the Menu soft button and choose Settings. Then choose Location & Security. On the Location and security-settings screen, in the My Location area, ensure that green check marks appear by all items in the list.

The names for the three items vary from phone to phone, but generally they cover these technologies:

Google Services: Allows software access to your location using Google technology.

GPS Services: Allows your phone to access the global positioning system (GPS) satellites, though it's not pinpoint accurate. That's why you need to activate more than this service to fully use your phone's location abilities.

Network Services: Allows the phone to use signals from the cell towers to triangulate your position and refine the data received from GPS Services.

Further, you can activate the phone's Wi-Fi feature for location information that's even more exact. See Chapter 19 for information on turning on the phone's Wi-Fi setting.

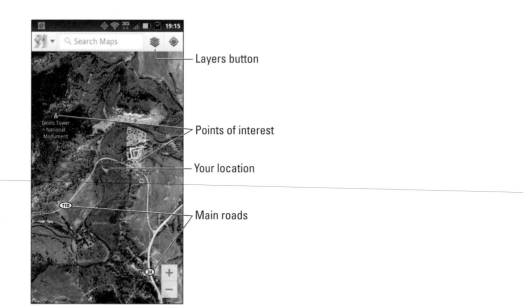

Layers button

Points of interest

Your location

Main roads

Figure 14-2: The satellite layer.

To remove a layer, choose it from the Layers menu; any active layer appears with a green check mark to its right. To return to Street view, remove all layers.

✔ Most features found on the Layers menu originated in the Google Labs. To see new features that may be added to the Maps app, visit the Labs by pressing the Menu soft button in the Maps app. Choose Settings and then Labs to pore over potential new features.

✔ The phone warns you whenever various applications access its Location feature. The warning is nothing serious — the phone is just letting you know that an app is accessing the phone's physical location. Some folks may view this action as an invasion of privacy; hence the warnings. I see no issue with letting the phone know where you are, but I understand that not everyone feels that way. If you'd rather not share location information, simply decline access when prompted.

It Knows Where You Are

War movies sometimes have this cliché scene: Some soldiers are looking at a map. They wonder where they are, when one of them says, "We're not even on the map!" Such things never happen on your phone's Maps app. That's because it always knows where you are.

Finding out where you are

The Maps app shows your location as a blue dot or compass arrow on the screen. But *where* is that? I mean, if you need to phone a tow truck, you can't just say, "I'm the blue triangle on the orange slab by the green thing."

Well, you *can* say that, but it probably won't do any good.

To find your current street address, or any street address, long-press a location on the Maps screen. Up pops a bubble, similar to the one shown in Figure 14-3, that gives your approximate address.

If you touch the address bubble (refer to Figure 14-3), you see a screen full of interesting things you can do, as shown in Figure 14-4.

When you're searching for a location, the distance and general direction are shown next to the Street view preview (refer to Figure 14-4). Otherwise, if you're just finding out where you are, the distance and direction information isn't necessary.

The What's Nearby command displays a list of nearby businesses or points of interest, some of them shown on the screen (refer to Figure 14-4) and others available by touching the What's Nearby command.

Choose the Search Nearby item to use the Search command to locate businesses, people, or points of interest near the given location.

Touch the bubble to see more info.   Long-press a location to see its address.

Figure 14-3: Finding an address.

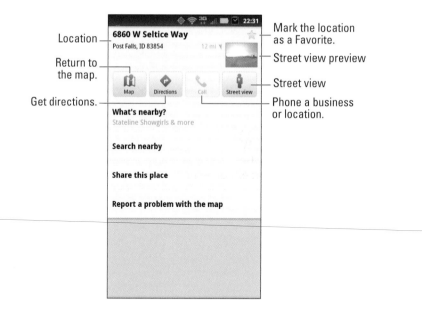

Location — 6860 W Seltice Way / Post Falls, ID 83854 — 12 mi — Mark the location as a Favorite.

Street view preview

Return to the map. — Map

Get directions. — Directions

Call — Street view — Phone a business or location.

What's nearby?
Stateline Showgirls & more

Search nearby

Share this place

Report a problem with the map

Figure 14-4: Things to do when you find a location.

What's *really* fun to play with is the Street View command. Choosing this option displays the location from a 360-degree perspective. In Street view, you can browse a locale, pan and tilt, or zoom in on details to familiarize yourself with an area, for example — whether you're familiarizing yourself with a location or planning a burglary.

Helping others find your location

Some Android phones let you use the Text Messaging app to send your current location to a friend. If your pal has a phone with smarts similar to those of your Android phone, they can use the coordinates to get directions to your location. Maybe they'll even bring tacos!

To send your current location in a text message, obey these steps:

1. **Start a new text message to the person desperately wanting to know where you are.**

   Refer to Chapter 9 for information on text messaging.

2. **Press the Menu soft button and choose the Insert command.**

3. **Choose Location and then choose Current Location.**

   Your current location appears on the map preview screen, along with your current address (if it's known).

4. **Touch the Attach Location button.**

   The street address (if available) is inserted into the message, along with a short URL link to your location on a map.

5. **Edit the message to add more details, such as "Bring tacos," and touch the Send button to send it.**

A recipient who receives the text message can touch the link to open your location in the Maps app. When the location appears, the recipient can follow my advice in the later section "Getting directions" to reach your location. Don't loan them this book either — have them buy their own copy. And bring tacos. Thanks.

Find Things

The Maps app can help you find places in the real world, just as the Browser app helps you find places on the Internet. Both operations work basically the same way:

Open the Maps app and press the Search soft button. You can type a variety of terms into the Search box, as explained in this section.

Looking for a specific address

To locate an address, type it into the Search box; for example:

```
1600 Pennsylvania Ave., Washington, D.C. 20006
```

Touch the Search button to the right of the Search box, and that location is then shown on the map. The next step is getting directions, which you can read about in the later section "Getting directions."

 ✔ You don't need to type the entire address. Oftentimes, all you need is the street number and street name and then either the city name or zip code.

 ✔ If you omit the city name or zip code, the Maps app looks for the closest matching address near your current location.

Finding a business, restaurant, or point of interest

You may not know an address, but you know when you crave sushi or Hungarian or perhaps the exotic flavors of Suriname. Maybe you need a hotel or a gas station, or you have to find a place that fixes dentures. To find a business entity or a point of interest, type its name in the Search box; for example:

```
movie theater
```

This command flags movie theaters on the current Maps screen or nearby.

Specify your current location, as described earlier in this chapter, to find locations near you. Otherwise, the Maps app looks for places near the area you see on the screen.

Or you can be specific and look for businesses near a certain location by specifying the city name, district, or zip code, such as

```
sushi 92123
```

After typing this command and touching the Search button, you see a smattering of coffee huts and restaurants found in my old neighborhood in San Diego, similar to the ones shown in Figure 14-5.

To see more information about a result, touch its cartoon bubble, such as the one for Tony's Sushi, shown in Figure 14-5. The screen that appears offers more information, and perhaps even a web address and phone number. You can touch the Get Directions button (refer to Figure 14-4) to get directions; see the later section "Getting directions."

 ✔ Every letter or dot on the screen represents a search result (refer to Figure 14-5).

 ✔ Use the zoom controls or spread your fingers to zoom in to the map.

✒ You can create a contact for the location, storing it as a part of your Contacts list: After touching the location balloon, scroll down the information screen and choose the command Add As a Contact. The contact is created using data that's known about the business, including its location and phone number and even a web page address — if that information is available.

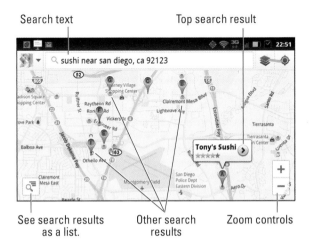

Search text   Top search result

See search results   Other search   Zoom controls
as a list.   results

Figure 14-5: Search results for sushi in San Diego, California.

Searching for interesting places

Maybe you don't know what you're looking for. Maybe you're like my teenage sons, who stand in front of the open refrigerator, waiting for the sandwich fairy to hand them a snack. The Maps app features a sort of I-don't-know-what-I-want-but-I-want-something fairy. It's the Places command.

Touch the Map Features button (refer to Figure 14-1), and choose the Places command to see the Places screen. It shows categories of places near you: restaurants, coffee shops, bars, hotels, attractions, and more. Touch an item to see matching locations in your vicinity.

Your phone may also feature the Places app, which takes you directly to the Places screen.

Locating a contact

You can hone in on where your contacts are located by using the map. This trick works when you've specified an address for the contact — either home or work or another location. If so, your phone can easily help you find that location or even give you directions.

The secret to finding a contact's location is the little icon by the contact's address. It may look like a tiny postcard, similar to the one shown in the margin. Anytime you see this icon or a similar one, you can touch it to view that location by using the Maps app. On some phones, you may find a command by the contact's address, such as View Home Address or View Work Address.

Your Phone Is Your Copilot

Finding a location is only half the job. The other half is getting there. Thanks to its various direction and navigation features, the Maps app stands at the ready, waiting to be your copilot. It's just like having a backseat driver, but one who knows where they're going and — *bonus* — who has a Mute option.

Getting directions

One command that's associated with location displays in the Maps app is Get Directions. Here's how to use it:

1. Touch the location's cartoon bubble displayed by an address, a contact, or a business or from the result of a map search.

2. Touch the Directions button.

You see the Directions screen, shown in Figure 14-6. The information is already filled out, including your current location (shown as My Location in the figure) as the starting point.

Transportation method

Choose a new starting location or destination.

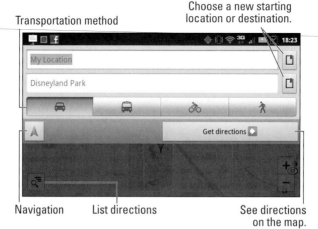

Navigation   List directions   See directions on the map.

Figure 14-6: Going from here to there.

3. **Choose a method of transportation.**

   The four methods are car, public transportation, bicycle, and walking, as shown in Figure 14-6.

4. **Touch the Get Directions button.**

   You see a map with a blue line detailing your journey. Use the zoom controls to make the map larger, if necessary.

5. **Follow the blue line.**

 If you'd rather see a list of directions, touch the List button on the map (refer to Figure 14-6). You can switch back to Map view (the one with the blue line) by touching the Map button, shown in the margin.

   ✐ The Maps app alerts you to toll roads on the specified route. As you travel, you can choose alternative, nontoll routes, if they're available. You're prompted to switch routes during navigation; see the next section.

   ✐ You may not get perfect directions from the Maps app, but for places you've never visited, it's a useful tool.

   ✐ To receive vocal directions, touch the Navigation button (refer to Figure 14-6) or just read the next section.

Navigating to your destination

Maps and lists of directions are so 20th century. I don't know why anyone would bother, especially when your Android phone features a digital copilot, in the form of voice navigation.

To use navigation, choose the Navigation option from any list of directions. Or touch the Navigation button, as shown earlier, in Figure 14-6. You can also enter the Navigation app directly by choosing it from the Map Features menu (refer to Figure 14-1), or open the Navigation app found on the Apps menu. Yes, sometimes it seems that you need navigation directions merely to find the Navigation feature.

In Navigation mode, your phone displays an interactive map that shows your current location and turn-by-turn directions for reaching your destination. A digital voice tells you how far to go and when to turn, for example, and gives you other nagging advice, such as to sit up, be nice to other drivers, and call your mother once in a while.

After choosing Navigation, sit back and have the phone dictate your directions. You can simply listen or glance at the phone for an update on where you're heading.

To stop navigation, press the Menu soft button and choose the Exit Navigation command.

- ✔ To remove the navigation route from the screen, exit Navigation mode: Press the Menu soft button, and choose the Exit Navigation command.

- ✔ The phone stays in Navigation mode until you exit. The Navigation notification can be seen atop the touchscreen when you're in Navigation mode.

- ✔ When you tire of hearing the navigation voice, press the Menu soft button and choose the Mute command.

- ✔ I refer to the navigation voice as "Gertrude."

- ✔ You can press the Menu soft button while navigating and choose Route Info to see an overview of your journey.

- ✔ When viewing the Route Info screen, touch the Gears button to see a handy pop-up menu. From this menu, you can choose options to modify the route so that you avoid highways or toll roads, for example.

- ✔ The neat thing about Navigation is that whenever you screw up, a new course is immediately calculated.

- ✔ Your cellular provider may have preinstalled another navigation app in addition to the one described in this section, such as the VZ Navigation app found on Verizon phones. After selecting Navigation, you may be prompted to choose between the Maps app and the cellular provider's app.

- ✔ In Navigation mode, your phone consumes a lot of battery power. I highly recommend that you plug the phone into your car's power adapter (its "cigarette lighter") for the duration of the trip.

Pics and Vids

*H*aving a camera in a phone is nothing new. It was the second thing that Alexander Graham Bell thought of, right after the busy signal. Sadly, it proved somewhat impractical because cameras and phones of the 1890s weren't really portable. And it was difficult to talk on the phone and hold still for 60 seconds to get the best exposure.

Not until the end of the 20th century did the marriage of the cell phone and digital camera become successful. Though it may seem like an odd combination, it's quite handy to have the phone act as a camera, because most people always keep their phones with them. That way, should you chance upon Bigfoot or a UFO, you can always take a picture or video — even when there's no cell signal, which is often the case when I try to capture Bigfoot on video.

The Phone's Camera

A camera snob will tell you that no true camera has a ringtone. You know what? He's correct: Phones don't make the best cameras. Regardless, you phone has a camera. Figuring out how the camera works is this section's topic.

Using the Camera app

To use your phone as a camera, you must do two things. First, hold the phone away from your face. That's because the phone has no viewfinder. Nope — the image preview shows up on the touchscreen.

The second thing you need to do is run the Camera app, which is how the phone is controlled on Android phones. (Your phone may use a different name, though *Camera* is the most common.) You'll find the Camera app on the Home screen or, like every other app on the phone, on the App menu.

The screen you see when you start the Camera app varies, depending on your phone's make and model. Even then, the Camera app gets updated, so it may not look the same today as it will months hence. Figure 15-1 shows the Camera app on the Motorola Droid 3, which contains common features found on most Camera apps.

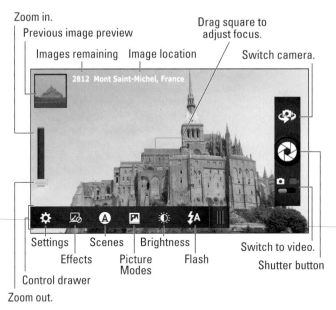

Zoom in.
Previous image preview
Drag square to adjust focus.
Images remaining   Image location
Switch camera.
2812 Mont Saint-Michel, France
Settings   Scenes   Brightness
Effects   Picture Modes   Flash
Switch to video.
Shutter button
Control drawer
Zoom out.

Figure 15-1: Your phone as a camera.

Here are some things to look for on your phone's Camera app screen:

Shutter button: Touch this button to snap the picture. Some phones feature a physical Camera button, which also can be pressed to take the picture.

Switch camera: For phones with front and rear cameras, touching this button switches between cameras. How can you tell which is which? When you see yourself, the front-facing camera is active.

Switch to Video: The Camera app is also used to record videos. This button switches between Still and Video modes.

Zoom controls: You may find the zoom controls on the screen as a slider (refer to Figure 15-1) or as + (zoom in) and – (zoom out) buttons. On some phones, pressing the Volume Up and Volume Down buttons zooms in and out.

Focus square: The more sophisticated phone cameras feature a graphic square that you can drag around the touchscreen. It's the focus square that's used to change the camera's focus.

Previous image: You can touch the tiny preview of the previous still image (or video) to review the image in Full Screen mode, share the image, delete it, or do a number of thrilling things.

Control drawer and related options: The various settings and controls for the Camera app are often found in a control drawer or in a slide-out or pop-up gizmo.

Random information: Text on the screen can tell you the image resolution, the number of images you can store on the phone, location information, camera settings, and other tidbits.

Your phone may not have all these items, and it may have more. The common features are covered in the sections that follow.

- The phone's camera uses a *digital* zoom, where the image is magnified using software. That's opposed to an *optical* zoom, which is done by adjusting the camera lens.

- If the onscreen controls disappear, touch the screen again to bring them back.

- Pressing the Menu soft button displays the control drawer. If not, a menu of options pops up.

Snapping a picture

To take a picture, point the camera at the subject and touch the Shutter button, either the touchscreen shutter button (refer to Figure 15-1) or the phone's physical shutter button, if it has one.

After you touch the Shutter button, the camera focuses, you may hear a mechanical shutter sound play, and the flash may go off. You're ready to take the next picture.

To preview the image you just snapped, touch the little icon that appears in the upper-left corner of the screen (refer to Figure 15-1).

> ✔ The camera focuses automatically, though you can drag the focus square around the touchscreen to specifically adjust the focus (refer to Figure 15-1).

> ✔ You can take as many pictures with your phone as you like, as long as you don't run out of storage for them on the phone's internal storage or MicroSD card.

> ✔ If your pictures appear blurry, ensure that the camera lens on the back of the phone isn't dirty.

> ✔ Use the Gallery app to preview and manage your pictures. See the later section "Your Digital Photo Album" for more information about the Gallery.

Deleting an image immediately after you take it

Sometimes, you just can't wait to delete an image. Either an annoyed person is standing next to you, begging that the photo be deleted, or you're just not happy and you feel the urge to smash into digital shards the picture you just took. Hastily follow these steps:

1. **Touch the image preview that appears in the upper-left corner of the screen (refer to Figure 15-1).**

   After touching the preview, you see the full-screen image.

2. **Press the Menu soft button and choose the Delete command.**

3. **Touch the OK button to confirm.**

   The image has been banished to bit hell.

If these steps don't do the job, remember that you can always delete (and manage) your images by using the Gallery app. See the later section "Deleting an image or a video."

Setting the flash

Three flash settings are controlled by the Camera app. Table 15-1 lists them, along with icons commonly used to represent the settings. The icons used on your phone may not look exactly like those shown in the table.

Table 15-1		Typical Camera Flash Settings
Setting	*Icon*	*Description*
Auto		The flash activates during low-light situations, but not when it's bright out.
On		The flash always activates.
Off		The flash never activates, even in low-light situations.

To change or check the flash setting, open the control drawer, shown earlier, in Figure 15-1. You should find the "flash command" button there. If not, the button may be found directly on the touchscreen or by pressing the Menu soft button.

✔ A good time to turn on the flash is when taking pictures of people or objects in front of something bright, such as Aunt Betty holding her prized peach cobbler in front of a nuclear explosion.

✔ Icons representing the flash setting may appear on the screen when using the Camera app, or they may replace the flash command button on the control drawer.

The Phone's TV Studio

When the action is hot — when you need to capture more than a moment (and maybe the sounds) — switch the phone's camera into Video mode. Doing so may not turn you into the next Steven Spielberg, because I hear he uses an iPhone to make his films.

Recording video

Your phone features the Camcorder app, which is used to record video. It's the same app as the Camera app, switched into a special video mode. In fact, you don't have to start the Camcorder app: Simply start the Camera app, and touch the switch (refer to Figure 15-1) with your finger to start shooting "vids."

Figure 15-2 shows the Camcorder app's interface. As with the Camera app, what you see on your phone's touchscreen may be subtly different. For example, not every Android phone has a front-facing camera, so there may be no Switch Camera command available. Also, the control drawer may look different or simply not even be there.

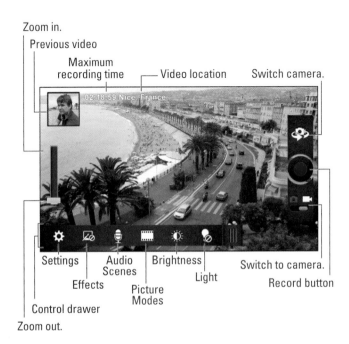

Zoom in.
Previous video
Maximum recording time — Video location   Switch camera.

Settings   Audio   Brightness   Switch to camera.
           Scenes   Light   Record button
      Effects   Picture
               Modes
Control drawer
Zoom out.

Figure 15-2: Your phone is a video camera.

Start shooting the video by pressing the Record button, as illustrated in Figure 15-2.

While the phone is recording, the Shutter button changes to the Stop button. To stop recording, touch that button.

- Hold the phone steady! The camera still works when you whip around the phone, but wild gyrations render the video unwatchable.

- The video's duration depends on its resolution (see the next section) as well as on the amount of storage available on your phone. The maximum recording time is shown on the screen before you shoot (refer to Figure 15-2). While you record, the elapsed time appears.

✔ In addition to using the zoom controls on the screen, you might be able to use the phone's volume buttons to zoom in or out as you record video.

✔ Recorded video is saved in the phone's storage — primarily, the MicroSD card. The storage capacity is what limits your recording time, so be wary: The more videos you store on your phone, the less space you have to store other things (music, pictures, and contacts, for example).

Setting video quality

The Camcorder app may have a command concealed somewhere for setting the video resolution. I mention this only because choosing high-quality or high-definition (HD) mode isn't always the best option. For example, video you shoot for YouTube need not be of HD quality. Multimedia text messaging (known as *MMS*) video should be of very low quality, or else the video doesn't attach to the message. Also, HD video uses up a heck of a lot more storage space.

The methods by which your phone's Camcorder app changes resolutions may vary. I would look first to the control drawer, for either a Resolution command or Settings command. If that doesn't work, press the Menu soft button and look for the command there.

Don't be surprised if you have limited resolution choices; not every phone's camera has a wide variety of options in that area. Here's a sampling of common video resolution settings and my recommendations for using them:

HD+ (1080p): The highest-quality setting is best suited for videos you plan to show on a large-format TV or computer monitor. It's useful for video editing or for showing important events, such as alien invasions.

High Definition (720p): The second-highest-quality setting, which would be a good choice if you need to record longer but still want high quality.

DVD (720 x 480): This option has good quality for shooting videos when you don't know where they'll end up.

VGA (640 x 480): This setting, good for quality Internet video, doesn't enlarge well.

CIF (352 x 288): This choice is good for medium-quality YouTube and web videos. The files are small, and they load quickly over an Internet connection. This setting isn't good for viewing videos in a larger format.

QVGA (320 x 240): This setting is designed for use with text-messaging video attachments.

Check the video quality *before* you shoot! Especially if you know where the video will end up (on the Internet, on a TV, or in an MMS message), it helps to set the quality first.

Your Digital Photo Album

The pictures and videos you take with your phone don't simply disappear after you click the shutter button. Though you can generally preview a previously shot picture or video, the place you go to look at the entire gamut of visual media is the app named Gallery.

Okay, well, your phone may not call it the Gallery, but you'll still have an app you can use to review pictures and videos — not only those you take with the phone but potentially also those synchronized from your social networking sites, online photo-sharing web albums, and media copied over from your computer.

Visiting the Gallery app

You can start the Gallery app by locating its icon, either on the Home screen or the App menu. How the Gallery looks varies from phone to phone, but generally the images are organized by albums, or "piles." Choosing a pile displays a scrolling list of thumbnail images. Touch a thumbnail to see the individual full-screen image.

Figure 15-3 shows a typical Gallery app with images organized into albums, or piles.

Videos appear in Full-Screen mode, but with the Play button superimposed. Touch the Play button to view the video. Other video controls may also appear on the screen, which let you pause, fast-forward, or adjust the video playback.

 ✔ Press the Back soft button to back out of viewing an image and return to the album. Likewise, press the Back soft button to return to the main Gallery library screen after you're done viewing an album.

 ✔ Many albums are automatically created for you. The Gallery app may also allow you to create your own albums to further organize your media. You can create a new album by choosing the New Album (or similar) command after pressing the Menu soft button. You might also be able to create an album by long-pressing an image and choosing the Add to Album command.

Images and videos
taken by the camera

Videos synced
with doubleTwist

Main Gallery screen   Go to the camera.

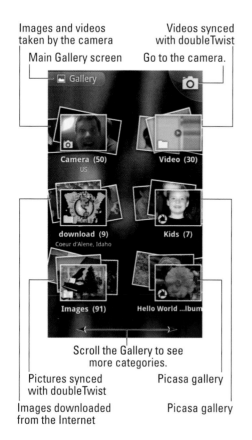

Scroll the Gallery to see
more categories.

Pictures synced   Picasa gallery
with doubleTwist

Images downloaded   Picasa gallery
from the Internet

Figure 15-3: The Gallery app might look like this.

Editing images

The best tool for image editing is a computer amply equipped with photo-editing software, such as Photoshop or one of its less expensive alternatives. Even so, it's possible to use the Gallery app to perform some minor photo surgery. Two popular tasks are cropping and rotating.

To *crop* an image, which is to remove a portion of the image to concentrate on a specific part, heed these steps:

1. **Open the Gallery app, and display the image you want to crop.**

2. **Press the Menu soft button and choose Edit.**

3. **Choose the Crop command from the Edit menu.**

   For an alternative, you may have to long-press the image and choose Edit and then Crop.

4. **Use the onscreen controls to crop the image.**

   Refer to Figure 15-4 for help with using the onscreen controls, though the controls you see on your screen may be subtly different.

5. **Touch the Save button to crop the image.**

   The image's size and content are changed immediately.

Some versions of the Gallery app automatically recognize human faces. It's possible to touch a face in an image when using the crop tool and have it automatically frame the person's face.

You cannot undo a crop.

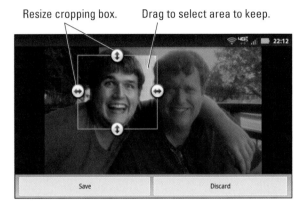

Figure 15-4: Cropping an image.

To rotate an image clockwise or counterclockwise, follow these steps:

1. **Display the image in the Gallery app.**

2. **Press the Menu soft button, and then choose Edit and then Rotate.**

   Or you may have to long-press the image, choose the Edit command, and then choose a specific Rotate command.

In some cases, a gizmo appears on the screen, which you control to rotate the image. You may also have to touch either the Apply or Save button when you're done rotating.

Not all images can be rotated, such as images synchronized from web albums or social networking sites.

Deleting an image or a video

To prune media that you no longer want in the Gallery, summon it on the screen by itself. Press the Menu soft button and choose the Delete command. Or, alternatively, long-press the image and choose the Delete command.

You're prompted before the image is removed; touch the OK button to delete the image. It's gone.

- ✐ There's no way to undelete an image you've removed from the Gallery.

- ✐ Some images cannot be edited, such as images brought in from social networking sites or from online photo-sharing albums.

Sharing your images

Images don't need to be bottled up inside your phone. Nope — you can take advantage of the Share command or Share button to liberate images and videos, setting them free on the Internet for others to enjoy.

The Share command or Share button is available when you view a full-screen image in the Gallery. You may see the Share button (shown in the margin) when you touch the screen. Or you may have to press the Menu soft button to choose the Share command.

After you touch the Share button or choose the Share command, you see a menu chock-full of methods or apps you can use to share the image or video. The variety of items depends on the apps installed on your phone as well as on which accounts you've added. Here's a run-through of some popular sharing options:

Photo/Video Share: These items work in conjunction with social networking sites as well as with any photo-sharing or hosting sites. You must set up your account on the phone for these options to work: Refer to Chapter 12 to add social networking.

Email and Gmail: Choosing Email or Gmail for sharing sends the media file from your phone as a message attachment. Fill in the To, Subject, and Message text boxes as necessary. Touch the Send button to send the media.

Picasa: The Picasa photo-sharing site is one of those free services that comes with your Google account. Choose this option to upload a photo to your Picasa account: Type a caption, choose an online album, and then touch the Upload button.

Print to Retail: The image is beamed to a local photo developer. This option may not be available on every phone.

Bluetooth: The image is sent *(uploaded)* to a Bluetooth printer. The printer must be paired and ready to use, similar to using other Bluetooth devices with the phone, as discussed in Chapter 19.

Text Messaging: Media can be attached to a text message, which then becomes the famous MMS, or multimedia message, that I write about in Chapter 9.

YouTube: The YouTube sharing option appears whenever you choose to share a video from the Gallery. See the later section "Uploading a video to YouTube."

Additional options may appear on the menu, depending on which apps you have on the phone or which special features have been added by the manufacturer or cellular provider. For example, if you have the Facebook app or a Twitter client, these items appear on the bottom part of the sharing menu.

  ✔ You need to set up your Picasa account before you can use the Share button to instantly upload your pictures. You get a free Picasa account with your Google account, so visit the `http://picasaweb.com` site to get started. You may also have to add your Picasa account to the phone's inventory of accounts. The methods work similar to adding social networking accounts, covered in Chapter 12.

  ✔ Some images and videos are too large to send as multimedia text messages. The phone may offer to automatically resize the images in some but not all, cases.

  ✔ Not every cell phone has the ability to receive multimedia text messages.

Uploading a video to YouTube

The best way to share a video is to upload it to YouTube. As a Google account holder, you also have a YouTube account. You can use the YouTube app on your phone to upload videos to the Internet, where everyone can see them and make rude comments about them. Here's how:

 1. **Activate the phone's Wi-Fi.**

    The best way to upload a video is to turn on the Wi-Fi connection. You can use the 4G signal, if you have a 4G phone, but you see a warning about data usage surcharges, which is a distinct possibility when you upload a video. My advice: Use Wi-Fi.

    See Chapter 19 for information on how to turn on the Wi-Fi connection.

2. **From the Apps Menu screen, choose the Gallery app.**

3. **View the video you want to upload.**

   Or simply have the video displayed on the screen.

4. **Touch the Share button, and choose YouTube from the menu.**

5. **Fill in the blanks to describe the video.**

   For example, you can type the video's title, replacing whatever random text is put there by the phone. You can touch the More Details button and type a description, specify whether to make the video public or private, add tags, or change other settings.

6. **Touch the Upload button.**

   You return to the Gallery as the video is being uploaded. It continues to upload, even if the phone gets bored and falls asleep.

To view your video, open the YouTube app on the App menu, press the Menu soft button, and choose the My Channel command. If necessary, choose your Google account from the pop-up list. Your video should appear in the Uploads list.

You can share your video by sending its YouTube web page link to your pals. I confess that using a computer for this operation is easier than using your phone: Log in to YouTube on a computer to view your video. Use the Share button that appears near the video to share it via e-mail or Facebook or other methods.

See Chapter 17 for more information on using YouTube on your Android phone.

16

O Sweet Music!

In This Chapter

- Checking into music on your phone
- Listening to a song
- Copying music from your computer
- Purchasing music
- Organizing your music into playlists
- Making a new playlist
- Using your phone as a radio

Your Android phone can make music. I'm not talking about the dialpad, either: Back in the 1970s, when "push-button" phones became popular, people realized that the sound created from dialing certain numbers sounded like popular tunes. My parents' home number sounded like *Yankee Doodle*. But that's not the kind of music I'm referring to when it comes to your phone today.

Just like those popular mobile-music gizmos that rhyme with "pie rod," your Android phone can play music. You can listen to songs you buy online, synchronize them from your computer, or find music on the Internet. Some phones can even listen to FM radio. So wherever you go with your phone, which should be everywhere, you also have your music library.

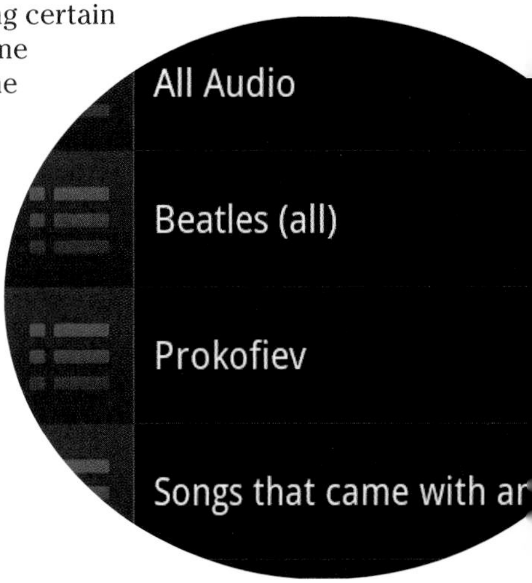

All Audio
Beatles (all)
Prokofiev
Songs that came with ar

The Hits Just Keep On Comin'

Your Android phone is ready to entertain you with music whenever you want to hear it. Simply plug in the headphones, summon the music-playing app, and choose tunes to match your mood. It's truly blissful — well, until someone calls you and the phone ceases being a musical instrument and returns to being the ball-and-chain of the modern digital era.

Browsing the music library

You'll probably find two music-playing apps on your Android phone. The first was probably added by the cellular provider or phone manufacturer. The second, which is recommended, is the Play Music app provided by Google. If you don't have the Play Music app, you can obtain it from the Google Play Store; see Chapter 18.

Figure 16-1 shows the Play Music app in two orientations: portrait view and landscape view. It also shows two categories: Albums and Recent.

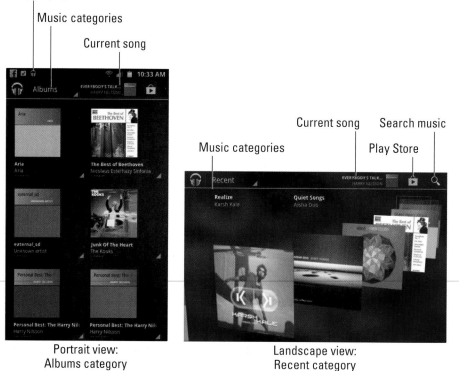

Figure 16-1: The Music library.

The Play Music app organizes by category the music stored on your phone, as shown in Figure 16-1:

Recent: Music you've purchased or transferred into your phone is displayed in this category.

Artists: Songs are listed by recording artist or group. Choose this category, and then choose an artist to see their albums. Choosing an album displays the songs for that album. Some artists may have only one song, not in any particular album.

Albums: Songs are organized by album. Choose an album to list its songs.

Songs: All songs are listed alphabetically.

Playlists: Only songs you've organized into playlists are listed by their playlist names. Choose a playlist name to view songs organized in that playlist. The section "Organize Your Tunes," later in this chapter, discusses playlists.

Genres: Tunes are organized by their themes, such as classical, rock, or irritating. Not every phone may have this category.

These categories merely represent ways that the music is organized — ways to make tunes easier to find when you may know an artist's name but not an album title or when you may want to hear a song but not know who recorded it.

- Music is stored on your phone's internal storage as well as on the MicroSD card.

- The size of the phone's storage limits the total amount of music you can keep on your phone. Also, consider that pictures and videos stored on your phone horn in on some of the space that can be used for music.

- See the later section "More Music for Your Phone" for information on getting music into your phone.

- Album artwork generally appears on imported music as well as on music you purchase online. If an album has no artwork, it cannot be manually added or updated (at least, not by using the Play Music app).

- When your phone is unable to recognize an artist, it uses the title Unknown Artist. This happens with music you copy manually to the phone. Music that you purchase, or import or synchronize with a computer, generally retains the artist and album information. (Well, the information is retained as long as it was supplied on the original source.)

Playing a tune

To listen to music on your phone, you first find a song in the Music app's library, as described in the preceding section. After you find the song, you touch its title. The song plays in another window, similar to the one shown in Figure 16-2.

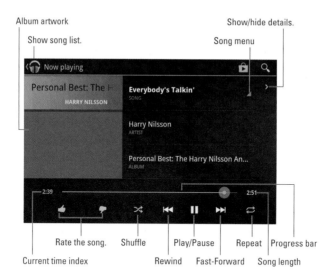

Album artwork

Show song list.

Show/hide details.

Song menu

Rate the song.   Shuffle   Play/Pause   Repeat   Progress bar

Current time index   Rewind   Fast-Forward   Song length

Figure 16-2: A song is playing.

While the song is playing, you're free to do anything else with the phone. In fact, the song continues to play even if the phone goes to sleep.

After the song is done playing, the next song in the list plays.

The next song doesn't play if you have the Shuffle button activated (refer to Figure 16-2). In that case, the phone randomizes the songs in the list, so who knows which one is next?

The next song also might not play if you have the Repeat option on: The three repeat settings are illustrated in Table 16-1, along with the shuffle settings. To change settings, simply touch either the Shuffle or Repeat button.

Table 16-1		Shuffle and Repeat Button Icons
Icon	**Setting**	**What Happens When You Touch the Icon**
	Shuffle Is Off	Songs play one after the other
	Shuffle Is On	Songs are played in random order

Icon	Setting	What Happens When You Touch the Icon
	Repeat Is Off	Songs don't repeat
	Repeat All Songs	All songs in the list play over and over
	Repeat Current Song	The same song plays over and over

To stop the song from playing, touch the Pause button (refer to Figure 16-2).

 When music plays on the phone, a notification icon appears, similar to the one shown in the margin. Use this notification to quickly summon the Play Music app, to see which song is playing or to pause the song.

Information about the song that's playing might also appear on the phone's lock screen. In fact, you may be able to use the music controls on the phone's lock screen without unlocking the phone.

✔ The volume is set by using the Volume switch on the side of the phone: Up is louder, down is quieter.

✔ Determining which song plays next depends on how you chose the song that's playing. If you choose a song by artist, all songs from that artist play, one after the other. When you choose a song by album, that album plays. Choosing a song from the entire song list causes all songs in the phone to play.

✔ To choose which songs play after each other, create a playlist. See the section "Organize Your Tunes," later in this chapter.

✔ After the last song in the list plays, the phone stops playing songs — unless you have the Repeat option on, in which case the song or list plays again.

More Music for Your Phone

Though the odds are good that your phone came with no music preinstalled, some resellers may have preinstalled a smattering of tunes, which merely lets you know how out of touch they are musically. Regardless, you can add music to your phone in a number of ways, as covered in this section.

Borrowing music from your computer

Your computer is the equivalent of the 20th century stereo system — a combination tuner, amplifier, and turntable, plus all your records and CDs. If you've already copied your music collection to your computer, or if you use your computer as your main music-storage system, you can share that music with your Android phone.

In Windows, you can use a music jukebox program, such as Windows Media Player, to synchronize music between your phone and the PC. Here's how it works:

1. **Connect the phone to the PC.**

   Specific phone-computer connection information is found in Chapter 20.

2. **Pull down the USB Connection notification.**

3. **Choose the item to mount the phone into your computer's storage system as a portable media player.**

   Not every phone has a specific media player option. Sometimes it's called Windows Media Sync or Media Sync. It may simply be named Mount. If necessary, touch the OK button to confirm your connection choice.

   It's not entirely necessary to connect your phone to the computer and have it pretend to be a portable media player. By choosing this option, you're simply making it easier for the computer to share music. Honestly, any of the USB connection options should work.

4. **On your PC, start Windows Media Player.**

   You can use most any media program, or "jukebox." These steps are specific to Version 12 of Windows Media Player, though they're similar to the steps you take in any media-playing program.

   If you see a device window for your phone in Windows 7, choose the item Manage Media on Your Device.

5. **If necessary, click the Sync tab in Windows Media Player.**

   Figure 16-2 shows the Motorola Droid Bionic in the Sync list on the right side of the Windows Media Player. Your phone should show up in the same place, though the computer may not be smart enough to recognize it by its brand name.

6. **Drag to the Sync area the music you want to transfer to your phone (refer to Figure 16-3).**

7. **Click the Start Sync button to transfer the music.**

Your Android phone

Click to sync.   Sync tab

Your phone's "drive"   Drag music to here.

Music to sync

Figure 16-3: Windows Media Player meets Android phone.

8. Close the Windows Media Player when you're done with the transfer.

Or keep it open — whatever.

9. Unmount your phone from the PC's storage system.

Refer to Chapter 20 for specific unmounting instructions, also known as turning off USB storage.

When you have a Macintosh, or if you detest Windows Media Player, you can use the doubleTwist program to synchronize music between your phone and your computer. For information, refer to the section in Chapter 20 about synchronizing with doubleTwist.

✔ The phone can store only so much music! Don't be overzealous when copying over your tunes. In Windows Media Player (refer to Figure 16-3), a capacity-thermometer thing shows you how much storage space is used and how much is available on your phone. Pay heed to the indicator!

✔ You cannot use iTunes to synchronize music with Android phones.

✔ Okay, I lied in the preceding point: You *can* synchronize music using iTunes, but only when you install the iTunes Agent program on your PC. You then need to configure the iTunes Agent program to use your Android phone with iTunes. After you do that, iTunes recognizes the phone and lets you synchronize your music. Yes, it's technical; hence the icon in the margin.

✔ Most Android phones cannot access their storage (music, photos, contacts) while mounted to a computer for music syncing. You can access this information after you unmount the phone from the computer.

Getting music from the Google Play Store

It's possible to get your music from the same source where you buy your apps, the Google Play Store. Here's how it works:

1. **Open the Play Store app on your phone.**

   You can quickly get to the Google Play Music store by touching the Play Store button in the Play Music app (refer to Figure 16-1).

2. **Choose the Music category.**

3. **Use the Search command to locate music you want, or just browse the categories.**

Keep an eye out for free music offers at the Play Store. It's a great way to pick up some free tunes.

Eventually you'll see a page showing details about the song or album, similar to what's shown in Figure 16-4. Choose a song from the list to hear a preview. The button next to the song or album indicates the purchase price, or it says FREE for free music.

More songs by this artist

Return to the music store.   Search.

Share this item. | Buy this item.

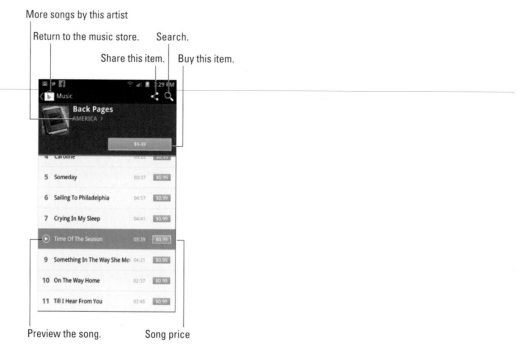

Preview the song.   Song price

Figure 16-4: Buying music at the Google Play Store.

4. **Touch the price button to purchase a song or album.**

   Don't worry, you're not buying anything yet.

5. **Choose your credit card or payment source.**

   If a credit card or payment source doesn't appear, choose the option to add a payment method. Sign up with Google Checkout and submit your credit card or other payment information.

6. **Touch the Accept & Buy button.**

   The album or song is downloaded into your phone.

A Google Play Music notification appears when the album or song has completed transfer into your phone. You can then use the Play Music app to listen to the new music; you'll find it quickly by choosing the Recent category from the Play Music app's main screen.

- ✔ All music sales are final. Don't blame me; I'm just writing down Google's current policy for music purchases.

- ✔ If you plan on downloading an album or multiple songs, connect to a Wi-Fi network. That way you won't run the risk of a data surcharge on your cellular plan. See Chapter 19 for information on activating your phone's Wi-Fi.

- ✔ The Google Play Music notification icon is the same that appears when you download a new app for your phone. The notification name, however, is Google Play Music.

- ✔ You'll eventually receive a Gmail notice regarding the purchase. The Gmail message lists a summary of your purchase.

- ✔ Music you purchase from the Google Play Music store is available on any mobile Android device with the Play Music app installed, providing you use the same Google account on that device. You can also listen to your tunes by visiting the music.google.com site on any computer connected to the Internet.

- ✔ For more information on the Google Play Store, see Chapter 18.

Organize Your Tunes

A *playlist* is a collection of tunes you create. You build the list by combining songs from an album or artist or from whatever music you have on your phone. You can then listen to the playlist and hear the music you want to hear in the order you want to hear it. That's how to organize your phone's music.

Reviewing your playlists

Any playlists you've already created, or that have been preset on your phone, appear under the Playlists category in the Play Music app. Playlists appear on the screen, similar to what's shown in Figure 16-5.

To listen to a playlist, long-press the playlist name and choose the Play command from the menu that appears.

Music categories   Add playlist.

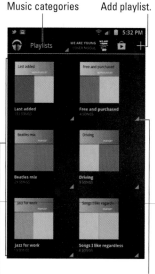

Playlists   Playlist menu

Figure 16-5: Playlists in the Play Music app.

You can also touch a playlist name to open the playlist and review the songs that are listed. You can touch any song from the list to start listening to that song.

A playlist is a helpful way to organize music when a song's information may not have been completely imported into your phone. For example, if you're like me, you probably have a lot of songs by "Unknown Artist." The quick way to remedy this situation is to name a playlist after the artist and then add those unknown songs to the playlist. The next section describes how it's done.

Building playlists

The Play Music app features one playlist that's already set up for you — the Last Added playlist, shown in Figure 16-5. This playlist contains all the songs you've purchased for, or imported to, your phone. Obviously, having more playlists would be a good idea.

To create a new playlist, follow these steps:

1. **Ensure that the Playlist category is selected.**

2. **Touch the Add Playlist button, or press the Menu soft button and choose the New Playlist command.**

   The Add Playlist button is shown in Figure 16-5.

3. **Type a descriptive name for the new playlist.**

   Short names are best.

4. **Touch the OK button.**

   The playlist is created, but it's empty. The next step is to add music to the playlist.

5. **Long-press the song you want to stick in a playlist.**

   Use the Music app to locate the song; you don't have to play the song — just locate its name on the screen.

6. **Choose Add to Playlist.**

7. **Choose a playlist from the Add to Playlist menu.**

   The song you long-pressed (refer to Step 5) is added to the playlist.

You can continue adding songs to as many playlists as you like. Adding songs to a playlist doesn't noticeably affect the phone's storage capacity.

✔ To remove a song from a playlist, long-press the song in the playlist and choose the command Remove from Playlist. Removing a song from a playlist doesn't delete the song from your phone. (See the next section for information on deleting songs from the Music library.)

✔ To delete a playlist, long-press its name in the list of playlists. Choose the Delete command. Touch the OK button to confirm. Though the playlist is removed, none of the songs in the playlist has been deleted.

Deleting music

To purge unwanted music from your phone, follow these brief, painless steps:

1. **Long-press the music that offends you.**

    It can be an album, a song, or even an artist.

2. **Choose Delete.**

    A warning message appears.

3. **Touch the OK button.**

    The music is gone.

Music you've purchased from the Play Store must be deleted on the web at `music.google.com`. Also, some music in the Play Music app might continue to be available on other Android devices you own or on the web.

One day, as a man walked through a cemetery, he heard a noise coming from Beethoven's tomb. So he quickly alerted the authorities. They opened the tomb and inside they found Beethoven madly erasing manuscript paper. The man asked, "What are you doing?" Beethoven replied, "Decomposing."

Your Phone Is a Radio

Music can be an impulsive thing, more often than not. Truly, for you to be able to listen to the proper song to match your current mood, your phone would have to sport one huge music library. Or perhaps not, especially when you can turn your Android phone into a radio.

Listening to FM radio

Several Android phones have the ability to pick up FM broadcast signals. Armed with the right app, you can use your phone to listen to the radio. It's a nifty trick, but not every phone comes with the proper software.

To see whether your phone can listen to the radio, look at the App menu for an FM radio app. I've seen the apps FM Player and FM Radio on a few Android phones, so look for something starting with the letters *FM*.

The FM radio apps magically pull radio signals from the air and put them into your ear. Kids: That's the way Mom and Dad listened to music back when they were teenagers.

- The FM radio apps require you to plug a headset into your phone. (If you forget, the app bugs you about it.) The phone's radio hardware requires the headset's wire to act as an antenna.

- Radio apps scan the airwaves for stations, creating presets for you. Some of the smarter apps note your location and the station's call letters and maybe even their broadcast schedules.

Streaming music from the Internet

Though they're not broadcast radio stations, some sources on the Internet — *Internet radio* sites — play music. Your Android phone may have come with a few Internet radio apps preinstalled. If so, great. If not, I can recommend these three:

- TuneIn Radio
- Pandora Radio
- StreamFurious

 The TuneIn Radio app gives you access to hundreds of Internet radio stations broadcasting around the world. They're organized by category, so you can find just about whatever you want. Many radio stations are also broadcast radio stations, so the odds are good that you can find a local station or two.

Pandora Radio lets you select music based on your mood, and it customizes, according to your feedback, the tunes you listen to. The app works like the Internet site www.pandora.com, in case you're familiar with it. The nifty thing about Pandora is that the more you listen, the better the app becomes at finding music you like.

 StreamFurious streams music from various radio stations on the Internet. Though not as customizable as Pandora, StreamFurious uses less bandwidth, so you can enjoy your music without having to risk running up digital cellular surcharges.

All these apps are available at the Google Play Store. They're free, though paid versions might also be available.

✔ Always listen to Internet radio when your phone is connected to the Internet via a Wi-Fi connection. Streaming music can use a lot of your cellular data plan's data allotment.

✔ See Chapter 18 for more information about the Play Store.

✔ Internet music of the type delivered by the apps mentioned in this section is referred to by nerds as *streaming music*. That's because the music arrives on your phone as a continuous download from the source. Unlike music you download and save, streaming music is played as it comes in and isn't stored long-term.

Apps Various and Sundry

*W*hen cell phones started to become sophisticated, manufacturers began installing a few basic apps. Those early apps were nothing to sneeze at. In fact, I remember my first cell phone that came with apps on it; I never touched them. Still, it's kind of traditional for a phone to come with an alarm clock, a calculator, a calendar, and perhaps a few games. Your Android phone is no different, and this chapter covers those basic apps.

The Alarm Clock

Your Android phone keeps constant and accurate track of the time, which is displayed at the top of the Home screen and also when you first wake up the phone. When you'd rather have the phone wake you up, you can take advantage of the Clock app, which might also be called Alarm or Alarm & Timer or a similar name.

The Clock app features a basic display, which shows the time and temperature and gives you access to music or perhaps a slideshow. Figure 17-1 shows a typical Clock app.

Phone is plugged in, and
the battery is 100% charged.

Current time and date

Dim the display.

100%

10:21 AM

Sunday, April 25

45° 55°
37°

Coeur d'Alene

Set or review
alarms.

Start photo
slideshow.

Open Music
app.

Go to Home
screen.

Weather info
(Touch to display more.)

Figure 17-1: A typical clock app.

To set an alarm, follow these steps:

1. **Touch the Alarm button in the Clock app.**

   If your phone's Clock app lacks the Alarm button, press the Menu soft button.

2. **Choose Add Alarm.**

3. **Describe the alarm.**

   Give the alarm a name, choose a time, set a sound, determine whether the phone vibrates, and set repeat options.

   Because the alarm name appears when the alarm goes off, I set the name to remind me of the reason I'm getting up (or being alarmed). If I need to go to the airport, for example, the alarm name is Get to the Airport!

4. **Touch the Done button to create the alarm.**

   The alarm appears in a list on the main Alarm Clock screen, along with any other available alarms.

Alarms must be set, or else they won't trigger. To set an alarm, touch it in the Alarms list. (Place a check mark in the gray box). When the alarm is set, the Alarm notification icon might appear in the status area atop the touchscreen. The icon is your clue that an alarm is set and ready to trigger.

✔ For a larger time display, you can add the Clock widget to the Home screen. Refer to Chapter 22 for more information about widgets on the Home screen.

✔ Turning off an alarm doesn't delete the alarm.

✔ To delete an alarm, long-press it from the list and choose the Delete Alarm command, or touch the red X button to remove it. Touch the OK button to confirm.

✔ The alarm doesn't work when you turn off the phone. The alarm goes off, however, when the phone is sleeping.

✔ So tell me: Do alarms go *off*, or do they go *on*?

The Calculator

The Calculator is perhaps the oldest of all traditional cell phone apps. It's probably also the least confusing and frustrating app to use.

Start the Calculator app by choosing its icon from the App menu. The Calculator appears, as shown in Figure 17-2.

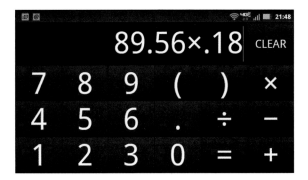

Figure 17-2: The Calculator.

✔ You can swipe the screen (refer to Figure 17-2) to the left to see a panel of strange, advanced mathematical operations you'll probably never use.

✔ Long-press the calculator's text (or results) to cut or copy the results.

✔ I use the calculator most often to determine my tip at a restaurant. In Figure 17-2, a calculation is being made for an 18 percent tip on a tab of $89.56.

The Date Book

I was never big on keeping a date book. Instead, I had a wall calendar upon which I wrote important dates. Well! Think of the money I'm saving on wall calendars because my Android phone has the Calendar app!

Understanding the Calendar

Thanks to your phone being a Google phone, it takes advantage of Google Calendar on the Internet. If you have a Google account (and I'm certain that you do), you already have an account with Google Calendar. You can visit Google Calendar by using your computer to go to this web page:

```
http://calendar.google.com
```

If necessary, log in using your Google account. You can use Google Calendar to keep track of dates or meetings or whatever else occupies your time. You can also use your phone to do the same thing, thanks to the Calendar app.

- ✔ I recommend that you use the Calendar app on your phone to access Google Calendar. It's a better way to access your schedule on the phone than using the Browser app to get to Google Calendar on the web.

- ✔ You can install the Calendar widget on the Home screen for quick access to looming appointments. See Chapter 22 for details on adding widgets to the Home screen.

Browsing dates and appointments

To see your schedule or upcoming important events, or to know which day of the month it is, summon the Calendar app. Touch the Launcher button at the bottom of the Home screen to display a list of all apps on the phone; choose the one named Calendar.

The first screen you see is most likely the monthly calendar view, which may look something like Month view, shown in Figure 17-3. The calendar looks like a typical monthly calendar, with the month and year at the top. Scheduled appointments appear as colored highlights on various days.

Use the View button (refer to Figure 17-3) to view your appointments by week or day. Or if your version of the Calendar app lacks such a button, press the Menu soft button to choose Month, Week, or Day.

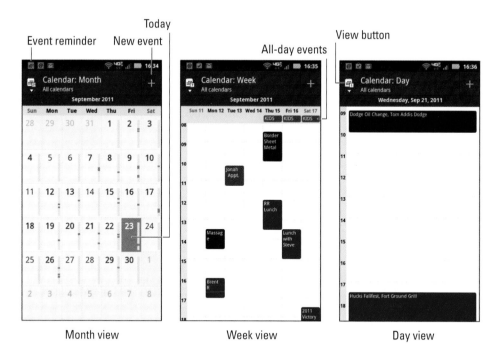

Figure 17-3: The Calendar's Month view.

Agenda view might also be available, which shows your appointments in a list format.

You can hop quickly to today's date by choosing from the View button the command Show Today. Or when your phone has no View button, press the Menu soft button and choose the Today command.

✔ See the later section "Creating a new event" for information on reviewing and creating events, as well as for information about color-coded calendars.

✔ Use Month view to see an overview of what's going on, but use Week view or Day view to see your appointments.

✔ I check Week view at the start of every week to remind me of what's coming up.

✔ Events on the calendar are color-coded, which not only helps you organize events but also shows and hides different types of events. To control the colors and event categories in the Calendar app, press the Menu soft button and choose Settings and then Manage Calendars.

✔ Use your finger to flick the Week view and Day view up or down to see your entire schedule, from midnight to midnight.

✔ Navigate the days, weeks, or months by flicking the screen with your finger. Months scroll up and down; weeks and days scroll from left to right.

✔ To go to a specific date, press the Menu soft button and choose the Go to Date command. Use the onscreen gizmo to enter a date, and then touch the Go button.

Checking your schedule

To see all upcoming events, choose Agenda from the View button's menu (refer to Figure 17-3). Or you might find the Agenda command by pressing the Menu soft button. Rather than list a traditional calendar, the Agenda screen lists only those dates with events and the events themselves.

To see more detail about an event, touch it. Details about the event appear on the screen. The quality of the details depends on how much information you entered when the event was created. At minimum, the event has a name and time.

If you specify an event location, you can touch that location to view on the Maps app where the event takes place. From there, you can easily get directions, as described in Chapter 14.

Creating a new event

The key to making the Calendar app work is to add events: appointments, things to do, meetings, or full-day events such as birthdays and colonoscopies. To create a new event, follow these steps in the Calendar app:

1. **Select the day for the event.**

   Use Month view or Week view, and touch the day of the new event.

   To save time, use Day view and touch the hour at which the event starts.

2. **Touch the New Event button (refer to Figure 17-3), or press the Menu soft button and choose the New Event command.**

   The Create Event screen appears, where you add details about the event.

3. Choose the Calendar event.

Calendars are best set up on the Internet using a computer. Basically, they let you organize your events by category and color. Also, you can show or hide individual calendar categories when you have a particularly busy schedule.

4. Type the event name.

For example, type **Mammogram**.

5. Set the event's start and end times.

Use the control gizmo on the screen to specify times. Or when an event is scheduled to last all day, such as when your mother-in-law comes to visit for an hour, touch the All Day button to put a check mark there.

At this point, you've entered the minimum amount of information for creating an event. Any details you add are okay but not necessary.

6. Fill in other fields to further describe the event.

For example, you can touch the Where field to enter a location. The location can be used by the Maps app to help you get to your appointment. My theory is that you should specify a location as though you're typing something to search for on the map. See Chapter 14 for more information on the Maps app.

A good item to set is the event reminder. That way, the phone signals you for an impending date or appointment.

7. Touch the Save button to create the new event.

You can change an event at any time: Simply touch the Edit Event button when viewing the event.

To remove an event, long-press it in Week view or Day view. Choose the Delete Event command. Touch the OK button to confirm.

✔ It's possible to create repeating events, such as weekly or monthly meetings, anniversaries, and birthdays. Use the Repetition button or Repeat button to create ongoing, scheduled events.

✔ When you've set a reminder for an event, the phone alerts you. At minimum, you may see the Calendar Reminder notification, similar to the one shown in the margin. The phone can also be set to sound a ringtone or vibrate for impending appointments.

✔ To deal with an event notification, pull down the notifications and choose the event. You can touch the Dismiss button to remove event alerts.

✔ Alerts for events are set by pressing the Menu soft button in the Calendar app and choosing the Settings command. Use the Select Ringtone option to choose an audio alert. Use the Vibrate option to control whether the phone vibrates to alert you of an impending event.

The eBook Reader

An *eBook* is an electronic version of a book. The words, formatting, figures, pictures — all that stuff is simply stored digitally so that you can read it on something called an eBook reader. Your phone may have come with eBook reader software, in which case you're ready to start reading. If not, the software can be obtained from the Google Play Store. Two of the more popular eBook readers are Google Play Books and the Amazon Kindle app, both discussed in this section.

✔ The advantage of an eBook reader is that you can carry an entire library of books with you without developing back problems.

✔ Rather than buy a new book at the airport, consider getting an eBook instead, though you can still read a paper book during takeoff and landing.

✔ Lots of eBooks are free, such as quite a few of the classics, including some that aren't boring. Current and popular titles cost money, though the cost is often cheaper than the book's real-world equivalent.

✔ Magazine and newspaper subscriptions are also available for eBook readers.

✔ Not every title is available as an eBook.

Reading Google Books

The Play Books app allows you to read eBooks purchased at the Google Play Store. The app organizes the books into a library and displays the books for reading on your phone.

If your phone doesn't already have the Play Books app, you can find it at the Play Store or scan the QR code in the margin. Or you can just get a book at the Play Books Store, in which case the phone begs you to automatically install the Play Books app.

The reading experience happens like this:

1. **Open the Play Books app.**

   If you're prompted to turn on synchronization, touch the Turn On Sync button.

   You see your eBook library, which lists any titles you've obtained for your Google Play Books account. Or when you're returning to the Play Books app after a break, you see the current page of the eBook you were last reading.

2. **Touch a book to open it.**

3. **Start reading.**

   Use Figure 17-4 as your guide for reading a Google Play Books eBook. Basically, you swipe the pages from left to right.

Touch here to see onscreen information.

Touch here to turn back a page.

Book title and author (onscreen information)

Drag to jump to a page.

Page count and progress indicator (onscreen information)

Touch here to turn to the next page.

Figure 17-4: Reading an e-book in the Play Books app.

Also see Chapter 18 for information on purchasing books at the Google Play Store.

Synchronization allows you to keep copies of your Google Play Books on all your Android devices as well as on the `http://books.google.com` website.

Using the Amazon Kindle app

The good folks at Amazon recognize that you probably don't want to buy a Kindle eBook reader gizmo, because you already have a nifty portable do-everything device in your Android phone. Therefore, the Kindle app serves as your eBook reader software and also provides access to the vast library of existing Kindle titles at Amazon (`www.amazon.com`).

If you don't have the Kindle app on your phone, you can obtain it at the Google Play Store, discussed in Chapter 18. Or you can scan the QR code in the margin to quickly download a copy.

Upon starting the Amazon Kindle app, you see the Registration screen. Log in using your e-mail address and Amazon password.

If you already have an Amazon Kindle account, after touching the Register button, your phone synchronizes with your existing Kindle library.

Choose a book from the Kindle bookshelf and start reading. The eBook-reading operation works on the Kindle similarly to the Google Books app (refer to Figure 17-4), though on the Kindle you can highlight text, bookmark pages, look up word in a dictionary, and do other keen stuff that Google will no doubt add to a future update of its Books app.

  ✔ Books for the Kindle app are purchased at the Kindle store using your existing Amazon account. In the Kindle app, press the Menu soft button and choose Kindle Store.

  ✔ Yes, you need an Amazon.com account to purchase eBooks (or even download freebies), so I highly recommend that you visit Amazon to set up an account if you don't already have one.

  ✔ To ensure that you get your entire Kindle library on your phone, turn on the Wi-Fi connection (see Chapter 19), press the Menu soft button, and choose the Archived Items command.

The Game Machine

For all its seriousness and technology, one of the best uses of a smartphone is to play games. I'm not talking about silly arcade games (though I admit that they're fun). No, I'm talking about some serious portable gaming.

To whet your appetite, your Android phone may have come with a small taste of what the device can do in regard to gaming; look for preinstalled game apps on the Apps menu. If you don't find any, hordes are available at the Google Play Store (refer to Chapter 18).

Game apps use phone features such as the touchscreen or the accelerometer to control the action. It takes some getting used to, especially if you regularly play using a game console or PC, but it can be fun.

The Video Player

The first commercially available television sets were about 12 inches across. Today, the screens can be 72 inches across or more. In a dramatic reversal of this trend, your Android phone has the ability to let you view movies, TV shows, and Internet video on its relatively diminutive screen.

Watching YouTube

The cheapest — and by that, I mean free — way to view video on your phone is to access YouTube. It's the Internet phenomenon that proves Andy Warhol right: In the future, everyone will be famous for 15 minutes. Or in the case of YouTube, they'll be famous on the Internet for the duration of a 10-minute video. That's because YouTube is *the* place on the Internet for anyone and everyone to share their video creations.

To view the mayhem on YouTube, or to contribute something yourself, start the YouTube app, which might be found on the Home screen but most definitely dwells on the App menu. The main YouTube screen is depicted in Figure 17-5.

Upload a video.

Touch a video to watch it.   Get information.

Figure 17-5: YouTube.

To view a video, touch its name or icon in the list.

To search for a video, press the Search soft button while using the YouTube app. Type or dictate what you want to search for, and then peruse the results.

Turn the phone to Landscape mode to view a full-screen video. You can touch the screen to see the onscreen video controls.

✔ Use the YouTube app to view YouTube videos rather than use the Browser app to visit the YouTube website.

✔ Because you have a Google account, you also have a YouTube account. I recommend that you log in to your YouTube account when using the YouTube app: Press the Menu soft button, and choose the command My Channel. Log in, if necessary. Otherwise, you see your account information, videos, and video subscriptions, if you have them.

✔ Not all YouTube videos can be viewed on mobile devices.

✔ You can touch the Upload button (refer to Figure 17-6) to shoot and then immediately send a video to YouTube. Refer to Chapter 15 for information on recording video.

Renting movies

Movies that you rent at the Google Play Store can be viewed on your phone for as long as 24 hours after you first start the film. The process involves renting the film at the Play Store and then using the Play Movies app to watch it.

If your phone comes without the Play Movies app preinstalled, you're prompted to download it automatically whenever you rent and start a video. Or, if you like, you can save time by downloading the app ahead of time, either from the Play Store directly (see Chapter 18) or by scanning the QR code in the margin.

Here are the general steps you take to rent and view a video on your phone:

1. **Visit the Google Play Store; open the Play Store app on your phone.**

2. **Choose the Movies category.**

   All movies are rentals.

3. **Browse or search for a movie.**

4. **Touch the movie's Rent button, which also lists the rental price.**

   You aren't charged for touching the Rent button. Instead, you see more details, such as the rental terms. After you choose a rental, you have 30 days to watch it. But once you start watching the film, you have only a 24-hour period during which you can pause and resume.

5. **Choose a payment method.**

   If you don't yet have an account set up at Google Checkout, you can configure one by touching the Add Payment Method button. Otherwise, choose your Google Checkout credit card, as shown on the screen.

6. **Touch the Accept & Buy button to rent the movie.**

7. **Touch the Play button to view the movie.**

If you don't already have the Videos app, you're prompted to download it: Follow the directions on the screen.

The movie is *streamed* to your phone, which means that it's sent as you watch it. Therefore, I highly recommend two things when you're ready to watch: First, plug your phone into a power source. Second, turn on the Wi-Fi network so that you don't incur data overages.

You don't have to view the movie right away. You can wait as long as 30 days. When you're ready, start the Videos app and choose your rental from the My Rentals list.

You can also start the Videos app from the App menu to review and view your rentals, as well as any personal videos you've installed on your phone.

Some Android phones feature an HDMI output jack. You can connect a special (and not cheap) HDMI cable to the phone, which connects it to an HDMI TV set or computer monitor. That way, you can view your rental on a larger screen. Chapter 20 discusses the HDMI connection for phones that feature HDMI output.

18

More Apps

Your Android phone may have come packed with diverse and interesting apps, or it may have only a paltry selection of tepid sample apps. Regardless of the assortment, you're in no way limited to the original collection. That's because hundreds of thousands of different apps are available for your phone: productivity apps, references, tools, games, and more. They're all found at the central shopping place for all Android phones, the place commonly called the Google Play Store.

Google Voice
Google Inc.
★★★★✦

Movies
Flixster Inc.
★★★★✦

Manual updates

TV Listings for Android
tv24
✦★★✦

Welcome to the Play Store

The Google Play Store is one of the things that make owning an Android phone rewarding. You can not only visit the Play Store to obtain more apps for your phone but also go shopping for music, books, and videos (films and TV shows). Someday, Google might even sell food and clothing at the Play Store. Until then, the selection seems adequate and satisfying.

✔ The Google Play Store was once known as the *Android Market*. You may still see it referred to as such in various documentation.

✔ You don't even need to know what you want at the Play Store; like many a mindless, ambling shopper, you can browse until the touchscreen is smudged and blurry with your fingerprints.

✔ You obtain items from the Play Store by *downloading* them into your phone. This file transfer works best at top speeds; therefore, you should:

✔ Connect to a Wi-Fi network if you plan to obtain apps, books, or movies at the Google Play Store. Wi-Fi not only gives you speed but also helps you avoid data surcharges. See Chapter 19 for details on connecting your phone to a Wi-Fi network.

✔ The Play Store app is frequently updated, so its look may change from the one you see in this chapter. Updated information on the Play Store can be found on my website:

        www.wambooli.com/help/phone

Visiting the Play Store

New apps, music, books, and videos await delivery into your phone, like animated vegetables shouting, "Pick me! Pick me!" To get to them, open the Play Store icon, which can be found on the Home screen or accessed from the App menu.

After opening the Play Store app, you see the main screen, similar to the one shown on the left in Figure 18-1. You can browse for apps, music, books, and movie rentals. The categories are listed on the screen, and the other parts of the screen highlight popular or recommended items. These recommendations are color-coded to let you know what they represent: green for apps, orange for music, blue for books, and red for video rentals.

Find items by choosing a category from the main menu (refer to Figure 18-1). The next screen lists popular and featured items, plus categories you can browse by swiping the screen from right to left. The category titles appear toward the top of the screen.

When you have an idea of what you want, such as an app's name or even what it does, searching works fastest: Touch the Search button at the top of the Market screen (refer to Figure 18-1). Type all or part of the app's name, book or movie title, or perhaps a description. Touch the keyboard's Search button or Go button to begin your search.

To see more information about an item, touch it. Touching something doesn't buy it, but instead displays a more detailed description, screen shots, a video preview, comments, plus links to similar items.

✔ The first time you enter the Android Market, you have to accept the terms of service; touch the Accept button.

✔ Books and videos you get from the Market are viewed from the Books app and Videos app, respectively. See Chapter 17 for information.

✔ Music you obtain from the Play Store is accessed through the Play Music app, not any other music-playing app on your phone. See Chapter 16 for information on the Play Music app.

Go up one level.   App title   Top Paid category

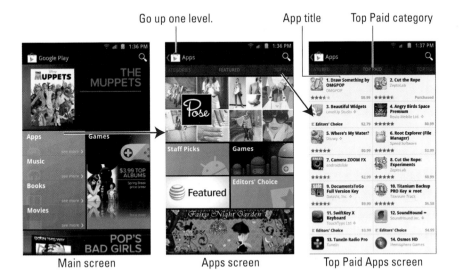

Main screen   Apps screen   Top Paid Apps screen

Figure 18-1: The Google Play Store.

Finding apps at the Play Store

The most common and traditional items to hunt down at the Google Play Store are more apps for your phone. As this book goes to press, more than 500,000 apps are available at the Play Store. That's good news. Better news: Most of the apps are free. Even the paid apps have "lite" versions that you can try without having to pay.

✔ Apps you download are added to the App menu, made available like any other app on your phone.

✔ You can be assured that all apps that appear in the Play Store can be used on your Android phone. There's no way to download or buy something that's incompatible with your phone.

✔ Pay attention to an app's ratings. Ratings are added by people who use the apps, like you and me. Having more stars is better. You can see additional information, including individual user reviews, by choosing the app.

✔ Another indicator of an app's success is the number of times it has been downloaded. Some apps have been downloaded more than 10 million times. That's a good sign.

✔ In addition to getting apps, you can download widgets and wallpapers for your phone's Home screen. Just search the Play Store for *widget* or *live wallpaper.*

✔ See Chapter 22 for more information on widgets and live wallpapers.

Getting a free app

After you locate an app you want, the next step is to download it. Follow these steps:

1. **If possible, activate the phone's Wi-Fi connection to avoid incurring data overages.**

   See Chapter 19 for information on connecting your phone to a Wi-Fi network.

2. **Open the Play Store app.**

3. **Locate the app you want, and open its description.**

   You can browse for apps or use the Search button to find an app by name or job description.

4. **Touch the Download button.**

   The button is found at the bottom of the app's list o' details. Free apps feature the Download button. Paid apps have a button with the app's price on it. (See the next section for information on buying an app.)

   Touching the button doesn't immediately download or install the app.

   After touching the Download button, you're alerted to any services that the app uses. The list of permissions isn't a warning, and it doesn't mean anything bad. The app's developer is simply informing you which of your phone's features the app uses.

5. **Touch the Accept & Download button to begin the download.**

   As the app is downloaded, you see the progress bar dance across the screen. When it's done, the app has been installed.

6. **Touch the Open button to run the app.**

   Or, if you were doing something else while the app was downloading and installing, choose the Installed App notification, as shown in the margin. The notification features the app's name, with the text `Successfully Installed` beneath it.

At this point, what happens next depends on the app you've downloaded. For example, you may have to agree to a license agreement. If so, touch the

I Agree button. Additional setup may involve setting your location, signing in to an account, or creating a profile, for example.

After the initial setup is complete, or if no setup is necessary, you can start using the app.

- ✒ The new app's icon is placed on the App menu, along with all the other apps on the phone.

- ✒ Peruse the list of services that an app uses (refer to Step 4 in the preceding step list) to look for anything unusual or out of line with the app's purpose. For example, an alarm clock app that uses your Contacts list and the text messaging service is a red flag, especially if it's your understanding that the app doesn't need to text-message your contacts.

- ✒ You can also place a shortcut icon for the app on the Home screen. See Chapter 22.

- ✒ Chapter 26 lists some Android apps that I recommend, all of which are free.

Buying an app

Some great free apps are available, but many of the apps you dearly want probably cost money. It's not a lot of money, especially compared to the price of computer software. In fact, it seems odd to sit and stew over whether paying 99 cents for a game is "worth it."

I recommend that you download a free app first, to familiarize yourself with the process.

When you're ready to pay for an app, follow these steps:

1. **Activate the phone's Wi-Fi connection.**

2. **Open the Play Store app.**

3. **Browse or search for the app you want, and choose the app to display its description.**

   Review the app's price.

4. **Touch the Price button.**

   For example, if the app costs 99 cents, the button reads $0.99.

5. **Choose your credit card.**

   The card must be on file with Google Checkout. If you don't yet have a card on file, choose the option Add Payment Method. Choose Add Card, and then fill in the fields on the Credit Card screen to add your payment method to Google Checkout.

6. **Touch the Accept & Buy button.**

   Your payment method is authorized, and the app is downloaded and installed.

The app can be accessed from the App menu, just like all other apps available on your phone. Or if you're still at the app's screen in the Play Store, touch the Open button.

Eventually, you receive an e-mail message from Google Checkout, confirming your purchase. The message explains how to apply for a refund from your purchase. Generally speaking, you can open the app's Info screen (see the later section "Controlling your apps") and touch the Refund button to get your money back.

Be quick on that refund: Some apps allow you only 15 minutes to get your money back. Otherwise, the standard refund period is 24 hours. You know when the time is up because the Refund button changes its name to Uninstall.

Also see the section "Removing apps," later in this chapter.

Manage Your Apps

The Google Play Store is not only where you buy apps — it's also the place you return to for performing app management. This task includes reviewing apps you've downloaded, updating apps, organizing apps, and removing apps that you no longer want or that you severely hate.

Reviewing your downloaded apps

If you're like me, and if I'm like anyone (and my editor says that I'm not), you probably sport a whole host of apps on your Android phone. It's kind of fun to download new software and give your phone new abilities. To review the apps you've acquired, follow these steps:

1. **Start the Play Store app.**

2. **Press the Menu soft button and choose My Apps.**

3. **Scroll your installed apps.**

The list of installed apps should look similar to the one shown on the left in Figure 18-2. If you swipe the screen left, you'll see the list of all apps you've ever obtained at the Play Store, shown in the right in Figure 18-2.

Besides reviewing the list, you can do other things with an installed app, as covered in the sections that follow.

TIP

Never buy an app twice

Any apps you've already purchased in the Google Play Store — say, for another phone or mobile device — are available at no charge for downloading on your current Android phone. Simply find the app and touch the Install button, and then touch Accept & Download.

You can review any already purchased apps in the Play Store: Touch the Menu soft button, and choose My Apps. At the bottom of the list, under the heading Not Installed, you'll find any apps you've already purchased at the Play Store.

Paid app, previously downloaded, not installed

Update all apps configured for automatic updating.   App installed on your phone

Touch to see more information or to open or uninstall.

Touch to update.

Free app, previously downloaded, not installed

Installed apps

All your apps

Figure 18-2: Apps installed and downloaded.

The list of downloaded apps is accurate in that it represents apps you've downloaded. Some apps in the all apps list, however, might not be installed on your phone: They were downloaded, installed, and then removed. To review all apps installed on the phone, see the section "Controlling your apps," later in this chapter.

Sharing an app

When you love an app so much that you can't contain your glee, feel free to share the app with your friends. You can easily share a link to the app in the Play Store by obeying these steps:

1. **Visit the app on your My Apps list.**

   Refer to the preceding section. Or, the app doesn't have to be on your list of apps; it can be any app in the Market. You just need to be viewing the app's Description screen.

2. **Touch the Share button.**

   A menu appears, listing various apps and methods for sharing the app's Google Play Store link with your pals.

3. **Choose a sharing method**

   For example, choose Text Messaging to send a link to the app in a text message.

4. **Use the chosen app to send the link.**

   What happens next depends on which sharing method you've chosen.

The result of completing these steps is that your friend receives a link. They can touch the link on their phone, or no another mobile Android device, and be whisked instantly to the Google Play Store, where they can view the app and easily install it on their gizmo.

Methods for using the various items on the Share menu are found throughout this book.

Updating an app

One nice thing about using the Google Play Store to get new software is that the phone notifies you of new versions of the apps you download. Whenever a new version of any app is available, you see it flagged for updating, as shown in Figure 18-2. Updating the app to get the latest version is cinchy.

From the My Apps list (refer to Figure 18-2), touch the Update button to update all apps for which automatic updating is allowed.

Some apps must be updated individually. They're shown in Figure 18-2, in the Manual Updates area of the My Apps list. To update those apps, touch the green Update button found to the right of the app's name (refer to Figure 18-2). Touch the Update button on the app's Information screen, and then choose Accept & Download.

To make updating easier, open an app's Information screen and place a green check mark by the item Allow Automatic Updating.

✔ The updating process often involves downloading and installing a new version of the app. That's perfectly fine; your settings and options aren't changed by the update process.

✔ Updates to apps might also be indicated by the Updates Available notification icon, shown in the margin. Choose the Updates Available notification to be instantly whisked to the My Apps screen, where you can update your apps as described in this section.

Removing apps

You're free to remove any app you've added to your phone — specifically, the apps you've downloaded from the Play Store. To do so, heed these steps:

1. **Start the Play Store app.**
2. **Press the Menu soft button and choose My Apps.**
3. **Touch the app that offends you.**
4. **Touch the Uninstall button.**
5. **Touch the OK button to confirm.**

   The app is removed.

The app continues to appear on the My Apps (downloads) list even after it has been removed. After all, you downloaded it once. That doesn't mean that the app is installed.

✔ In most cases, if you uninstall a paid app right away, your credit card or account is fully refunded. The definition of "right away," which depends on the app, is stated on the app's Description screen. The return period can be anywhere from 15 minutes to 24 hours.

✔ You can always reinstall paid apps that you've uninstalled. You aren't charged twice for doing so.

✔ You may have a handful of apps that you cannot remove from your phone. They include certain basic Android apps (such as the Dialer and address book apps), but also some apps preinstalled by your cellular provider. Only if you hack into your phone by using the *rooting* process can you remove those apps. I don't recommend it.

Controlling your apps

Your Android phone has a technical area where you can review and manage all installed apps. To visit that place, follow these steps:

1. **At the Home screen, press the Menu soft button.**

2. **Choose Settings, and then choose Applications.**

3. **Choose Manage Applications.**

4. **Touch the All tab at the top of the screen.**

   A complete list of apps installed on your phone is displayed. Unlike the My Apps list in the Play Store app, only installed apps appear.

5. **Touch an application name.**

   The app's Info screen appears, showing lots of trivia about the app.

Among the trivia on the application's Info screen, you'll find some useful buttons. Among them, these are my favorites:

Force Stop: Touch this button to halt a program run amok. For example, I had to stop an older Android app that continually made noise and offered no option to exit.

Uninstall: Touch the Uninstall button to remove the app, which is another way to accomplish the steps described in the preceding section.

Move to Media Area/ SD Card: Touch this button to transfer the app from the phone's internal storage to the MicroSD card. Doing so can help reduce storage overload on the phone.

Move to Phone: Touch this button to transfer an app from the MicroSD card to the phone's internal storage. (This button replaces the Move to Media Area/SD Card button when an app is already dwelling on the MicroSD card.)

Share: Touch the Share button to send a text or e-mail message to a friend. In the message is a link that the recipient can use to install the app on their phone.

A controversy is brewing in the Android community about whether to store apps on the phone's internal storage or the MicroSD card. I prefer the internal storage because the app stays with the phone and is always available. Further, the shortcuts to apps stored internally don't disappear from the Home screen when you access the media card from your computer.

Part V
Nuts and Bolts

The 5th Wave   By Rich Tennant

"So, what kind of roaming capabilities does this thing have?"

PC Mode

Windows Media Sync

USB Mass Storage

Charge Only

*S*ome of the things you do with your phone you don't see in TV ads. That happy, smiling human using an Android phone is probably on a call — and by the looks of things, she's just won a boatload of money. Or you see Junior watching a video or playing a game. There's Grandma, video-chatting with a grandchild. Yes, your phone can do amazing feats, but it's also capable of things you probably won't see in the ads.

For example, you'll never see a Verizon ad with someone cheering their newly connected Bluetooth headset. AT&T won't run an ad showing someone swapping files between their phone and their computer. And Sprint would be reluctant to run an ad featuring a bemused 30-something browsing live wallpaper for her phone's Home screen. Yet all these wonderful activities are covered in this part of the book.

No Wires, Ever!

*T*here are varying degrees of mobility. *Portable* implies that something can be moved, but not how far or how easily. My first TV was a "portable," which meant that it had handholds on the sides; the TV weighed about 25 pounds. *Cordless* implies a degree of freedom beyond portable, but still requires a charging station. There's also a range beyond which cordless devices fail to communicate. *Wireless* is the best type of mobility. It implies freedom from wires, but also lightweight and tiny.

Your Android phone is truly wireless. Forget for a second that you have to plug in the thing to give it a charge. That's not really a hindrance. After the battery is charged, you can take your phone anywhere and use it wirelessly. You can access the cellular network, a Wi-Fi network, and even wireless gizmos and peripherals. This chapter describes the degrees to which you can make your phone wireless.

Android Wireless Networking

Though you can't see it, wireless communications is going on all around. No need to duck — wireless signals are intercepted only by items such as cell phones, tablets, and laptop computers. Your phone uses these signals to let you talk, and to communicate over the Internet and other networks.

Using the digital network

You pay your cellular provider a handsome fee every month. The fee comes in two chunks. One chunk (the less expensive of the two) is the telephone service. The second chunk is the data service, which is how your Android phone gets on the Internet. This system is the *cellular data network.*

Several types of cellular data network are available. When your phone uses one, a status icon appears atop the touchscreen, cluing you in to which network the phone is accessing. Here's the gamut:

4G: The fourth generation of wide-area data networks is comparable in speed to standard Wi-Fi Internet access. It's fast. It also allows for both data and voice transmission at the same time.

3G: The third generation of wide-area data networks isn't quite as fast as 4G, but it's moderately tolerable for surfing the web, watching YouTube videos, and downloading information from the Internet.

1X: The slowest data connection comes in several technical flavors, but they all represent the same thing: the original, slow data network.

Your phone always uses the best network available for its technology. So when you have a 4G phone and a 4G network is within reach, it's the network the phone uses for Internet communications. Otherwise, the 3G data network is chosen, followed by 1X. Or if you have a 3G phone, it uses the 3G network unless one isn't available, and then the 1X network is used.

- ✔ The icons representing the network speed vary from phone to phone and between the various cellular providers.

- ✔ When a data network isn't available, no icon appears on the status bar. In fact, it's entirely possible for the phone to have no data signal but still be able to make phone calls.

- ✔ The cellular data network icons come in two colors. When they're blue (or green, on certain phones), the phone can connect with the Internet and with Google services such as Gmail and Maps. When the icons are gray (or white), the Internet connection is available but the phone cannot reach Google services.

- ✔ Accessing the digital cellular network isn't free. You likely signed up for some sort of subscription plan for a certain quantity of data when you first received your Android phone. When you exceed that quantity, the costs can become prohibitive.

✔ The data subscription is based on the *quantity* of data you send and receive, not on its speed. At 4G speeds, the prepaid threshold can be crossed quickly.

✔ See Chapter 21 for information on how to avoid cellular data overcharges when taking your phone out and about.

Understanding Wi-Fi

Wi-Fi is the same wireless networking standard used by computers for communicating with each other and the Internet. Making Wi-Fi work on your Android phone requires two steps. First, you must activate Wi-Fi, by turning on the phone's wireless radio. The second step is connecting to a specific wireless network.

Turning on Wi-Fi

Follow these steps to activate Wi-Fi on your Android phone:

1. **At the Home screen, press the Menu soft button.**

2. **Choose Settings and then Wireless & Networks.**

3. **Choose Wi-Fi to place a green check mark by that option.**

   A green check mark indicates that the phone's Wi-Fi radio is now activated.

The next step is to connect the phone to a Wi-Fi network, which is covered in the next section.

Your phone may be blessed with the Power Control widget or perhaps a specific Wi-Fi widget, which you may find affixed to the Home screen. An example of what the widget might look like is shown in Figure 19-1.

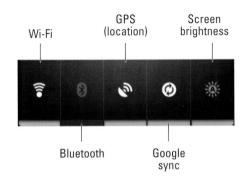

Figure 19-1: The Power Control widget.

Touch the Power Control widget's Wi-Fi button to turn on the phone's Wi-Fi abilities.

To turn off Wi-Fi, repeat the steps in this section. Doing so turns off the phone's Wi-Fi access, disconnecting you from any networks.

✔ Using Wi-Fi to connect to the Internet doesn't incur data usage charges.

✔ The Wi-Fi radio places an extra drain on the battery, but it's truly negligible. If you want to save a modicum of juice, especially if you're out and about and don't plan to be near a Wi-Fi access point for any length of time, turn off the Wi-Fi radio.

✔ Refer to Chapter 22 for information on adding widgets to your phone's Home screen. The Power Control widget or a Wi-Fi widget may be available, which you can use to quickly turn off or on the Wi-Fi radio.

Accessing a Wi-Fi network

After activating the Wi-Fi radio on your Android phone, you can connect to an available wireless network. Heed these steps:

1. **Press the Menu soft button while viewing the Home screen.**

2. **Choose Settings and then Wireless & Networks.**

3. **Choose Wi-Fi Settings.**

   You see a list of Wi-Fi networks displayed, as shown in Figure 19-2. If no wireless network is displayed, you're sort of out of luck regarding Wi-Fi access from your current location.

4. **Choose a wireless network from the list.**

   In Figure 19-2, I chose the Imperial Wambooli network, which is my office network.

5. **If prompted, type the network password.**

   Putting a green check mark in the box by the Show Password option makes it easier to type a long, complex network password.

   If the Wi-Fi network supports the WPS setup, you can connect by using the network PIN, pressing the connection button on the wireless router, or using whatever other WPS method is used by the router.

6. **Touch the Connect button.**

   You should be immediately connected to the network. If not, try the password again.

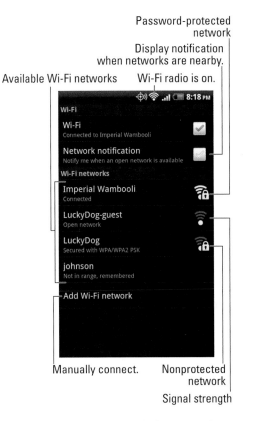

Password-protected network

Display notification when networks are nearby.

Available Wi-Fi networks   Wi-Fi radio is on.

Manually connect.   Nonprotected network

Signal strength

Figure 19-2: Hunting down a wireless network.

When the phone is connected, you see the Wi-Fi status icon appear atop the touchscreen, looking similar to the icon shown in the margin. This icon indicates that the phone's Wi-Fi is on — connected and communicating with a Wi-Fi network.

Some wireless networks don't broadcast their names, which adds security but also makes accessing them more difficult. In these cases, choose the Add Wi-Fi Network command (refer to Figure 19-2) to manually add the network. You need to input the network name, or *SSID,* and the type of security. You also need the password, if one is used. You can obtain this information from the girl with the pink hair and pierced lip who sold you coffee or from whoever is in charge of the wireless network at your location.

✔ Not every wireless network has a password.

✔ Some public networks are open to anyone, but you have to use the Browser app to get on the web and find a login page that lets you access the network: Simply browse to any page on the Internet, and the login page shows up.

✔ Security issues are paramount when you connect to public Wi-Fi networks, such as at coffee shops or libraries. It's possible, though rare, that other people on the Wi-Fi network can use "snooper" software to intercept passwords, credit card numbers, and other sensitive information. My advice: Wait to send this type of information until you're back home or at a more secure location.

✔ The phone automatically remembers any Wi-Fi network it's connected to as well as its network password. An example is the Johnson network, shown in Figure 19-2.

✔ To disconnect from a Wi-Fi network, simply turn off Wi-Fi on the phone. See the preceding section.

✔ A Wi-Fi network is faster than the 3G cellular data network, so it makes sense to connect by Wi-Fi if the only available network is 3G.

✔ Unlike a cellular data network, a Wi-Fi network's broadcast signal goes only so far. My advice is to use Wi-Fi when you plan to remain in one location for a while. If you wander too far away, your phone loses the signal and is disconnected.

Share the Connection

You and your Android phone can get on the Internet anywhere you receive a digital cellular signal. But pity the poor laptop that sits there, unconnected, seething with jealousy.

Well, laptop, be jealous no more! It's possible to share your phone's digital cellular signal in one of two ways. The first is to create a mobile *hotspot,* which allows any Wi-Fi–enabled gizmo to access the Internet via your phone. The second is a direct connection between your phone and another device, which is the *tethering* concept.

Sharing the digital cellular connection might not be an option for your phone. Further, sharing the connection may incur data surcharges or usage fees if your cellular contract doesn't allow for these services to be used.

Creating a mobile hotspot

The mobile hotspot feature allows your Android phone to share its cellular data connection by creating a Wi-Fi network. Other Wi-Fi devices — computers, laptops, other mobile devices — can then access that Wi-Fi network and use the phone's cellular data network. The process is referred to as *creating a mobile, wireless hotspot*, though no fire is involved.

To set up a mobile hotspot with your phone, heed these steps:

1. **Turn off the Wi-Fi radio.**

   There's no point in creating a Wi-Fi hotspot when one is already available.

2. **Plug the phone into a power source.**

   The mobile hotspot feature can draw a lot of power.

3. **From the App menu, open the Mobile Hotspot app.**

   The app may have another name, such as 4G Hotspot or 3G Hotspot.

   Upon opening the app, you may see text describing the process. If so, dismiss the text.

4. **Touch the box to place a green check mark by the Mobile Hotspot item.**

5. **Touch the OK button to dismiss the warning.**

6. **If you're prompted, accept the terms and conditions to subscribe to the service that gives your phone mobile hotspot abilities.**

   On my phone, the fee is about $30 a month. That's above and beyond the fee for my regular data plan.

7. **Name your mobile hotspot and change its password, if you so desire.**

   If you've not yet set up a mobile hotspot, you need to supply some information, such as the name of your hotspot and the password. You can change the name and password provided or keep them as is.

   Make a note of the password. You need it to log in to the mobile hotspot.

8. **Touch the OK button or the Save button to save your settings and start the hotspot.**

   You're done.

When the mobile hotspot is active, you see the Hotspot Active notification icon appear, similar to the one shown in the margin. You can then access the hotspot by using any computer or mobile device that has Wi-Fi capabilities.

To turn off the mobile hotspot, open the Mobile Hotspot app and remove the green check mark.

- ✐ The range for the mobile hotspot is about 30 feet. Items such as walls and tornados can interfere with the signal, rendering it much shorter.

- ✐ Data usage fees apply when you use the mobile hotspot, and they're on top of the fee your cellular provider may charge for the basic service. These fees can add up quickly.

- ✐ Don't forget to turn off the mobile hotspot when you're done using it.

Tethering the Internet connection

A more intimate way to share the phone's digital cellular connection is to connect the phone directly to a computer and activate the tethering feature. Not every Android phone has this ability.

Yes: I am fully aware that tethering goes against the wireless theme of this chapter. Still, it remains a solid way to provide Internet access to another gizmo, such as a laptop or desktop computer. Follow these steps to set up Internet tethering:

1. **Connect the phone to another mobile device by using the USB cable.**

2. **On the phone, at the Home screen, press the Menu soft button.**

3. **Choose Settings and then choose Wireless & Networks.**

4. **Choose Tethering & Mobile Hotspot.**

    On some phones, you may have multiple options rather than a single Tethering option. You may see the options Internet Connection Mode or Internet Pass-Through. The one you want is Internet Connection mode. (The other option, Internet Pass-Through, is where the phone uses the other device's Internet signal.)

5. **Place a green check mark by the item USB Tethering.**

    Internet tethering is activated.

The other device should instantly recognize the phone as a "modem" with Internet access. Further configuration may be required, which depends on the device using the tethered connection. For example, you may be prompted on the PC to locate and install software for your phone. Do so: Accept the installation of new software when prompted by Windows.

✔ There's no need to disable the Wi-Fi radio to activate USB tethering.

✔ Sharing the digital network connection incurs data usage charges against your cellular data plan. Be careful with your data usage when you're sharing a connection.

The Bluetooth Connection

One type of computer network you can confuse yourself with is Bluetooth. It has nothing to do with the color blue or any dental hygiene.

Bluetooth is a wireless protocol for communication between two or more Bluetooth-equipped devices. Your Android phone just happens to be Bluetooth-equipped, so it too can use Bluetooth devices, such as those earphone-speakers that make you look like you have a stapler stuck to your ear.

Activating Bluetooth

You must turn on the phone's Bluetooth networking before you can use one of those Borg-earpiece implants and join the ranks of walking nerds. Here's how to turn on Bluetooth:

1. **At the Home screen, press the Menu soft button.**

2. **Choose Settings and then Wireless & Networks.**

3. **Choose Bluetooth.**

   Or, if a little green check mark already appears by the Bluetooth option, Bluetooth is already on.

You can also turn on Bluetooth by using the Power Control widget (refer to Figure 19-1), if your phone has it floating somewhere on the Home screen. Just touch the Bluetooth button to turn it on.

To turn off Bluetooth, repeat the steps in this section.

   ✔ When Bluetooth is on, the Bluetooth status icon appears. It uses the Bluetooth logo, shown in the margin.

   ✔ Activating Bluetooth can quickly drain the phone's battery. Be mindful to use Bluetooth only when necessary, and remember to turn it off when you're done.

Using a Bluetooth headset

Bluetooth can be used to pair the phone with a variety of gizmos, including your computer (if it's Bluetooth-equipped) and even Bluetooth printers, as described in the later sidebar "Printing something from your phone." The most common Bluetooth gizmo to use with an Android phone remains a headset.

To make the Bluetooth connection between your phone and a set of those I'm-so-cool earphones, follow these steps:

1. **Ensure that Bluetooth is on.**

2. **Turn on the Bluetooth headset.**

3. **At the Home screen, press the Menu soft button and choose Settings.**

4. **Choose Wireless & Networks and then Bluetooth Settings.**

   The Bluetooth Settings screen appears.

Printing something from your phone

Not every Android phone is capable of printing. Those that can print often employ a Bluetooth connection to make printing happen. The operation works the same as for pairing a Bluetooth headset with your phone: You pair the Bluetooth printer. Then you use the Bluetooth item on the various Share menus to upload a document or image to the printer.

Yeah, it sounds easy, and it can be fun, but it can also be an ordeal to configure. Bluetooth-enabled printers are also quite rare. (Bluetooth printers feature the Bluetooth logo.)

Some cellular providers include Wi-Fi printing apps on their phones, such as the MOTOPRINT app found on certain Motorola Android phones.

You can use the app to locate printers shared on a Wi-Fi network. After the connection is established, you can print pictures or documents from your phone.

The Print to Retail option is also found on the Share menu on certain Android phones. This option allows you to upload a photo to a local printer, such as the photo department at your local Costco or Sam's Club. Not every Android phone has the Print to Retail feature.

Don't wallow in despair if your phone lacks the ability to print. You can always e-mail yourself documents or photos and then print them from your computer.

---

5. **Choose Scan for Devices.**

6. **If necessary, press the main button on the Bluetooth gizmo.**

   The main button is the one you use to answer the phone. You may have to press and hold the button.

   Eventually, the device should appear on the screen, or you see its code number.

7. **Choose the device.**

8. **If necessary, input the device's passcode.**

   It's usually a four-digit number, and quite often it's simply 1234.

When the device is connected, you can stick it in your ear and press its main Answer button when the phone rings.

After you've answered the call (by pressing the main Answer button on the earphone), you can chat away.

If you tire of using the Bluetooth headset, you can touch the Bluetooth button on the touchscreen to use the phone's own speaker and microphone. (Refer to Figure 5-2, in Chapter 5, for the location of the Bluetooth button.)

- You can turn the Bluetooth earphone on or off after it has been paired. As long as Bluetooth is on, the phone instantly recognizes the earphone when you turn it on.

- To unpair a device, locate it on the Bluetooth Settings screen. Long-press the device and choose either the Disconnect or Disconnect & Unpair command.

- Don't forget to turn off the earpiece when you're done with it. The ear-piece has a battery, and it continues to drain when you forget to turn the thing off.

Connect, Store, Share

1 don't believe that your computer is jealous of your phone. It might be. My phone is jealous of my laser printer, which I know because they refuse to talk with each other. But the computer? That situation was resolved by using the USB connection. Now the computer and cell phone are bosom buddies, connecting, chatting, and sharing long into the wee hours. Apparently, your Android phone is incredibly capable of sharing, and is even eager to share, information with your computer. This chapter explains how it works.

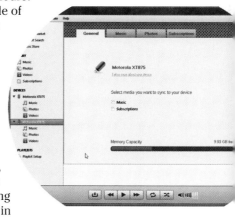

The USB Connection

The most direct way to mate an Android phone with a computer is to use a USB cable. Coincidentally, a USB cable comes with the phone. It's a match made in heaven, but, like many matches, it often works less than smoothly. Rather than hire a counselor to put the phone and computer on speaking terms, I offer you some good USB connection advice in this section.

Connecting the phone to a computer

Communication between your computer and your Android phone works faster when both devices are physically connected. This connection happens by using the USB cable: The cable's A end plugs into the computer. The other end, known as the *micro-USB connector,* plugs into the phone's USB hole.

Computer nerds call the USB hole a *port.*

The cable plugs in only one way, so you can't connect the computer and phone improperly (backward or upside down). That's good.

When your phone is connected via USB cable to a computer, you see the USB Connection notification icon appear, similar to the one shown in the margin. Refer to the next section to see what you can do with this notification to configure the USB connection.

✏ If possible, plug the USB cable into the computer itself, not into a USB hub. The phone-computer connection works best with a powered USB port.

✏ If you have no USB cable for your phone, you can buy one at any computer- or office-supply store. Get a USB-A-male-to-micro–USB cable.

✏ A flurry of activity takes place when you first connect an Android phone to a Windows PC. Notifications pop up about new software that's installed, or you may see the AutoPlay dialog box, prompting you to install software. Do so.

Configuring the USB connection

Upon the successful connection of your Android phone to a computer, you have the option of configuring the USB connection. A menu appears, either automatically or when you choose the USB notification. The menu may look similar to the one shown in Figure 20-1, though there are plenty of variations, depending on the phone's manufacturer.

The number and names of the items shown in the USB Connection menu vary. Here are the most useful choices:

Charge Only / None: Use this option when you want only to charge the phone and not have it communicate with the computer. Because there's no data connection, the Charge Only option may be titled None on certain phones.

USB Mass Storage / Disk Drive: When this option is chosen, the computer treats the phone as a removable storage device, such as a USB thumb drive or a media card.

Windows Media Sync / Media Sync: This option is used on a Windows PC to treat the phone as a media device, similar to a camera or an MP3 music player. It's ideal for synchronizing files.

Figure 20-1: The USB Connection menu.

Other, specific options may exist for your phone's USB connection menu. Though when you're in doubt, choosing one of these listed options should help you accomplish whatever task you had in mind for connecting the phone to the computer.

✓ HTC phones feature the HTC Sync item. To get that item to work, you must install the HTC Sync program on your Windows computer. Visit the website www.htc.com/www/help to install the HTC Sync program for HTC Android phones.

✓ If you have a Macintosh, use only the Charge Only and USB Mass Storage / Disk Drive USB settings. Other options may not be compatible with the Mac.

✓ After choosing the Media Sync or Mass Storage options, you see one or two AutoPlay dialog boxes on your Windows PC. You can choose how to deal with the phone by using the dialog box to choose an item such as Windows Media Player or Open Folder to View Files. Or just close the dialog box.

✓ The reason you may see two AutoPlay dialog boxes is that most Android phones feature two storage locations: internal storage and the MicroSD card. One AutoPlay dialog box appears for each storage location. See the later section "Phone Storage Mysteries" for additional information about the phone's storage.

✓ When you're done accessing information, you should properly unmount the phone from your computer system. See the next section.

✔ You may not be able to access the phone's storage while it's mounted into a computer storage system. Items such as your music and photos are unavailable until you disconnect the phone from the computer or choose the Charge Only / None setting for the USB connection.

✔ No matter which USB connection option you've chosen, the phone's battery charges whenever it's connected to a computer's USB port — as long as the computer is turned on, of course.

Disconnecting the phone from the computer

When you're using any USB connection option other than Charge Only / None, you must properly disconnect the phone from the computer. Never yank out the USB cable. Never! Never! *Never!* Doing so can damage the phone's storage, which is A Bad Thing. Instead, follow these steps to do things properly:

1. **Close whichever programs or windows are accessing the phone from the computer.**

2. **Properly unmount the phone from the computer's storage system.**

   On a PC, locate the phone's icon in the Computer window or the My Computer window. Right-click the icon, and choose either the Eject or Safely Remove command.

   On a Macintosh, drag the phone's Storage icon to the Trash.

3. **On your phone, pull down the notifications.**

4. **Choose USB Connection.**

5. **Choose the Charge Only or None setting.**

6. **Touch the OK button to confirm.**

   The phone's storage is unmounted and can no longer be accessed from your computer.

7. **If you like, unplug the USB cable.**

When you choose to keep the phone connected to the computer, the phone continues to charge. (Only when the computer is off does the phone not charge.) Otherwise, the computer and phone have ended their little *tête-à-tête,* and you and the phone are free again to wander the earth.

Synchronize Your Stuff

The synchronizing procedure involves hooking your Android phone to a computer and then swapping information back and forth. This process can be completed automatically by using special software, or it can be done manually. The manual method isn't pleasant, though oftentimes it's necessary.

Synchronizing with doubleTwist

One of the most popular ways to move information between your Android phone and a computer is to use the third-party utility doubleTwist. This amazing program is free, and it's available at www.doubletwist.com.

doubleTwist isn't an Android app. You use it on your computer, either a PC or a Macintosh. The app lets you easily synchronize pictures, music, videos, and web page subscriptions between your computer and its media libraries and any portable device, such as your phone. Additionally, doubleTwist gives you the ability to search the Google Play Store and obtain new apps for your phone.

To use doubleTwist, connect your phone to your computer as described earlier in this chapter. Choose either the Mass Storage / Disk Drive or Media Sync option; the phone's MicroSD card is added to your computer's storage system as a USB mass storage device. Start up the doubleTwist program if it doesn't start by itself. The simple doubleTwist interface is illustrated in Figure 20-2.

Items stored on your computer   Choose items to sync.

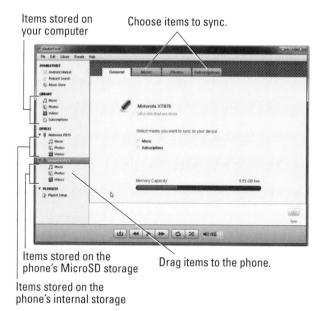

Items stored on the phone's MicroSD storage   Drag items to the phone.

Items stored on the phone's internal storage

Figure 20-2: The doubleTwist synchronization utility.

The way I use doubleTwist is to drag and drop media either from my computer to the phone or the other way around. Use the program's interface to browse for media, as shown in Figure 20-2.

- If you choose the Media Sync option, only the phone's MicroSD card is available in doubleTwist. When you choose the Mass Storage or Disk Drive connection option, you see both the internal and MicroSD storage areas available (refer to Figure 20-2).

- You cannot copy media purchased at the iTunes store from the Mac to an Android phone. Apparently, you need to upgrade to iTunes Plus before the operation is allowed.

- doubleTwist doesn't synchronize contact information. Contact information is automatically synchronized between your phone's address book and Google. For synchronizing vCards, see the next section.

- Information on synchronizing music between your computer and phone is covered in Chapter 16.

Doing a manual sync

When you can't get software on your computer to synchronize automatically, you have to resort to making the old manual connection. Yes, it can be complex. And bothersome. And tedious. But it's often the only way to get some information out of the phone and on to a computer, or vice versa.

Follow these steps to copy files between your computer and your Android phone:

1. **Connect the phone to the computer by using the USB cable.**

2. **Choose the USB Mass Storage or Disk Drive option for the USB connection.**

   Specific directions are offered earlier in this chapter.

3a. **On a PC, in the AutoPlay dialog box, choose the option Open Folder to View Files.**

   The option might instead read Open Device to View Files.

   You see a folder window appear, which looks like any common folder in Windows. The difference is that the files and folders in this window are on the phone, not on your computer.

   Use the second AutoPlay dialog box to repeat this process for the phone's other storage (internal or MicroSD).

3b. **On a Macintosh, open the Removable Drive icon (or icons) to access the phone's storage.**

   The Mac uses generic, Removable Drive icons to represent the phone's storage. If two icons appear, one represents the phone's internal storage, and the second is for the phone's MicroSD card or removable storage.

4. **Open a folder window on your computer.**

   It's either the folder from which you're copying files to the phone or the folder that will receive files from the phone — for example, the `Documents` folder.

   If you're copying files from the phone to your computer, use the `Pictures` folder for pictures and videos and the `Documents` folder for everything else.

5. **Drag the File icons from one folder window to the other to copy them between the phone and the computer.**

   Use Figure 20-3 as your guide.

Drag files to here to copy to the root.
The phone's internal storage is Drive I on this PC.
The phone's MicroSD is Drive H on this PC.

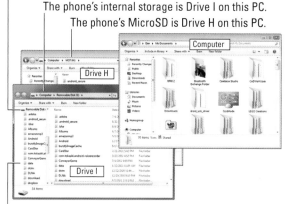

Specific folders on the phone

Figure 20-3: Copying files to the phone.

6. **When you're done, properly unmount the phone's storage from your computer's storage system and disconnect the USB cable.**

   You must eject the phone's Storage icon (or icons) from the Macintosh computer before you can turn off USB storage on the phone.

Any files you've copied to the phone are now stored on either the phone's internal storage or the MicroSD card. What you do with the files next depends on the reasons you copied the files: to view pictures, use the Gallery; to import vCards, use the Contacts app; to listen to music, use the Music Player — and so on.

✔ It doesn't matter to which storage location you copy files — internal storage or MicroSD card (removable storage). I recommend using the MicroSD card because the phone seems to prioritize its internal storage, and it can fill up quickly.

✔ Quite a few files can be found in the *root folder,* the main folder on the phone's MicroSD card, which you see when the phone is mounted into your computer's storage system and you open its folder.

✔ A good understanding of basic file operations is necessary to get the most benefit from transferring files between your computer and the phone. These basic operations include copying, moving, renaming, and deleting. It also helps to be familiar with the concept of folders. A doctorate in entanglement theory is optional.

Phone Storage Mysteries

Information stored on your phone (pictures, videos, music) is kept in two places: on the removable MicroSD card and on the phone's internal storage. That's about all you need to know, though if you're willing to explore the concept further — including the scary proposition of file management on a cell phone — keep reading.

Generally speaking, you use specific apps to access the stuff stored on your phone — for example, the Gallery app to view pictures or the Music app to listen to tunes. Beyond that, you can employ some nerdy apps to see where stuff dwells on your Android phone.

The first app, which is the least scary, is the Downloads app. It displays the Downloads screen, which is used to review the files you've downloaded from the Internet (via the web or an e-mail attachment) to your phone.

The second app, which is scary because it's a file management app and these apps aren't user friendly, is the Files app. It works like the File Explorer in Windows or the Finder on the Macintosh: Files and folders are displayed on the screen, with options for examining and manipulating those files.

Using the Files app works like this:

1. **Start the Files app.**

   It's found on the App menu. If it's not there, despair not: Plenty of file management apps are available at the Google Play Store. See the list at the end of this section for a good alternative.

2. **Choose which storage device to examine: Internal Phone Storage or SD Card.**

Where the phone's files lurk

Files on your phone don't just randomly float around, like marbles in a paper bag. Nope, just like your computer, files on the phone are organized into folders. Certain files wind up in specific locations on Android phones. The folders may have slightly different names, but generally speaking, you can find common files in these locations:

`/download`: This folder contains files you've downloaded using the Browser app.

`/dcim/camera`: Pictures and videos are stored in this folder.

`/music`: The Music app organizes your phone's music into this folder. Subfolders are organized by artist.

These folders can exist on either the internal storage or the MicroSD card. So when you can't find the file or folder you're looking for on one media, look in the other.

---

3. **Browse the files just as you would on a computer.**

   If you're familiar with computer file management, you'll be right at home amid the Folder and File icons: Touch a Folder icon to open it and see which subfolders and files dwell inside. Touch a File icon to preview it — if that's possible.

4. **To manage a file or folder, long-press it.**

   A menu appears where you can perform typical file management operations: delete, rename, copy, or move, for example.

You can press the Home soft button when you're done being frightened by file management in the Files app.

- ✔ Every storage location on the phone is a *volume*. It's the same term used on a computer: If your PC has two hard drives, for example, both of them are volumes.

- ✔ You can also examine files and folders on your phone by mounting the phone's storage to a computer system. This method is easier to manage because you have access to a full-size screen and keyboard; plus, a computer mouse to move things around. See the preceding section.

- ✔ If your Android phone lacks a Files app, consider picking up the Astro file manager at the Google Play Store. Astro has many of the features of the Files app, plus a few more that make it extremely popular among the Android phone nerd set. Scan the QR code in the margin, or refer to Chapter 18 for information on getting Astro for your phone.

Make the HDMI connection

A popular feature on several Android phones is the ability to connect the phone to an HDMI monitor. The phone must have an HDMI connector, and you need to buy an HDMI cable. After doing so, you can hunt down an HDMI monitor or computer and then plug the two gizmos into each other. In mere moments, you can watch a Gallery app slideshow or full-screen videos or movies, or simply enjoy the thrill of playing *Angry Birds* on the big screen.

HDMI stands for High Definition Multimedia Interface.

Here are the specific steps for doing the HDMI thing with your Android phone:

1. **Attach the HDMI cable to the HDMI monitor or TV set.**

   If it's an HDMI TV, make a note of the port number so that you can switch to that input channel for viewing the phone.

2. **Plug the HDMI cable into the phone's HDMI jack.**

   The jack looks similar to the micro-USB connector, and it may, in fact, be found right next to it.

3. **Choose which option you want for HDMI viewing.**

   Among the options you find displayed on the phone screen:

   Gallery: The Gallery app opens. You can start a slide show by choosing My Library and then pressing the Menu soft button and choosing the Slideshow command.

   Music: The Music app starts. Choose a playlist, an album, or an artist, and enjoy watching the Music app on the big screen. (The sound should play from the TV's speakers.)

   Mirror On Display: The screen output on your Android phone is duplicated on the HDMI TV or monitor. This option is the one you choose when you want to watch a full-size rented movie.

4. **Disconnect the HDMI cable when you're done.**

   There's no need to give any commands or officially touch a button; just unplug the cable.

If you change your mind about your choice in Step 3, pull down the notifications and choose the item Connected to HDMI Cable. Choose another option from the menu.

On the Road Again

*O*nce upon a time, in a land far, far away, can your Android phone still get a signal? And how far away is far? Sure, you can take your phone to outer Mongolia. It might even work there, connecting your phone calls and even letting you update your Facebook status. "I'm in outer Mongolia — Like!" Or what happens when you're sitting in the comfort of your own solarium and you want to call outer Mongolia? How far can you go with your phone?

Well, by gum! This chapter has the answers to all those questions.

Where the Android Phone Roams

The word *roam* takes on an entirely new meaning when applied to a cell phone. It means that your phone receives a cell signal whenever you're outside your cell phone carrier's operating area. In that case, your phone is *roaming*.

Roaming sounds handy, but there's a catch: It almost always involves a surcharge for using another cellular service — an *unpleasant* surcharge.

Relax: Your Android phone alerts you whenever you're roaming. The Roaming icon appears at the top of the screen, in the status area. The icon differs from phone to phone, but the letter *R* appears over the traditional signal bars. The lock screen may also announce that the phone is roaming whenever you're outside the standard signal area, possibly using another cellular provider's network.

There's little you can do to avoid incurring roaming surcharges when making or receiving phone calls. Well, yes: You can wait until you're back in an area serviced by your primary cellular provider. You can, however, altogether avoid using the other network's data services while roaming. Follow these steps:

1. **At the Home screen, press the Menu soft button.**

2. **Choose Settings.**

3. **Choose Wireless & Networks and then Mobile Networks.**

   On some Android phones, you may have to choose Battery & Data Manager and then Data Delivery.

4. **Ensure that the Data Roaming option isn't selected.**

   Remove the green check mark by Data Roaming.

Your phone can still access the Internet over the Wi-Fi connection when you're roaming. Setting up a Wi-Fi connection doesn't make you incur extra charges, unless you have to pay to get on the wireless network. See Chapter 19 for more information about Wi-Fi.

Another network service you might want to disable while roaming has to do with multimedia, or *MMS*, text messages. To avoid surcharges from another cellular network for downloading an MMS message, follow these steps:

1. **Open the phone's text messaging app.**

   See Chapter 9 to find out what the app may be named, though often it's Text Messaging.

2. **If the screen shows a specific conversation, press the Back soft button to return to the main messaging screen.**

   (It's the screen that lists all your conversations.)

3. **Touch the Menu soft button.**

4. **Choose the Settings command or the Messaging Settings command.**

5. **Remove the green check mark by the Auto-Retrieve or Roaming Auto-Retrieve command.**

   Or, if the item isn't selected, you're good to go — literally.

When the phone is roaming, you may see the text *Emergency Calls Only* displayed on the locked screen.

Airplane Mode

If you've been flying recently, you're already familiar with the cell phone airplane rules: Placing a call on your cell phone while on an airborne plane is strictly forbidden. That's because, if you did, the navigation system would completely screw up and the plane would invert and crash into a nearby mountain. The FCC is so certain of disaster that even if there are no mountains around, one will pop up the second you turn on your phone, and the plane will fireball into it.

Seriously, you're not supposed to use a cell phone when flying. Specifically, you're not allowed you make calls in the air. You can, however, use your Android phone to listen to music or play games or do anything else that doesn't require a cellular connection. The secret is to place the phone in *Airplane mode*.

The most convenient way to put any Android phone in Airplane mode is to press and hold the Power button. From the menu, choose Airplane Mode. You don't even need to unlock the phone to perform this operation.

The most inconvenient way to put the phone into Airplane mode is to follow these steps:

1. **At the Home screen, press the Menu soft button.**

2. **Choose Settings, and then choose Wireless & Networks.**

3. **Touch the square by Airplane Mode to set the green check mark.**

   When the green check mark is visible, Airplane mode is active.

When the phone is in Airplane mode, a special icon appears in the status area, similar to the one shown in the margin. You might also see the text *No Service* appear on the phone's locked screen.

To exit Airplane mode, repeat the steps in this section. On the Wireless & Network Settings screen, remove the green check mark by touching the square next to Airplane Mode.

Android phone air-travel tips

I don't consider myself a frequent flyer, but I travel several times a year. I do it often enough that I wish the airports had separate lines for security: one for seasoned travelers, one for families, and one, of course, for frickin' idiots. That last category would have to be disguised by placing a Bonus Coupons sign or a Free Snacks banner over the metal detector. That would weed 'em out.

Here are some of my cell phone and airline travel tips:

✓ **Charge your phone before you leave.** This tip probably goes without saying, but you'll be happier with a full cell phone charge to start your journey.

✓ **Take a cell phone charger with you.** Many airports feature USB chargers, so you might need just a USB-to-micro-USB cable. Still, why risk it? Bring the entire charger with you.

✓ **At the security checkpoint, place your phone in a bin.** Add to the bin all your other electronic devices, keys, brass knuckles, grenades, and so on. I know from experience that keeping your cell phone in your pocket most definitely sets off airport metal detectors.

✓ **When the flight crew asks you to *turn off* your cell phone for takeoff and landing, obey the command.** That's *turn off,* as in power off the phone or shut it down. It doesn't mean that you place the phone in Airplane mode. Turn it off.

✓ **Use the phone's Calendar app to keep track of flights.** The combination of airline and flight number can serve as the event title. For the event time, I insert takeoff and landing schedules. For the location, I add the origin and destination airport codes. Remember to input the proper time zones. Referencing the phone from your airplane seat or in a busy terminal is much handier than fussing with travel papers. See Chapter 17 for more information on the Calendar app.

✓ **Some airlines feature Android apps you can use while traveling.** Rather than hang on to a boarding pass printed by your computer, for example, you simply present your phone to the scanner.

✓ **Some apps you can use to organize your travel details are similar to, but more sophisticated than, using the Calendar app.** Visit the Google Play Store and search for *travel* or *airline* to find a host of apps.

REMEMBER

✓ Officially, your cell phone must be powered *off* when the plane is taking off or landing. See Chapter 2 for information on turning off the phone.

✓ Some Android phones feature Sleep mode, in which case you can place your phone into Sleep mode for the duration of a flight. The phone wakes up faster from Sleep mode than it does when you turn it on. See Chapter 2.

✓ Bluetooth networking is disabled in Airplane mode. See Chapter 19 for more information on Bluetooth.

✔ You can compose e-mail while the phone is in Airplane mode. The messages aren't sent until you disable Airplane mode and connect again with a data network. Unless:

✔ Many airlines now feature wireless networking onboard. You can turn on wireless networking for your Android phone and use a wireless network in the air: Simply activate the Wi-Fi feature, per the directions in Chapter 19, after placing the phone in Airplane mode — well, after the flight attendant tells you that it's okay to do so.

International Calling

You can use your cell phone to dial up folks who live in other countries. You can also take your cell phone overseas and use it in another country. Completing either task isn't as difficult as properly posing for a passport photo, but it can become frustrating and expensive when you don't know your way around.

Dialing an international number

A phone is a bell that anyone in the world can ring. To prove it, all you need is the phone number of anyone in the world. Dial that number using your phone and, as long as you both speak the same language, you're talking!

To make an international call with your Android phone, you merely need to know the foreign phone number. The number includes the international country-code prefix, followed by the number.

Before dialing the international country-code prefix, you must first dial a plus sign (+) when using the Dialer app. The + symbol is the *country exit code,* which must be dialed in order to flee the national phone system and access the international phone system. For example, to dial Finland on your phone, you dial +358 and then the number in Finland. The +358 is the exit code (+) plus the international code for Finland (358).

To produce the + code in an international phone number, press and hold the 0 key on the Dialer app's dialpad. Then input the country prefix and the phone number. Touch the Dial button (the green Phone icon) to complete the call.

✔ You also pay a surcharge for sending text messages abroad. You have to contact your cellular provider to see the text message rates. Generally, there are two rates, one for sending and another for receiving messages.

✔ If texting charges vex you, remember that e-mail has no associated per-message charge. There are also alternative ways to chat, such as Google Talk and Skype, both covered in Chapter 13.

- In most cases, dialing an international number involves a time zone difference. Before you dial, be aware of what time it is in the country or location you're calling.

- Dialing internationally also involves surcharges, unless your cell phone plan already provides for international dialing.

- The + character isn't a number separator. When you see an international number listed as 011+20+xxxxxxx, do not insert the + character in the number. Instead, dial +20 and then the rest of the international phone number.

- International calls fail for a number of reasons. One of the most common is that the recipient's phone company or service blocks incoming international calls.

- Another reason that international calls fail is the zero reason: Oftentimes, you must leave out any zero in the phone number that follows the country code. So, if the country code is 254 for Kenya and the phone number starts with 012, you dial +254 for Kenya and then 12 and the rest of the number. Omit the leading zero.

- Know which type of phone you're calling internationally — cell phone or landline. The reason is that an international call to a cell phone often involves a surcharge that doesn't apply to a landline.

Making international calls with Skype

One of the easiest, and cheapest, ways to make international calls on your Android phone is to use the Skype app. If the app isn't supplied on your phone, you have to install it from the Google Play Store: Search for *Skype* in the Play Store app, or use the QR code in the margin to download Skype to your phone.

I cover Skype in detail in Chapter 13, where the topic is free Internet calls as well as video chat. Because Skype uses the Internet, you can also use Skype to contact overseas Skype users without incurring any extra costs (well, beyond your normal data plan). You can, however, use Skype Credit in your Skype account to dial internationally, both from the United States to a foreign country as well as from a foreign country home.

To make an international call, log in to Skype as you normally would. At the main Skype screen, choose the Call Phone command. Punch in the number, including the plus sign (+) symbol for international access, as described earlier in this chapter and shown in Figure 21-1. Touch the green Call button to make the call.

After the call is connected by Skype, the phone's touchscreen looks similar to the way it looks when you regularly place calls. You can use the phone's dialpad, if necessary, mute the call, or put the phone on speaker, for example.

Choose a country.
Skype notification   Skype contacts

Dialpad   Press and hold to
insert a (+) in the number.

Figure 21-1: Calling internationally with Skype.

When you're finished with the call, touch the End button.

✔ You're always signed in to Skype unless you sign out. Pressing the Home soft button to switch to another app doesn't sign you out of Skype.

✔ To sign out of Skype, press the Menu soft button at the main Skype screen and choose Sign Out. If the Sign Out command isn't visible at first, touch the More command to find it.

✔ Check with your cellular provider to see whether you're charged connection minutes for using Skype. Even though the international call is free, you might still be dinged for the minutes you use on Skype to make the call.

Taking your Android phone abroad

The easiest way to use a cell phone abroad is to rent or buy one in the country where you plan to stay. I'm serious: Often, international roaming charges are so high that it's cheaper to simply buy a throwaway cell phone wherever you go, especially if you plan to stay there for a while.

When you opt to use your own phone rather than buy a local phone, things should run smoothly — if a compatible cellular service is in your location. Not every Android phone uses the same network and, of course, not every foreign country uses the same cellular network. Things must match before the phone can work. Plus, you may have to deal with foreign carrier roaming charges.

The key to determining whether your phone is usable in a foreign country is to turn it on. The name of that country's compatible cellular service should show up at the top of the phone, where the name of your carrier appears on the main screen. So where your phone once said *Verizon Wireless,* it may say *Wambooli Telcom* when you're overseas.

✔ You receive calls on your cell phone internationally as long as the phone can access the network. Your friends need only dial your cell phone number as they normally do; the phone system automatically forwards your calls to wherever in the world you are.

✔ The person calling you pays nothing extra when you're off romping the globe with your Android phone. Nope — *you* pay extra for the call.

✔ While you're abroad, you need to dial internationally. When calling the United States, you need to use a ten-digit number (phone number plus area code). You may also be required to type the country exit code when you dial.

✔ When in doubt, contact your cellular provider for tips and other information specific to whatever country you're visiting.

✔ Be sure to inquire about texting and cellular data (Internet) rates while you're abroad.

✔ Using an Android phone over a Wi-Fi network abroad incurs no extra fees (unless data roaming is on, as discussed earlier in this chapter). In fact, you can use the Skype app on your phone over a Wi-Fi network to call the United States or any international number at inexpensive rates.

22

Customize and Configure

In This Chapter

▷ Changing the Home screen background

▷ Putting your favorite apps on the Home screen

▷ Adding and removing icons and widgets

▷ Setting the phone's locks

▷ Silencing the phone

▷ Modifying phone settings

*W*ho in their right mind would want to customize a cell phone? I mean, what exactly can you do to the phone? A phone isn't like a hotrod, though you can give your phone a custom paint job. (I wouldn't recommend it.) You can use the Bedazzler™ on the phone. You can hire an artisan to make a tiny fur coat for your phone. True, that's an example of customizing your Android phone, but it's not the topic of this chapter.

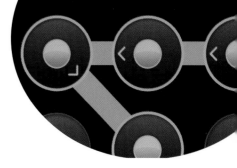

The customization of an Android phone doesn't involve sprucing up the phone's case, though if you're into such things, by all means — go for it. No, in this chapter, the topic is customizing the Android operating system itself. You can change the way the phone looks, change sounds, modify the Home screen, add security, and do a host of other things. The goal, as with any customization, is to make your phone your own.

It's Your Home Screen

The typical Android phone sports a roomy Home screen. It can have anywhere from five to nine or more Home screen panels. Of course, the phone comes preconfigured with an armada of icons and widgets festooning every panel. You can customize the panels by removing widgets and icons, especially those you seldom use, and replacing them with icons and widgets you frequently use. You can put a new wallpaper on the Home screen, including a fancy *live* wallpaper. Truly, you can make the Home screen look just the way you want.

For the most part, the key to changing the Home screen is the *long-press:* Press and hold your finger on a blank part of the Home screen (not on an icon). You see a pop-up menu appear, as shown in Figure 22-1. From the menu, you can begin your Home screen customization adventure, as discussed in this section.

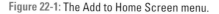

Figure 22-1: The Add to Home Screen menu.

> ✔ The Add to Home Screen menu doesn't appear when the Home screen panel is already full of icons or widgets.

> ✔ On some HTC phones, you customize the Home screen by touching the Personalize button, shown in the margin. From the Personalize menu, you can choose the same items shown in Figure 22-1.

> ✔ Some Android phones may offer additional Home screen customization options, such as multiple skins or designs for the Home screen. There may even be third-party methods for customizing the Home screen. This section, however, sticks with the traditional Android methods of modifying the Home screen.

Changing wallpaper

The Home screen has two types of backgrounds, or *wallpapers:* traditional and live. *Live* wallpapers are animated. A not-so-live wallpaper can be any image, such as a picture from the Gallery.

To set a new wallpaper for the Home screen, obey these steps:

1. **Long-press the Home screen.**

   The Add to Home Screen menu appears (refer to Figure 22-1).

2. **Choose the Wallpaper (or Wallpapers) command.**

3. **Another menu appears, listing various types of wallpaper.**

   Your choices are

   Gallery: Choose a still image that's stored in the Gallery app.

   Live Wallpapers: Choose an animated or interactive wallpaper from a list.

   Wallpapers: Choose a wallpaper from a range of stunning images (no nudity). These images are preinstalled by the phone's manufacturer, so this item may have the manufacturer's name in the title.

4. **Choose the wallpaper you want from the list.**

   For the Gallery option, you see a preview of the wallpaper, where you can select and crop part of the image.

   For certain live wallpapers, the Settings button may appear. The settings let you customize certain aspects of the interactive wallpaper.

5. **Touch either the Save, Set Wallpaper, or Apply button to confirm your selection.**

   The new wallpaper takes over the Home screen.

Live wallpaper is interactive, usually featuring some form of animation. Otherwise, the wallpaper image scrolls slightly as you swipe from one Home screen panel to another.

- If you need to change the wallpaper and all the Home screen panels are full of icons, press the Menu soft button and choose the Wallpaper command.

- The Zedge app has some interesting wallpaper features. Check it out at the Google Play Store; see Chapter 18.

- See Chapter 15 for more information about the Gallery, including information on how cropping an image works.

Adding apps to the Home screen

You need not live with the unbearable proposition that you're stuck with only the apps that come preset on the Home screen. Nope — you're free to add your own apps. Just follow these steps:

1. **Visit the Home screen panel on which you want to stick the app icon shortcut.**

   The screen must have room for the icon shortcut.

2. **Touch the Launcher button to display the App menu.**

3. **Long-press the icon of the app you want to add to the Home screen.**

4. **Choose the command Add to Home.**

   A copy of the app's icon is placed on the Home screen.

The app hasn't moved: What you see is a copy or, officially, a *shortcut.* You can still find the app on the App menu, but now the app is available — more conveniently — on the Home screen.

✔ On some HTC phones, you can add apps from the Personalize menu: Touch the Personalize button and choose the App command. Choose an app to add to the Home screen.

✔ Some Android phones feature the *Dock,* or a set of icons found at the bottom of every Home screen panel. To change an app icon on the Dock, long-press an existing Dock icon. Choose a new icon from the list.

✔ You cannot replace the Launcher icon on the Dock. I also highly recommend keeping the Dialer app on the Dock.

✔ See the later section "Rearranging and removing icons and widgets" for information on moving the app around on the Home screen or from one panel to another. That section also covers removing apps from the Home screen.

Slapping down widgets

The Home screen is the place where you can find *widgets,* or tiny, interactive information windows. A widget often provides a gateway into another app, or displays information such as status updates, the name of the song that's playing, or the weather. To add a widget to the Home screen, heed these steps:

1. **Switch to a Home screen panel that has room enough for the new widget.**

   Unlike app icons, some widgets can occupy more than a postage-stamp-size piece of real estate on the Home screen.

2. **Long-press the Home screen and choose the Widget (or Widgets) command.**

3. **From the list, choose the widget you want to add.**

   For example, choose the Power Control widget to get quick access to several popular phone features, such as Wi-Fi or Bluetooth or other settings you often turn on or off.

The widget is plopped on the Home screen.

The variety of available widgets depends on the applications you have installed. Some applications come with widgets, some don't.

> ✒ More widgets are available at the Google Play Store. See Chapter 18.

> ✒ To remove, move, or rearrange a widget, see the later section "Rearranging and removing icons and widgets."

Creating shortcuts

Besides widgets, everything on the Home screen is a shortcut. But the variety of shortcuts doesn't end with apps. You can add shortcuts to the Home screen that help you get at a phone feature or display an informational tidbit without digging deep in the phone. That's why they're called *shortcuts*.

For example, I have a shortcut on my Home screen that uses the Maps app Navigation feature to help me return to my house. I swear that I use the shortcut only when I'm sober.

To add a shortcut, long-press the Home screen and choose the Shortcuts command from the Add to Home Screen menu (refer to Figure 22-1). What happens next depends on which shortcut you choose.

For example, when you choose Bookmark from the Select Shortcut menu, you add a web page bookmark to the Home screen. Touch the shortcut to open the Browser app and visit that web page.

Choose the shortcut from the phone's address book to display information for a specific contact. There are shortcuts for the Music app and the Maps app (Direction & Navigation), shortcuts for various apps installed on your phone, and shortcuts to common phone settings such as battery use, Wi-Fi, and more.

 When your phone seems to lack the ability to create a specific shortcut, check out the Any Cut app. It's useful for creating shortcuts that may not be available otherwise. Check out Any Cut at the Google Play Store; see Chapter 18.

Rearranging and removing icons and widgets

Icons and widgets aren't fastened to the Home screen. If they are, it's day-old chewing gum that binds them, considering how easily you can rearrange and remove unwanted items from any Home screen panel.

Long-press an icon on the Home screen to move it. Eventually, the icon seems to lift and break free, as shown in Figure 22-2.

Drag to left panel.   Drag to right panel.

Icon being pressed

Trash

Figure 22-2: Moving an icon.

You can drag a free icon to another position on the Home screen or to another Home screen panel, or you can drag it to the Trash icon that appears on the Home screen, which deletes the shortcut (refer to Figure 22-2).

Widgets can also be moved or removed in the same manner as icons.

- ✓ The Trash icon can appear on the top or bottom of the screen. In Figure 22-2, it appears at the bottom of the screen.

- ✓ Dragging a Home screen icon or widget to the trash removes the icon or widget from the Home screen. It doesn't uninstall the application or widget; the app can still be found on the App menu, and the widget can once again be added to the Home screen.

- ✓ If the Home screen features the Dock, you can drag the icon to the Dock to stick it there, replacing whatever icon already dwells there; you cannot drag an icon off the Dock.

- ✓ When an icon hovers over the Trash icon, ready to be deleted, its color changes to red.

- ✓ See Chapter 18 for information on uninstalling applications.

Moving Home screen panels

Some Android phones allow you to rearrange the Home screen panels. You might even be allowed to add or remove panels. Such a feature is offered by the phone's manufacturer; it isn't a native part of the Android operating system.

 To see whether your phone lets you rearrange the Home screen panels, press the Home button twice to see the Home screen overview, similar to the one shown in Figure 22-3. Try dragging around a Home screen panel thumbnail. If it moves, as shown in the figure, you can rearrange the panels. If you can't — oh, well.

Long-press a Home screen
to pick it up and move it.

The center Home screen
is the main Home screen.

Insertion pointer shows where
Home screen will be moved.

Figure 22-3: Manipulating Home screens.

Press either the Back or Home soft button when you're done rearranging.

✏ Any Home screen can be moved to any other position. Figure 22-3 shows the seven Home screen positions. The Home screen in the center is the main Home screen.

✏ The main Home screen is the one you return to when you press the Home soft button.

✔ The methods for adding new Home screen vary, though a popular way to do so is simply to drag a Home screen icon left or right from the leftmost or rightmost Home screen panel, respectively. On some phones, this action automatically spawns a new Home screen panel. Again, this technique isn't part of the Android operating system, so it's not available to all phones.

Android Phone Locks

Your Android phone comes with a *lock,* the simple touchscreen gizmo you slide to unlock the phone and gain access to its information and features. For most folks, this lock is secure enough. For others, the lock is about as effective as using a kitten to frighten an intruder.

You can add three additional types of security locks to your phone: pattern, PIN, or password. The details are provided in this section.

Finding the screen locks

All screen locks on the phone can be found in the same location: on the Choose Screen Lock screen. Heed these steps to visit that screen:

1. **At the Home screen, press the Menu soft button.**

2. **Choose Settings.**

3. **Choose Location & Security.**

4. **If no additional lock is set, choose Set Up Screen Lock; otherwise, choose Change Screen Lock.**

If the screen lock is already set, you have to work the lock to proceed: Trace the pattern, or type the PIN or password. You then get access to the Screen Unlock Security screen, which shows four items: None, Pattern, PIN, and Password. Using these items is covered in the next few sections.

✔ The lock you apply affects the way you turn on and wake up your phone. See Chapter 2 for details.

✔ The locks don't appear when you answer an incoming phone call. You're prompted, however, to unlock the phone if you want to use its features while you're on a call.

✔ See the following sidebar, "The lock doesn't show up!" for information on setting the Security Lock timer, which affects when the screen locks appear after you put the phone to sleep.

The lock doesn't show up!

The lock screen shows up whenever you turn on the phone or wake it up from Sleep mode. Whether the lock appears after awakening the phone depends on how long the phone has been sleeping. If you awaken the phone right away, for example, the lock may not even show up. The timing depends on the Security Lock Timer setting.

The Security Lock Timer setting specifies how long the phone waits after being put to sleep before the screen lock appears. Initially, the timer is set to 20 minutes. You can set a shorter interval, which is more secure: From the Home screen, press the Menu soft button and choose Settings. Choose Location & Security, and then choose Security Lock Timer. Choose a new time-out value from the list.

Removing a lock

To disable the pattern, PIN, or password screen lock on your phone, choose the None option from the Screen Unlock Security screen. When None is chosen, the phone uses the standard slide lock, as described in Chapter 2.

Refer to the preceding section for information on finding the None option on your Android phone.

Creating an unlock pattern

The unlock pattern is perhaps the most popular, and certainly the most unconventional, way to lock an Android phone's screen. The pattern must be traced on the touchscreen to unlock the phone.

To set the unlock pattern, follow these steps:

1. **Summon the Screen Unlock Security screen.**

   Refer to the earlier section "Finding the screen locks."

2. **Choose Pattern.**

   If you haven't yet set a pattern, you may see the tutorial describing the process; touch the Next button to skip merrily through the dreary directions.

3. **Trace an unlock pattern.**

   Use Figure 22-4 as your guide. You can trace over the dots in any order, but you can trace over a dot only once. The pattern must cover at least four dots.

4. **Touch the Continue button.**

5. **Redraw the pattern again, just to confirm that you know it.**

6. **Touch the Confirm button, and the pattern lock is set.**

Start here...

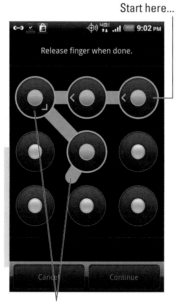

... and trace pattern.

Figure 22-4: Setting the unlock pattern.

Ensure that a check mark appears by the option Use Visible Pattern, found on the Location & Security Settings screen. That way, the pattern shows up when you need to unlock the phone. For even more security, you can disable this option, but you *must* remember how and where the pattern goes.

- To remove the pattern lock, set None as the lock type, as described in the preceding section.

- The pattern lock can start at any dot, not necessarily at the upper-right dot, shown in Figure 22-4.

- The unlock pattern can be as simple or as complex as you like. I'm a big fan of simple.

- Wash your hands! Smudge marks on the display can betray your pattern.

Setting a PIN

The *PIN lock* is a code between 4 and 16 numbers long. It contains only numbers, 0 through 9. To set the PIN lock for your Android phone, follow the directions in the earlier section "Finding the screen locks" to reach the Choose Screen Lock screen. Choose PIN from the list of locks.

Type your PIN twice to confirm to the doubting computer that you know it. The next time you need to unlock your phone, type the PIN on the keyboard and touch the Enter button (shown in the margin) to proceed.

Applying a password

Perhaps the most secure way to lock the phone's screen is to apply a full-on password. Unlike a PIN (refer to the preceding section), a *password* contains a combination of numbers, symbols, and uppercase and lowercase letters.

Set the password by choosing Password from the Choose Screen Lock screen; refer to the earlier section "Finding the screen locks" for information on getting to that screen.

The password you create must be at least four characters long. Longer passwords are more secure but easier to mistype.

You type the password twice to set things up, which confirms to the phone that you know the password and will, you hope, remember it in the future.

The phone prompts you to type the password whenever you unlock the screen, as described in Chapter 3. You also type the password whenever you change or remove the screen lock, as discussed in the section "Finding the screen locks," earlier in this chapter.

Various Phone Adjustments

Android phones feature a plethora of options and settings for you to adjust. You can fix things that annoy you or make things better to please your tastes. The whole idea is to make your phone more usable for you.

Stopping the noise!

Your phone features a bag of tricks designed to silence the phone. These techniques can come in quite handy, especially when a cell phone's digital noise can be outright annoying.

Vibration mode: You can make the phone vibrate for all incoming calls, which works in addition to any ringtone you've set (and still works when you've silenced the phone). To activate Vibration-all-the-time mode, follow these steps:

1. **At the Home screen, press the Menu soft button.**

2. **Choose Settings and then Sound.**

   3. **Choose Vibrate.**

   4. **Choose Always.**

Silent mode: Silent mode disables all sounds from the phone, except for music and YouTube and other types of media, as well as alarms that have been set by the Alarm (or Clock) and Calendar apps.

To enter Silent mode, follow Steps 1 and 2 in the previous set of steps and then place a check mark by the item Silent Mode.

Changing various settings

This section describes a smattering of settings you can adjust on the phone — all made from, logically, the Settings screen. To get there from the Home screen, press the Menu soft button and choose the Settings command.

You can also view the Settings screen by choosing the Settings app from the App menu.

Screen brightness: Choose Display, and then choose Brightness. Use the slider to adjust the touchscreen's intensity. Some phones feature the Automatic Brightness setting. It uses the phone's magical light sensor to determine how bright it is where you are.

Screen timeout: Choose Display, and then choose Screen Timeout. Select a time-out value from the list. This duration specifies when the phone goes into Snooze mode.

Ringer volume: Choose Sound, and then choose Volume. Use the sliders to specify how loud the phone rings for incoming calls (ringtones) and media and alarms. If you place a check mark by the Notifications item, the Ringtone setting also applies to notifications. Touch OK when you're done.

Keep the phone awake when plugged in: Choose Applications, and then choose Development. Place a check mark by the option Stay Awake.

Adjust the keyboards: Choose Language & Keyboard. Keyboard option names depend on what the phone's manufacturer calls the keyboard, and whether a physical ("device") keyboard is available. After choosing the proper keyboard-name option, you find a slew of interesting options that you can set when they please you or deactivate when they annoy you.

23

Maintenance, Troubleshooting, and Help

In This Chapter

▷ Checking the phone's battery usage

▷ Making the battery last

▷ Cleaning the phone

▷ Keeping the system up-to-date

▷ Dealing with problems

▷ Finding support

▷ Getting answers to common questions

Maintenance is that thing you were supposed to remember to do, but you didn't do, and that's why you need help and troubleshooting. Don't blame yourself; no one likes to do maintenance. Okay, well, I like maintaining my stuff. I even change the belt on my vacuum cleaner every six months. Did you know that the vacuum cleaner manual tells you to do so? Probably not, which is why I wrote this chapter: No, not to get you to maintain your vacuum cleaner, but to help you maintain your phone. Also thrown in (because most people forget maintenance) are the topics of troubleshooting and help. They all go together, for some reason.

Battery Care and Feeding

Perhaps the most important item you can monitor and maintain on your Android phone is its battery. The battery supplies the necessary electrical juice by which the phone operates. Without battery power, your phone is about as useful as a tin-can-and-a-string for communications. Keep an eye on the battery.

Monitoring the battery

Android phones display the current battery status at the top of the screen, in the status area, next to the time. The icons used to display battery status are similar to the icons shown in Figure 23-1. In some cases, the battery may point to the left rather than the right, or the Battery icon may be in a vertical orientation.

 Battery is fully charged and happy.

 Battery is being used and starting to drain.

Battery is getting low, so you should charge!

 Battery frighteningly low — stop using and charge at once!

 Battery is being charged.

Figure 23-1: Battery status icons.

You might also see the icon for a dead or missing battery, but for some reason I can't get my phone to turn on and display it.

You can check the specific battery level by following these steps:

1. **At the Home screen, press the Menu button.**
2. **Choose Settings.**
3. **Choose About Phone.**
4. **Choose Status.**

The top two items on the Status screen offer information about the battery:

Battery Status: This setting explains what's going on with the battery. It might say *Full* when the battery is full, *Discharging* when the battery is in use, or *Charging* when the battery is being charged. Other text may be displayed as well, depending on how desperate the phone is for power.

Battery Level: This setting reveals a percentage value describing how much of the battery is charged. A value of 100 percent indicates a fully charged battery. A value of 110 percent means that someone can't do math.

Later sections in this chapter describe activities that consume battery power and tell you how to deal with battery issues.

✔ Heed those low-battery warnings! The phone sounds a notification whenever the battery power gets low. (See the orange Battery icon shown earlier, in Figure 23-1). The phone sounds another notification whenever the battery gets *very* low. (See the red Battery icon in Figure 23-1).

✔ When the battery is too low, the phone shuts itself off.

✔ In addition to the status icons, the phone's notification light might turn a scary shade of red whenever battery juice is dreadfully low.

✔ The best way to deal with a low battery is to connect the phone to a power source: Either plug the phone into a wall socket, or connect the phone to a computer by using a USB cable. The phone charges itself immediately; plus, you can use the phone while it's charging.

✔ The phone charges more efficiently when it's plugged into a wall socket rather than a computer.

✔ You don't have to fully charge the phone to use it. If you have only 20 minutes to charge and the power level returns to only 70 percent, that's great. Well, it's not great, but it's far better than a 20 percent battery level.

✔ Battery percentage values are best-guess estimates. Just because you talked for two hours and the battery shows 50 percent doesn't mean that you're guaranteed two more hours of talking. Odds are good that you have much less than two hours. In fact, as the percentage value gets low, the battery appears to drain faster.

Determining what is sucking up power

A nifty screen on your Android phone lets you review which activities have been consuming power when the phone is operating from its battery. This informative screen is shown in Figure 23-2.

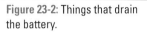

Figure 23-2: Things that drain the battery.

To get to this screen, follow these steps:

1. At the Home screen, press the Menu soft button.

2. Choose Settings and then About Phone.

3. Choose Battery Use.

You may have to choose the Battery command before you find the Battery Use item. Eventually, you see a screen similar to the one shown in Figure 23-2.

On some Android phones, you might find battery usage statistics by choosing Settings and then Battery & Data Manager. Touch the big Battery icon to see a screen similar to the one shown in Figure 23-2.

The number and variety of items listed on the Battery Use screen depend on what you've been doing with your phone between charges and how many different programs you're using.

Saving battery life

Here's a smattering of things you can do to help prolong battery life for your Android Phone:

Turn off vibration options. The phone's vibration is caused by a teensy motor. Though you don't see much battery savings by disabling the vibration options, it's better than no savings. To turn off vibration, follow these steps:

1. **At the Home screen, press the Menu soft button.**

2. **Choose Settings, and then choose Sound.**

3. **Choose Vibrate.**

4. **Choose Never.**

5. **Also on the Sound Settings screen: Remove the check mark by Haptic Feedback.**

   The Haptic Feedback option is what causes the phone to vibrate when you touch the soft buttons.

Additionally, consider lowering the volume of notifications by choosing the Volume option. This option also saves a modicum of battery life, though in my travels, I've missed important notifications by setting the volume too low.

Dim the screen. The display is capable of drawing down quite a lot of battery power. Though a dim screen can be more difficult to see, especially outdoors, it definitely saves on battery life.

You set the screen brightness from the Settings app: Choose Display, and then choose Brightness.

Turn off Bluetooth. When you're not using Bluetooth, turn it off. Or, when you *really* need that cyborg Bluetooth ear-thing, try to keep your phone plugged in. See Chapter 19 for information on turning off Bluetooth.

Turn off Wi-Fi. Wi-Fi networking on the phone keeps you on the Internet at top speeds but drains the battery. Because I tend to use Wi-Fi when I'm in one place, I keep my phone plugged in. Otherwise, the battery drains like my bank account at Christmas time. Refer to Chapter 19 for information on turning off the phone's Wi-Fi.

Disable automatic syncing. Your Android phone syncs quite often. In fact, it surprises me when I update something on the Internet and find my phone updated almost instantly. When you need to save battery power and frequent updates aren't urgent (such as when you're spending a day traveling), disable automatic syncing by following these steps:

1. **At the Home screen, press the Menu soft button.**

2. **Choose Settings, and then choose the Accounts command or the Accounts & Sync command.**

3. **Choose your Google account.**

4. **Remove the green check mark by each item.**

When saving battery juice isn't important, remember to repeat these steps to reenable background and automatic synchronization.

Get a bigger battery. Most Android phones have larger batteries available, which the nice people at the Phone Store will be more than happy to sell you. You may need to get a new back cover for your phone to accommodate the larger battery. Anyway, the folks at the Phone Store, or whatever online phone retailer you favor, know the details.

If you buy a larger battery — or any replacement battery, for that matter — ensure that the battery is manufacturer-compatible with your phone. Improper batteries can damage your phone. Heck, they can catch fire. So be careful when choosing a replacement battery.

Manage battery performance. Several Android phones come with battery-saving software built in. You can access the software from a special app or from the Settings screen. Similar to your computer, battery-performance management involves turning phone features on or off during certain times of the day.

If your phone lacks battery management software, you can pick up the Juice Defender app at the Google Play Store. Juice Defender comes in three flavors: Battery Saver, Plus, and Ultimate, depending on how intricately you want to tune your phone's power management. The QR code for the Battery Saver version of the app is shown in the margin.

Regular Phone Maintenance

There are only two basic tasks you can do for regular maintenance on an Android phone: Keep it clean, and keep important information backed up.

Where to find phone information

Who knows what evil lurks inside the heart of your phone? Well, the phone itself knows. You can view information about the battery, phone number, mobile network, and uptime, plus other information. To see this collection of trivia, summon the Settings app and choose About Phone and then Status.

For specific information about your account, such as minutes used and data transmitted, you have to visit the cellular service's website:

For AT&T, contact `www.att.com/ wireless`.

For Sprint, contact `www.sprint.com`.

For T-Mobile, contact `www.t-mobile.com`.

For Verizon, contact `www.verizon wireless.com`.

Keeping it clean

You probably already keep your phone clean. I must use my sleeve to wipe the touchscreen at least a dozen times a day. Of course, better than your sleeve is something called a *microfiber cloth*. This item can be found at any computer- or office-supply store.

✐ Never use ammonia or alcohol to clean the touchscreen. These substances damage the phone. Use only a cleaning solution specifically designed for touchscreens.

✐ If the screen continually gets dirty, consider adding a *screen protector*. This specially designed cover prevents the screen from getting scratched or dirty but also lets you use your finger on the touchscreen. Be sure that the screen protector is intended for use with your specific phone brand.

✐ You can also find customized cell phone cases, belt clips, and protectors, though I've found that these add-on items are purely for decorative or fashion purposes and don't even prevent serious damage if you drop the phone.

Backing up your phone

A *backup* is a safety copy of the information on your phone. It includes any contact information, music, photos, videos, and apps you've recorded, downloaded, or installed, plus any settings you've made to customize your phone. Copying this information to another source is one way to keep the information safe, in case anything happens to the phone.

On your Google account, information is backed up automatically. This information includes your Contacts list, Gmail messages, and Calendar app appointments. Because Android phones automatically sync this information with the Internet, a backup is always present.

To confirm that your Google account information is being backed up, heed these steps:

1. **From the Home screen, touch the Launcher button.**
2. **Choose My Accounts.**
3. **Choose your Google account.**
4. **Ensure that a green check mark appears by every option.**

   When no check mark is there, touch the gray square to add one.

If you have more than one Google account synchronized with the phone, repeat these steps for every account.

Updating the system

Every so often, a new version of your phone's operating system becomes available. It's an *Android update* because *Android* is the name of the phone's operating system, not because your phone thinks that it's a type of robot.

Whenever an automatic update occurs, you see an alert or a message appear on the phone, indicating that a system upgrade is available. You have three choices:

- ✔ Install Now
- ✔ Install Later
- ✔ More Info

My advice is to choose Install Now and get it over with — unless you have something (a call, a message, or another urgent item) pending on the phone, in which case you can choose Install Later and be bothered by the message again.

You can manually check for updates: From the Settings screen, choose About Phone, and then choose System Updates. You might also check for the Software Update item on the Settings screen. When your system is up-to-date, the screen tells you so. Otherwise, you find directions for updating the system.

Help and Troubleshooting

Things aren't as bad as they were in the old days. Back then, you could try two sources for help: the atrocious manual that came with your electronic device or a phone call to the guy who wrote the atrocious manual. It was unpleasant. Today, things are better. You have many resources for solving issues with your gizmos, including your Android phone.

Getting help

Some phone manufacturers, as well as cell phone providers, offer more help than others. Though it's not part of the standard Android operating system, some phones come with the Help app. It may be called Help or Help Center or something similar, and it may not be the kind of avuncular, well-written help you get from this book, but it's better than nothing.

A Guided Tour or Tutorial app may also be available, which helps you understand how to work some of the phone's interesting features.

Of course, none of the information found in an Android app helps you when you can't get turn on the phone. That's why books such as the one you're reading right now will probably never go out of style.

Fixing random and annoying problems

Aren't all problems annoying? There isn't really such a thing as a welcome problem, unless the problem is welcome because it diverts attention from another, preexisting problem. And random problems? If problems were predictable, they would serve in office. Or maybe they already are?

Here are some typical problems and my suggestions for a solution:

You have general trouble. For just about any problem or minor quirk, consider restarting the phone: Turn off the phone, and then turn it on again. This procedure will most likely fix a majority of the annoying and quirky problems you encounter when using an Android phone.

Some Android phones feature the Restart command on the Phone Options menu: Press and hold the Power Lock button to see this menu. If a Restart command is there, use it to restart the phone and (you hope) fix whatever has gone awry.

When restarting doesn't work, consider turning off the phone and removing its battery. Wait about 15 seconds, and then return the battery to the phone and turn on the phone again.

The data connection needs to be checked. Sometimes the data connection drops but the phone connection stays active. Check the status bar. If you see bars, you have a phone signal. When you don't see either the 4G, 3G, 1X, or Wi-Fi icon, the phone has no data signal.

Occasionally, the data signal suddenly drops for a minute or two. Wait and it comes back around. If it doesn't, the cellular data network might be down, or you may simply be in an area with lousy service. Consider changing your location.

For wireless connections, you have to ensure that the Wi-Fi is set up properly and working. Setup usually involves pestering the person who configured the Wi-Fi signal or made it available, such as the cheerful person in the green apron who serves you coffee.

The phone's storage is busy. Most often, the storage — internal or MicroSD card — is busy because you've connected the phone to a computer and the computer is accessing the phone's storage system. To "unbusy" the storage, unmount the phone or stop the USB storage. See Chapter 20.

When the phone's storage remains busy, consider restarting the phone, as described earlier in this section.

An app has run amok. Sometimes, apps that misbehave let you know. You see a warning on the screen announcing the app's stubborn disposition. Touch the Force Close button to shut down the errant app.

When you see no warning or an app appears to be unduly obstinate, you can shut 'er down the manual way, by following these steps:

1. **At the Home screen, press the Menu soft button.**
2. **Choose Settings, and then choose Applications.**
3. **Choose Manage Applications.**
4. **Touch the Running tab at the top of the Manage Applications screen.**
5. **Choose the application that's causing you distress.**

   For example, a program might not start or might say that it's busy or has another issue.

6. **Touch either the Stop or Force Stop button.**

   The program stops.

After stopping the program, try opening it again to see whether it works. If the program continues to run amok, contact its developer: Open the Play Store app, press the Menu soft button, and choose My Apps. Open the app you're having trouble with, and choose the option Send Email. Send the developer a message describing the problem.

The phone's software must be reset (a drastic measure). When all else fails, you can do the drastic thing and reset all the phone's software, essentially returning it to the state it was in when it first arrived. Obviously, you need not perform this step lightly. In fact, consider finding support (see the next section) before you start:

1. **At the Home screen, press the Menu soft button.**
2. **Choose Settings, and then choose Privacy.**
3. **Choose Factory Data Reset.**

   By itself, the Factory Data Reset option merely resets the phone's software. The information you have on the phone's storage (internal and MicroSD card) remains. That way, the pictures, videos, music, and other information saved on the phone's storage aren't erased. That is, unless you:

4. **Optionally, place green check marks by any Erase options for the phone's internal storage and MicroSD card.**

   Erasing these options isn't required in order to fix phone problems. The only time I've used them is when I've sold a phone or traded it in.

5. **Touch the Reset Phone button.**

6. **Touch the Erase Everything button to confirm.**

All the information you've set or stored on the phone is purged.

Again, *do not* follow these steps unless you're certain that they will fix the problem or you're under orders to do so from someone in tech support.

Getting support

Never discount these two sources of support: your cellular provider and the phone's manufacturer. Even so, I recommend phoning your cellular provider first, no matter what the problem.

Contact information for both the cellular provider and phone manufacturer is found in the material you received with the phone. I recommended that you save those random pieces of paper from Chapter 1. You obviously have read it and have followed my advice, so you can easily find that information.

Okay, so you don't want to go find the box, or you didn't heed my admonition and you threw out the box. In that event, Table 23-1 lists contact information on U.S. cellular providers. The From Cell column has the number you can call using your Android phone; otherwise, you can use the toll-free number from any phone.

Table 23-1		U.S. Cellular Providers	
Provider	**From Cell**	**Toll-Free**	**Website**
AT&T	611	800-331-0500	www.att.com/esupport
Sprint Nextel	*2	800-211-4727	mysprint.sprint.com
T-Mobile	611	800-866-2453	www.t-mobile.com/Contact.aspx
Verizon	611	800-922-0204	http://support.vzw.com/clc

Your cellular provider's help line might already be found in the phone's address book. Look for it there if it's not listed above.

In Table 23-2, you can find contact information for various Android handset manufacturers.

Table 23-2	Android Phone Manufacturers
Manufacturer	**Website**
HTC	www.htc.com/www/help
LG	www.lg.com/us/support
Motorola	www.motorola.com
Samsung	www.samsung.com/us/mobile/cell-phones

If you have an issue using the Google Play Store, you can visit its support website:

```
http://support.google.com/googleplay
```

Android Phone Q&A

I love Q&A! That's because not only is it an effective way to express certain problems and solutions but some of the questions might also cover topics I've been wanting to ask.

"The touchscreen doesn't work!"

The touchscreen, such as the one used on your phone, requires a human finger for proper interaction. The phone interprets complicated electro-magnetic physics between the human finger and the phone to determine where the touchscreen is being touched.

You cannot use the touchscreen when you're wearing gloves, unless they're specially designed gloves that claim to work on touchscreens. Batman wears this type of glove, so it probably exists in real life.

The touchscreen might also fail when the battery power is low or when the phone has been physically damaged.

"The screen is too dark!"

Modern cell phones feature a teensy light sensor on the front. The sensor is used to adjust the touchscreen's brightness based on the amount of ambient light at your location. If the sensor is covered, the screen can get very, very dark.

Ensure that you don't unintentionally block the light sensor. Avoid buying a case or screen protector that obscures the sensor.

If you'd rather manually set screen brightness, from the Home screen press the Menu soft button. Choose Settings, Display, Brightness. Remove the check mark by Automatic Brightness, and then use the slider to manually set the touchscreen's intensity.

"The battery doesn't charge"

Start from the source: Is the wall socket providing power? Is the cord plugged in? The cable may be damaged, so try another cable.

When charging from a USB port on a computer, ensure that the computer is turned on. Computers provide no USB power when they're turned off.

"The phone gets so hot that it turns itself off!"

Yikes! An overheating phone can be a nasty problem. Judge how hot the phone is by seeing whether you can hold it in your hand: When the phone is too hot to hold, it's too hot. If you're using the phone to fry an egg, the phone is too hot.

Turn off the phone. Take out the battery and let it cool.

If the overheating problem continues, have the phone looked at for potential repair. The battery might need to be replaced.

"The phone won't do Landscape mode!"

Not every app takes advantage of the phone's ability to orient itself in Landscape mode. On certain Android phones, the Home screen doesn't "do landscape" unless it's placed into a car mount or unless the phone has a physical keyboard that works in Landscape mode.

One program that definitely does Landscape mode is Browser, described in Chapter 11. So just because an app doesn't enter Landscape mode doesn't mean that it *can* enter Landscape mode.

Android phones have a setting you can check to confirm that landscape orientation is active: From the App menu, choose Settings and then Display. Ensure that a check mark appears by the Auto-Rotate Screen option. If not, touch the square to put a green check mark there.

Part VI
The Part of Tens

The 5th Wave   By Rich Tennant

"Well, here's what happened—I forgot to put it on my AK Notepad."

Camera (50)
US

Video (30)

download (9)

Kids (7)

The number of lists of ten items you can find is amazing. You may be familiar with the Ten Commandments and the ten plagues of ancient Egypt. Beethoven composed ten violin sonatas. In American football, you advance ten yards to a first down. There are ten pins in bowling. And need I mention that you have ten fingers and ten toes? Yep, ten is a famous number.

In a For Dummies book, it's a tradition to end the book with The Part of Tens. This part contains chapters that list ten items apiece. The items aren't necessarily the top ten items, but they're items that expand further the good and whole-some information presented throughout this book.

24

Ten Tips, Tricks, and Shortcuts

In This Chapter

▷ Turning off animations

▷ Installing a wireless battery charger

▷ Unlocking dirty words on voice input

▷ Putting a new word in the dictionary

▷ Adding direct-dial and direct-text screen shortcuts

▷ Using Quick Launch

▷ Dictating orders to your phone

▷ Configuring a navigation shortcut

▷ Finding a lost phone

▷ Nerding out with Task Manager

A tip is a handy suggestion, something spoken from experience or insight, and something you may not have thought of yourself. A *trick* is something that's good to know, something impressive or unexpected. And a *shortcut* is the path you take through the graveyard because it's a lot faster — not minding that the groundskeeper may, in fact, be a zombie.

Though I'd like to think that everything I mention in this book is a tip, trick, or shortcut for using your Android phone, there's even more information I can offer. This chapter provides ten tips, tricks, and shortcuts to help you get the most from your phone.

Disable Animations

Who doesn't want a faster phone? Well, people who don't care about all the onscreen animations. Though this trick doesn't truly speed up your phone, by disabling animations you help your phone have a peppier feel to it. Heed these directions:

1. **At the Home screen, press the Menu soft button.**

2. **Choose Settings and then Display.**

3. **Choose Animation and then No Animations.**

The disabled animations are mostly screen transitions, such as the fade-in effect when you return to the Home screen. It may not be much, but when I disabled animation on my phone, I had a sudden feeling of intense power and well-being. Though that may not happen to you, disabling animations is worth a try.

Get a Wireless Charging Battery Cover

When you want to go truly wireless (I mean, forgo all wires — period), you can get the wireless charging battery cover for your Android phone. Though not every phone may have an official, manufacturer-blessed wireless charging battery cover, many do, and the Phone Store is the first place to look for them.

You get two toys with the wireless charging battery cover. The first is the cover itself. The second is a charging pad. With the cover installed, you simply set the phone on the pad to charge it. A battery inside the back cover lines up the phone for perfect charging.

Voilà! No more wires. Ever.

Add Spice to Dictation

I feel that too few people use dictation, despite how handy it can be — especially for text messaging. Anyway, if you've used dictation, you might have noticed that it occasionally censors some of the words you utter. Perhaps you're the kind of person who doesn't put up with that kind of s###.

Relax. You can lift the vocal censorship ban by following these steps:

1. **At the Home screen, press the Menu soft button.**

2. **Choose Settings, and then choose Voice Input and Output.**

3. **Choose Voice Recognizer Settings.**

4. **Remove the check mark by the option Block Offensive Words.**

And just what are offensive words? I would think that *censorship* is an offensive word. But no, apparently only a few choice words fall into this category. I won't print them here, because the phone's censor retains the initial letter and generally makes the foul language easy to guess. D###.

Can you go completely wireless?

When you wave bye-bye to the USB cord for charging purposes, thanks to the wireless charging battery cover, it brings you one step closer to that nirvana of being completely wireless. Is it possible?

Beyond charging the phone, the only other reason to connect by wire is to share files with a computer or to send the phone's video to an HDMI monitor or TV (if it's capable of such a feat). It's possible to exchange files wirelessly between a computer and a phone by using Bluetooth. Some Android phones feature the Files app with its Shared Folders option, which lets you access a computer's file system over a Wi-Fi network. DLNA-capable phones can view media from a PC by using the Wi-Fi network.

So the technical answer is Yes — it's entirely possible to configure your Android phone to be completely wireless. But the realistic answer is that wires are still necessary for certain tasks, simply because the wireless method of file transfer or broadcasting video isn't as easy as the wire-based method. For now.

Add a Word to the Dictionary

Betcha didn't know that your phone sports a dictionary. The dictionary is used to keep track of words you type — words that may not be recognized as being spelled properly.

Words unknown to the phone are highlighted on the screen. Sometimes, the word is shown in a different color or on a different background or even underlined in red. To add that word to the phone's dictionary, long-press it. You see the Add Word to Dictionary command, which sticks the word in the phone's dictionary.

To review or edit the phone's dictionary, follow these steps:

1. **At the Home screen, press the Menu soft button.**
2. **Choose Settings.**
3. **Choose Language & Keyboard.**
4. **Choose User Dictionary.**

   The command may not be obvious on some phones: Try choosing the keyboard first, and then choose either the Dictionary or User Dictionary command.

When the dictionary is visible, you can review words, edit them, remove them, or manually add new ones. To edit or delete a word, long-press it. To add a word, choose the Add New button or, if you can't see that button, press the Menu soft button and choose either the Add or Add New command.

Create Direct-Dial and Direct Text-Message Shortcuts

For the folks you contact most frequently, you can create Home screen contact shortcuts. Here's how:

1. **Long-press the Home screen.**

   Choose a Home screen panel that has room for at least one icon.

2. **Choose either the Shortcuts or Shortcut command.**

3. **Choose Direct Dial.**

4. **Choose the contact you want to direct-dial.**

   Contacts with multiple phone numbers have more than one listing.

A shortcut to that contact's phone number (with the contact's picture, if they have one) appears on the Home screen. Touching the shortcut instantly dials the contact's phone number.

Just as you can create a direct-dial shortcut (shown in the preceding section), you can create an icon to directly text-message a contact. The difference is that you choose Direct Message rather than Direct Dial in Step 3.

See Chapter 9 for more information about text messaging.

Take Advantage of the Quick Launch Feature

If your Android phone features a physical keyboard, you're in for a treat: You can assign app shortcuts to the 36 keys on that keyboard. That's one shortcut per letter key, A through Z, plus 10 for the numbers 1 through 9 and 0. The keyboard shortcuts make up the Quick Launch function. Setting them up works like this:

1. **At the Home screen, press the Menu soft button.**

2. **Choose Settings, and then choose Applications.**

3. **Choose Quick Launch.**

   You see various entries titled Assign Application, followed by the 36 keys from the keyboard, A through Z, and then 0 through 9. If an app is already assigned to a key, you see the app listed. Otherwise, you see the text *No Shortcut.*

4. **Choose a letter to assign an app to that key.**

   For example, choose the C key.

5. **Select an app to assign to the Quick Launch key.**

   Pluck an app from the scrolling menu, such as Calculator.

6. **Repeat Steps 4 and 5 to assign more apps to Quick Launch keys.**

 To use a Quick Launch shortcut, press and hold the Search key on the device keyboard, and then touch the Quick Launch key shortcut, such as Search+C to launch the app associated with the C key.

To reassign an app to a key, repeat the steps in this section and choose a new app in Step 5.

To remove an app from a key, long-press its entry on the Quick Launch screen. Touch the OK button to confirm that that you're clearing the key.

Control the Phone with Your Voice

Not every Android phone may have this feature, but it's worth checking out: Peruse the Apps menu for the Voice Search app. If you find it, great: You can use this app to dictate commands to your phone. I just tried this trick for my son, and he was duly impressed: I uttered, "Listen to the Beatles." In less than five seconds, my phone began playing the *White Album.*

Here are just a few of the phrases you can utter into the phone after starting the Voice Search app and seeing the Speak Now prompt:

- Watch a video
- Listen to *(artist, album, song)*
- Send e-mail to *(contact)*
- Set alarm for *(time)*
- Go to *(address, map location)*

Alas, try as I might, the phone never responds when I say, "Make me a sandwich!"

Get Somewhere Quickly

I normally use the following shortcut on all my phones, but on my latest Android phone, I forgot. Silly me. The trick: Put a shortcut icon on the Home screen for your home location. That way, you can touch the shortcut to instantly have the phone help you navigate home. And I don't use the shortcut for those late nights when I'm being chased by an angry mob.

To create a location shortcut for your home or office, heed these steps:

1. **Long-press the Home screen.**

   Ensure that you're using a Home screen panel that has room for a new icon.

2. **Choose the Shortcuts or Shortcut command.**

3. **Choose Directions & Navigation**.

   A special screen appears where you can enter location information.

4. **Type a destination address.**

   Type the address exactly as though you were searching for a location by using the Maps app. For your home or office, type the street address and zip code.

5. **Choose a method of transportation.**

6. **Type a name for the shortcut.**

   The name appears below the shortcut's icon on the Home screen, so keep the name short and descriptive.

7. **Choose an icon.**

   All the icons are dull and generic, so it doesn't matter which you select.

8. **Touch the Save button.**

   The shortcut icon is created and pasted to the Home screen.

You can use this technique to create a Home screen shortcut for any location: your favorite coffee hangout, a pizza joint, the parole office, or any place you frequent. To use the icon, touch it. The phone instantly launches the Maps app and sets you on a course for the destination you typed in Step 4.

Find Your Lost Cell Phone

Someday, you may lose your beloved Android phone. It might be for a few panic-filled seconds, or it might be for forever. The hardware solution is to weld a heavy object to the phone, such as an anvil or a rhinoceros, yet that strategy kind of defeats the entire mobile/wireless paradigm. (Well, not so much the rhino.) The software solution is to use a cell phone locator service.

Cell phone locator services employ apps that use a phone's cellular signal as well as its GPS to help locate the missing gizmo. These types of apps are available at the Google Play Store. I've not tried them all, and many of them require a subscription service or registration at a website to complete the process.

Here are some suggestions for cell phone locator apps:

- Wheres My Droid
- Lookout Mobile Security
- Mobile Phone Locator

The first word of the Wheres My Droid app has no apostrophe. I mention it because the lack of an apostrophe bugs the bejeebers out of my editor.

Visit the Task Manager

If you want to get your hands dirty with some behind-the-scenes stuff on your Android phone, Task Manager is the app to open. It's not for everyone, so feel free to skip this section if you want to use your phone without acquiring any computer nerd sickness that you have otherwise successfully avoided.

The Task Manager app is found on the App menu. It may not be found on your Android phone. If so, you can avoid looking at Figure 24-1, which illustrates the Task Manager's main screen.

The Task Manager window shows all the phone's currently running apps, along with trivial information about each one: The CPU item shows how much processor power the app is consuming, and the RAM item shows how much storage the app occupies.

You can use Task Manager to kill off tasks that are hogging up too much CPU time or memory or that simply bug the stuffing from your couch. As illustrated in Figure 24-1, you touch items you want to kill off and then touch the End Apps button. The apps are silently snuffed out.

A nifty feature in Task Manager is the Auto-End list. When apps have been assigned to this list, they automatically exit two minutes after the display times out. To add apps to the list, select them from the main screen (refer to Figure 24-1) and touch the Add to Auto-End button at the bottom of the screen.

- There's no need to kill off an app flagged as "not running."
- Task Manager doesn't delete apps; it merely stops them from running. To delete an app, use the Google Play Store, as discussed in Chapter 18.

Selected apps

Menu shows up only
when items are selected.

Running apps

Figure 24-1: Managing tasks.

✔ Also see Chapter 23 on using the Force Stop button to kill an app run amok.

✔ The Android operating system does an excellent job of managing apps. If resources are needed for another app, Android automatically closes any open apps as needed. There's no need to futz with Task Manager, unless you just enjoy messing with such a thing.

Ten Things to Remember

*1*f only it were easy to narrow to ten items the list of all the things I want you to remember when using your Android phone. So even though you'll find in this chapter ten good things not to forget, don't think for a moment that there are *only* ten. In fact, as I remember more, I'll put them on my website, at www.wambooli.com. Check it for updates about your phone and perhaps for even more things to remember.

Lock the Phone on a Call

Whether you dialed out or someone dialed in, after you start talking, you should lock your phone: Press the Power Lock button. By doing so, you ensure that the touchscreen is disabled and the call isn't unintentionally disconnected.

Of course, the call can still be disconnected by a dropped signal or by the other party getting all huffy and hanging up on you, but by locking the phone, you prevent a stray finger or your pocket from disconnecting (or muting) the phone.

Landscape Orientation

The natural orientation of the typical Android phone is vertical — its *portrait* orientation. Even so, that doesn't mean you have to use an app in portrait orientation.

Turning the phone to its side makes many apps appear wider, such as the Browser app and the Maps app. It's often a better way to see things, to see more available items on certain menus, and, if you're using the onscreen keyboard, to give you larger key caps on which to type.

Not every app supports landscape orientation.

Recent Apps

There's no point having to switch between an app and the Home screen or between an app and the Apps menu. The better solution is to use the Recent Apps feature, to not only switch between apps but also to summon any app you've recently opened.

To quickly access the apps you've recently opened on your phone, press and hold the Home button. You see a screen listing the last several apps you've opened or used. Choose one.

Keyboard Suggestions

Don't forget to take advantage of the suggestions that appear above the keyboard when you're typing text. In fact, you don't even need to touch a suggestion: To replace your text with the highlighted suggestion, simply touch the space key. Zap! The word appears.

The setting that directs the keyboard to make suggestions work is Show Suggestions. To ensure that this setting is active, obey these steps:

1. **At the Home screen, press the Menu soft button.**

2. **Choose Settings.**

3. **Choose Language & Keyboard.**

4. **Choose your phone's keyboard from the list.**

   The standard keyboard is named Android Keyboard, though your manufacturer may call it a specific name, such as the Multi-Touch Keyboard or Touch Input or something equally random.

5. **Ensure that a check mark appears by the option Show Suggestions.**

Things That Consume Lots of Battery Juice

Three items on your phone suck down battery power faster than an 18-year-old fleeing the tyranny of high school on Graduation Day:

- Navigation
- Bluetooth
- Wi-Fi networking

Navigation is certainly handy, but because the phone's touchscreen is on the entire time and dictating text to you, the battery drains rapidly. If possible, try to plug the phone into the car's power socket when you're navigating. If you can't, keep an eye on the battery meter.

Both Bluetooth and Wi-Fi networking require extra power for their wireless radios. When you need that level of speed or connectivity, they're great! I try to plug my phone into a power source when I'm accessing Wi-Fi or using Bluetooth. Otherwise, I disconnect from those networks as soon as I'm done, to save power.

- Technically speaking, using Wi-Fi doesn't drain the battery as drastically as you would think. In fact, the Wi-Fi signal times itself out after about 15 minutes of non-use. So it's perfectly okay to leave Wi-Fi on all day — you experience only a modicum of battery loss because of it. Even so, I'm a stickler for turning off Wi-Fi when I don't use it.

- See Chapter 23 for more information on managing the phone's battery.

Check for Roaming

Roaming can be expensive. The last non-smartphone (dumbphone?) I owned racked up $180 in roaming charges the month before I switched to a better cellular plan. Even though you too may have a good cell phone plan, keep an eye on the phone's status bar. Ensure that when you're making a call, you don't see the Roaming status icon on the status bar atop the touchscreen.

Well, yes, it's okay to make a call when your phone is roaming. My advice is to remember to *check* for the icon, not to avoid it. If possible, try to make your phone calls when you're back in your cellular service's coverage area. If you can't, make the phone call but keep in mind that you will be charged roaming fees. They ain't cheap.

Use the + Symbol When Dialing Internationally

I suppose that most folks are careful when dialing international numbers. On an Android phone, you can use the + key to replace the country's exit code. In the United States, the code is 011. So whenever you see an international number listed as 011-xxx-xxxxxxx, you can instead dial +xxx-xxxxxxx, where the x characters represent the number to dial.

See Chapter 21 for more information on international dialing.

Properly Access Phone Storage

To access the phone's storage area from your computer, you must properly mount the phone's storage. For most Android phones, that includes two storage locations: internal storage and the MicroSD card.

After the storage is mounted, you can use your computer to access files — music, videos, still pictures, contacts, and other types of information — stored on your phone.

When the phone's storage is mounted on a computer storage system, you cannot access phone storage by using the phone. If you try, you see a message explaining that the storage is busy.

When you're done accessing the phone's storage from your computer, be sure to stop USB storage: Pull down the USB notification and choose either the Charge Only or None setting. Touch the OK button. (See Chapter 20 for more details.)

Do not simply unplug the phone from the USB cable when the computer is accessing the phone's storage. If you do, you can damage the phone's storage and lose all information stored there.

Snap a Pic of That Contact

Here's something I always forget: Whenever you're near one of your contacts, take the person's picture. Sure, some people are bashful, but most folks are flattered. The idea is to build up your Contacts list so that all contacts have photos. Receiving a call is then much more interesting when you see the caller's picture displayed, especially a silly picture (or an embarrassing one).

When taking the picture, be sure to show it to the person before you assign it to the contact. Let them decide whether it's good enough. Or if you just want to be rude, assign a crummy-looking picture. Heck, you don't even have to do that: Just take a random picture of anything and assign it to a contact: A plant. A rock. Your dog. But, seriously, the next time you meet up with a contact, keep in mind that the phone can take that person's picture.

See Chapter 15 for more information on using the phone's camera.

The Search Command

Google is known worldwide for its searching abilities. By gum, the word *google* is now synonymous for searching. So, please don't forget that your Android phone, which uses the Google Android operating system, has a powerful Search command.

The Search command is not only powerful but also available all over. The Search soft button can be pressed at any time, in just about any program, to search for information, locations, people — you name it. It's handy. It's everywhere. Use it.

26

Ten Worthy Apps

In This Chapter

- AK Notepad
- CardStar
- Dolphin Browser
- Gesture Search
- Google Finance
- Google Sky Map
- Movies
- SportsTap
- Voice Recorder
- Zedge

*N*othing stirs up controversy like stating that ten Android apps are more worthy than the 500,000-plus apps available at the Google Play Store. Even so, when I started out with my first Android phone 20 years ago, I wanted to see a list of worthy apps, or even apps recommended by friends. Lamentably, that was a long time before anyone else had an Android phone, so I was forced to wait. Thanks to the suggestions in this chapter, you don't have to wait to get started with apps on your Android phone.

AK Notepad

It's odd, but for some reason, your Android phone may not come with a note-taking app. Some do, most don't. Anyway, a good choice for an app to fill that void is AK Notepad: You can type or dictate short messages and memos, which I find handy.

For example, before a recent visit to the hardware store, I made (dictated) a list of items I needed by using AK Notepad. I also keep some important items as notes — things that I often forget or don't care to remember, such as frequent-flyer numbers, my dress-shirt-and-suit size (like I ever need that info), and other important notes I might need handy but not cluttering my brain.

 Perhaps the most important note you can make is one containing your contact information. A note labeled In Case You Find This Phone on my phone contains information about me in case I ever lose my phone and someone is decent enough to search it for my information. (Also see Chapter 24 for information on finding lost phones.)

CardStar

 The handy CardStar app answers the question "Why do I have all these store-rewards cards?" They're not credit cards — they're marketing cards designed for customer loyalty programs. Rather than tote those cards around in your wallet or on your keychain, you can scan a card's bar code using your phone and save the "card" on the phone.

After you store your loyalty cards in the phone, you simply run the CardStar app to summon the appropriate merchant. Show the checkout person your phone, or scan the bar code yourself. CardStar makes it easy.

Dolphin Browser

 Though I don't mind using the Browser app that comes with my phone, it's universally despised by many Android users. A better and more popular alternative is Dolphin Browser.

Like many popular computer browsers, Dolphin Browser features a tabbed interface, which works much better than the silly multiple-window interface of the standard Browser app.

Gesture Search

 The Gesture Search app provides a new way to find information on your phone. Rather than use a keyboard or dictate, you simply draw on the touchscreen the first letter of whatever you're searching for.

TIP

Get thee a bar code scanner app

Many apps from the Google Play Store can be quickly accessed by scanning their bar code information. Scanning with what? Why, your phone, of course!

By using a bar code scanner app, you can instantly read in and translate bar codes into links to that app at the Play Store.

Plenty of bar code apps are out there, though I use one called Barcode Scanner. It's easy: Run the app. Point the phone's camera at a bar code and, in a few moments, you see a link or an option for what to do next. To get an app, choose the Open Browser option, which opens the Play Store app on your phone.

You can use the Barcode Scanner app to take advantage of the various QR Code icons that appear in this chapter, as well as throughout this book. To install an app, choose the option Open Browser.

Start the Google Search app to begin a search. Use your finger to draw a big letter on the screen. After you draw a letter, search results appear on the screen. You can continue drawing more letters to refine the search or touch a search result.

Gesture Search can find contacts, music, apps, and bookmarks in the Browser app.

Google Finance

 The Google Finance app is an excellent market-tracking tool for folks who are obsessed with the stock market or want to keep an eye on their portfolios. The app offers you an overview of the market and updates to your stocks, as well as links to financial news.

To get the most from this app, configure Google Finance on the web, using your computer. You can create lists of stocks to watch, which are then instantly synchronized with your Android phone. You can visit Google Finance on the web at

```
www.google.com/finance
```

As with other Google services, Google Finance is provided to you for free, as part of your Google account.

Google Sky Map

 Ever look up into the sky and say, "What the heck is that?" Unless it's a bird, an airplane, a satellite, a UFO, or a superhero, Google Sky Map helps you find what it is. You may learn that a particularly bright star in the sky is, in fact, the planet Jupiter.

Google Sky Map app is elegant. It basically turns your Android phone into a window you can look through to identify objects in the night sky. Just start the app, and hold the phone up to the sky. Pan the phone to identify planets, stars, and constellations.

 Google Sky Map promotes using the phone without touching its screen. For this reason, the screen goes blank after a spell, which is merely the phone's power-saving mode. If you plan some extensive stargazing with Google Sky Map, consider resetting the screen time-out. Refer to Chapter 2 for details.

Movies

 The Movies app is your phone's gateway to Hollywood. It lists currently running films and films that are opening, and it has links to your local theaters with showtimes and other information. It's also tied into the popular Rotten Tomatoes website for reviews and feedback. If you enjoy going to the movies, you'll find the Movies app a valuable addition to any Android phone.

SportsTap

 I admit to not being a sports nut, so it's difficult for me to identify with the craving to have the latest scores, news, and schedules. The sports nuts in my life, however, tell me that the very best app for that purpose is a handy thing named SportsTap.

Rather than blather on about something I'm not into, I'll just ask that you take my advice and obtain SportsTap. I believe you'll be thrilled.

WARNING!

Avoiding Android viruses

How can you tell which apps are legitimate and which might be viruses or evil apps that do odd things to your phone? Well, you can't. In fact, most people can't, because most evil apps don't advertise themselves as such.

The key to knowing whether an app is evil is to look at what it does, as described in Chapter 18. If a simple grocery-list app uses the phone's text messaging service and the app doesn't need to send text messages, it's suspect.

In the history of the Android operating system, only a handful of malicious apps have been distributed, and most of them were found in Asia. Google routinely removes these apps from the Play Store, and a feature of the Android operating system even lets Google remove apps from your phone. So you're relatively safe.

Generally speaking, avoid porn and "hacker" apps and apps that use social engineering to make you do things on your phone that you wouldn't otherwise do, such as text an overseas number to see racy pictures of politicians or celebrities.

Voice Recorder

The typical Android phone has the hardware necessary to record your voice or other sounds. An app that can accomplish this task is Voice Recorder. It has an elegant and simple interface: Touch the big Record button to start recording. Make a note for yourself, or record a friend doing his Daffy Duck impression.

Previous recordings are stored in a list on the Voice Recorder main screen. Every recording is shown with its title, the date and time of the recording, and the recording duration.

Zedge

The Zedge app is a helpful resource for finding wallpapers and ringtones for your Android phone. It's a sharing app, so you can access wallpapers and ringtones created by other Android phone users as well as share your own.

Zedge features an easy-to-use interface, plus lots of helpful information on what it does and how it works.

Index